MEAD AND
MERLEAU-PONTY

MEAD AND MERLEAU-PONTY

Toward a Common Vision

SANDRA B. ROSENTHAL
PATRICK L. BOURGEOIS

STATE UNIVERSITY OF NEW YORK PRESS

Published by
State University of New York Press, Albany

© 1991 State University of New York

For information, address State University of New York
Press, State University Plaza, Albany, N.Y., 12246

Production by E. Moore
Marketing by Fran Keneston

Library of Congress Cataloging-in-Publication Data

Rosenthal, Sandra B.
    Mead and Merleau-Ponty : toward a common vision / Sandra B.
Rosenthal, Patrick L. Bourgeois.
        p. cm.
    Includes bibliographical references and index.
    ISBN 0–7914–0789–6 (alk. paper).—ISBN 0–7914–0790–X (pbk. :
alk. paper)
        1. Mead, George Herbert, 1863–1931.   2. Merleau-Ponty, Maurice,
1908–1961.   I. Bourgeois, Patrick L.   II. Title.
    B945.M464R67   1991
    191—dc20   90–20226
                                                                                    CIP

10 9 8 7 6 5 4 3 2 1

In Memory of
Stanford H. Rosenthal
Our great fan and cheerleader

And

To
Alvin J. Holloway, S.J.
For over twenty good years of leadership and friendship;
and for the many more to come.

CONTENTS

ACKNOWLEDGMENTS

This book has been supported by a grant from the National Endowment for the Humanities, an independent federal agency. We are deeply grateful for this support.

We would like to express our appreciation also to those at Loyola responsible for providing concurrent sabbaticals during which background work was done for this book.

Thanks are due to the editors of the following journals for permission to republish parts of these articles. "Scientific Time and the Temporal Sense of Human Existence: Merleau-Ponty and Mead," *Research in Phenomenology*, (1990) Vol. XX. "Role Taking, Corporeal Intersubjectivity, and Self: Mead and Merleau-Ponty," *Philosophy Today*, (1990) Vol. XXXIV. "Meaning and Human Behavior: Mead and Merleau-Ponty," *The Southern Journal of Philosophy*, (1988) Vol. XXVI. "The Field of Perception and the Dimensions of Human Activity: Mead and Merleau-Ponty," *The Southern Journal of Philosophy* (1990) Vol. XXVIII. "Sensation, Perception and Immediacy: Mead and Merleau-Ponty," *Southwest Philosophy Review*, (1990) Vol. VI.

On a more personal note, we wish to acknowledge our indebtedness and gratitude to John Lachs for living the life of true philosophic community with gusto and authenticity.

And, this joint project, like our previous ones, owes much to the active encouragement, stamina, and patience of Stan and Mary. We know that the legacy of Stan's enthusiasm and vitality will pervade our future endeavors as well.

INTRODUCTION

The philosophies of both G. H. Mead and Maurice Merleau-Ponty are the product of, and actively direct, the respective courses of their different traditions. Mead's philosophy is firmly rooted within the mainstream of classical American pragmatism. He maintained an ongoing philosophic exchange with John Dewey over a period of many years, and as part of the Chicago school of pragmatism was influenced from various directions by scholars working in the context of this tradition. His appropriation of pragmatism, however, took it in new directions, and the originality of his ideas contributed greatly to its further development. Merleau-Ponty's philosophy is both the result of, and an influence upon phenomenology and existential philosophy. For, while he was clearly influenced by such writers as Kierkegaard, Marcel, Heidegger, Sartre, and Husserl, it is equally clear that he was one of the leading formative proponents of phenomenology, philosophy of existence, and existential phenomenology. It is to his philosophy that the term "existential phenomenology" applies better than to any other philosophy.

Although phenomenology and pragmatism have developed as entirely independent philosophical traditions, there has been a growing awareness on the part of philosophers working both in classical American pragmatism and in European phenomenology that important similarities and clarifying insights are to be gained through the comparative study of these two movements. And, within their respective movements, Mead and Merleau-Ponty have each received a great deal of attention recently. There is a developing interest in Mead's philosophy both in Europe and in the United

States, as is evident from new studies on Mead, some of which have been done by Germans interested in American philosophy as such. There is renewed and ongoing interest in Merleau-Ponty in the United States, Canada, and Europe, as can be seen by journal articles and books recently written or translated, and by the recent discussions that attempt to interpret his works as a whole. Further, there have been fleeting yet persistent hints of their philosophic kinship. For example, John McDermott, as early as 1976, in focusing on developing sensibilities in grasping interpersonal relations on "both a theoretical and a practical level," cites both Mead and Merleau-Ponty as relevant to this emerging trend.[1] And, McDermott renews the theme of the link between Merleau-Ponty and American philosophy in general in his most recent book.[2] Again, Joseph Margolis provides hints of a kinship between Mead and Merleau-Ponty concerning a contemporary view of the self, though this insight is not one that he pursues.[3] Oddly, in spite of the growing interest in the relation between pragmatism and phenomenology in general, as well as in Mead and Merleau-Ponty within their respective traditions, and in spite of briefly stated insights concerning their similar interests, there has been virtually no sustained attempt to explore their philosophical affinities.

Maurice Natanson's book on Mead, which is unique in focusing on Mead from the direction of phenomenology, is highly perceptive on many issues.[4] Nonetheless he tends to evaluate Mead's theories only against the traditional Husserlian or Schutzian phenomenology, viewing Mead's rejection of transcendental phenomenology in favor of distinctively pragmatic doctrines as a philosophical "naivete" rooted in his naturalistic approach. Because of such attempts either to criticize Mead in terms of phenomenology, or totally assimilate his position to that of phenomenology, Hans Joas, in his recent book, indicates a basic disdain for attempts to relate Mead to phenomenology,[5] though what lies implicit in his references to this tradition in general is the framework of Husserlian philosophy.

Joas's negative attitude in this area is indicative of two points that have hindered approaches to the relationship between Mead and Merleau-Ponty. First, this kind of adverse reaction can easily occur when scholars working within one tradition see a philosopher in whom they are interested evaluated from the framework of, or reduced to, an alien tradition. A real exchange must be built upon respect for the uniqueness and integrity of each distinctly different position while recognizing converging interests and points of contact in responding to enduring philosophical problems. It should be an occasion not for melting down one framework to the other, but rather for the two positions to be fed in such a way as to clarify for themselves their own positions and deepen their own insights.

Second, the remarkable and fruitful relationships between Mead and Merleau-Ponty have gotten buried under the weight of arguments and claims explicitly or implicitly using Husserlian phenomenology as the model for phenomenology in general. Though the phenomenological return to lived experience has first passed through the phase of transcendental idealism, as evidenced in the writings of Husserl, such idealism is rejected in the philosophy of Merleau-Ponty, and the richness of human experience finds its location within the natural world.

Just as the pragmatist must overcome the tendency to read into Merleau-Ponty's philosophy the very subjectivist, transcendentalist, and idealist elements he rejects in his own unique appropriation of phenomenology, so too the phenomenologist must resist the tendency to read into Mead's pragmatic focus on the method of experimental inquiry the very reductionisms that he, as well as pragmatism in general, so strongly rejects. Though Mead views scientific method or the method of experimental inquiry as operative in all human activity, his concern is precisely with the creative, anticipatory dynamics of scientific experimentalism as method. There is no attempt to replace lived experience with scientific explanation. Rather, the very dynamics of scientific inquiry negate this possibility.

Indeed, Mead and Merleau-Ponty are, each from within a different context, reacting against a tradition of philosophy culminating in the modern worldview with its illicit reification of scientific contents and the inadequate understanding of humans and nature to which this gave rise. Both return to the richness of lived experience within nature, and in such a return, reveal the impossibility of making the contents of science the ultimate building blocks of reality or knowledge. The implications of this return unite Mead and Merleau-Ponty in a shared rejection of substance philosophy as well as the spectator theory of knowledge in favor of a focus on the ultimacy of temporal process and the constitutive function of social praxis. They both attempt to integrate the characteristics of consciousness that emerge from its natural empirical conditions with the idea of consciousness as the tissue of significations, the field of meanings by which humans are intentionally bound to their world. Further, this intentional link is rooted, for Mead and for Merleau-Ponty alike, in the total corporeal dimension of existence, which is best understood in terms of the dynamics of human activity or the structure of human behavior. This in turn leads them to radically new, insightful, at times converging, at times complementary, but always compatible, visions of the nature of selfhood, language, freedom, and time itself, as well as of the nature of the relation between the so-called tensions of appearance and reality, sensation and object, the individual and the community, freedom and constraint, continuity and creativity, among others.

Neither position can be understood as an eclectic synthesizing of traditional alternatives. As Mead so well warns, in a statement which is echoed in various ways by both philosophers throughout their respective works, and which is applicable, with appropriate revisions of terms, to just about all the standard alternatives relevant to the issues they explore, "There is an old quarrel between rationalism and empiricism which can never be healed as long as either sets out to tell the whole story of reality. *Nor is it possible to divide the narrative between them.*"[6] Indeed, Mead and Merleau-Ponty, in their respective returns to lived experience, each engage in a shattering attack on virtually all the assumptions governing the philosophical tradition and the kinds of alternatives to which they gave rise, as well as the assumptions of what is often considered mainstream philosophy today. This attack becomes even more effective when the strengths of each of their respective positions are used to illuminate and expand various facets of the other, in turn clarifying a shared contemporary vision which draws them ever closer.

The writing of this work follows two other coauthored books which we have published in the past: *Pragmatism and Phenomenology: A Philosophical Encounter,*[7] and *Thematic Studies in Phenomenology and Pragmatism.*[8] The first of these studies attempts to provide a broad, general overview of the relation between pragmatism and phenomenology, while the second focuses on the more in-depth analysis of particular themes within these two traditions in general. This third book, then, by concentrating on an author from each tradition, logically follows these other two. Further, it accords with them in taking a systematic rather than developmental approach to the positions involved.

1. THE STRUCTURE OF BEHAVIOR AND THE CONTENT OF PERCEPTION: CONVERGING PERSPECTIVES

THE BASIC APPROACHES of Mead and Merleau-Ponty to the examination of meaning and human behavior may at first glance seem mutually exclusive. For Mead's pragmatic focus emphasizes the relation between organic activity and behavioral environment, while Merleau-Ponty's phenomenological focus stresses prereflective awareness as an intentionally unified field. Further, Mead, usually considered a social behaviorist or a behavioral psychologist, appropriates behaviorism in a positive way, redirecting it within a nonreductive, holistic context, whereas Merleau-Ponty's aim is to show how the scientific treatments of experience by physiology and experimental psychology, because of their reductionistic inadequacies, demand a rejection of behavioristic interpretations in favor of a phenomenological approach. It will become clear in the ensuing analysis, however, that the seeming contrast represents two different emphases operative within a common general context. The phenomenology of Merleau-Ponty incorporates the behavioral aspect emphasized by Mead. And Mead's position contains a phenomenological dimension, for there emerges within the context of behavior the very structure of the experiential intentional link upon which Merleau-Ponty focuses. The following discussion will first turn to Mead's approach.

The usual characterization of Mead as a behavioral psychologist or sociologist can be misleading in two directions. It can falsely bring to mind shades of reductionism. And it can just as falsely hide a phenomenological dimension to Mead's thought, a dimension not usually associated with behavioristic approaches of any type. Turning to the first issue, Mead's social behaviorism, in contrast to a Watsonian behaviorism, views behavior as explaining mind or consciousness without explaining it away. Mead does not reduce mental functions, mind, or consciousness to reductionist bodily behavior; rather he approaches these dimensions of human existence through a focus on objectively observable behavior, or behavior observed "from the outside." As Mead notes,

> Watson apparently assumes that to deny the existence of mind or consciousness as a psychical stuff, substance, or entity is to deny its existence altogether and that a naturalistic or behavioristic account of it as such is out of the question. But, on the contrary, we may deny its existence as a psychical entity without denying its existence in some other sense at all; and if we then conceive it functionally, and as a natural[1] rather than a transcendental phenomenon, it becomes possible to deal with it in behavioristic terms.[2]

For Mead, behaviorism is a methodological, not an ontological, position.[3] As he notes of behaviorism in a "wider sense," it "is simply an approach to the study of the experience of the individual from the point of view of his conduct, particularly, but not exclusively, the conduct as it is observable by others."[4] In viewing behaviorism in terms of an observational methodology rather than a reductionist ontology, the nature of the behavior studied changes radically. It is no longer the behavior characterized through the illicit reifications of the contents of science, but a structure of behavior which is guided throughout by active selectivity.

Mead distinguishes the physical or physiochemical, the vital, and the mental in terms of three different levels of system. A physical or physiochemical system does not as such involve life; a biological system per se does not involve mind. Partaking in more than one of these systems gives rise to emergent properties. As Mead clarifies, "I have defined emergence as the presence of things in two or more different systems, in such a fashion that its presence in the later system changes its character in the earlier system or systems to which it belongs."[5] The appropriation of the earlier by the later system restructures the earlier. Far from being reducible to something earlier, the later has transformed the earlier, not just added on to it. The human, as belonging to more than one system, incorporates emergent qualities which vitiate all forms of reductionism.

Mead holds that the behavior which gives rise to mentality is rooted in the most rudimentary of biological activity. Even in the biological system as such, in the operation of lower animals, the animal endows the environment with characters, thus affecting it even as it affects the animal. There is an essential reciprocity between the organism and its environment. In the primitive biological adjustment, the stimulus serves as a stimulus in its role as answering the needs of the organism. The organism "chooses" the stimuli to which it will be sensitive and the character of the stimuli is partially determined by this choosing. Embedded in the very life process, then, is to be found a continual adjustment of organism and environment as a unified field. All living organisms, "from cells to humans," are in anticipatory interaction with an environment.[6] From this context, Mead stresses that the life process is such that it must "confer its characters within its whole field of operation."[7] There is a mutual determination of life and environment. Thus he approvingly quotes Dewey's criticism of the reflex arc in favor of a circuit:

> Failing to see the unity of activity, no matter how much it may prate of unity, it still leaves us with sensation or peripheral stimulus; ideal or central process (the equivalent of attention); and motor response, or act, as three disconnected existences, having somehow to be adjusted to each other.[8]

The selective activity embodied in the life process contains the rudiments of intelligence, for "intelligence finds its simplest expression in the appropriateness of the responses of a living form to the environment in the carrying-out of its living process."[9] Indeed, such intelligence is almost coextensive with life, for it belongs not only to animal forms but also to vegetable forms.[10] And even rudimentary animal intelligence, as intelligence, embodies the pragmatic understanding of the nature of experience as experimental—as incorporating the rudimentary dynamics of experimental or scientific or instrumental method—for "if we look upon the conduct of the animal form as a continual meeting and solving of problems, we can find in this intelligence, even in its lowest expression, an instance of what we call 'scientific method'. . . . The animal is doing the same thing the scientist is doing."[11] Here also, it will be seen, are to be found the rudimentary origins of the phenomenological dimensions of experience as the experience of meaningful things within a world, for selective tendencies, as attitudes of response, enter into the very character of the world of human experience. The ensuing discussion will turn to this phenomenological dimension.

It is important to stress that the intent here is not to equate Mead's biological focus with his pragmatic focus as one strand, then to locate the phenomenological focus as a separate strand external to his pragmatism. Maurice Natanson continually finds conflicts and contradictions in Mead's thought because he sets up a sharp distinction between human action as biological and as constitutive, and views these as conflicting strands in Mead's thought: a pragmatic strand on the one hand, and a latent and inadequately developed phenomenological strand on the other.[12] Rather, the point is that Mead's pragmatic focus incorporates both dimensions—the biological and the phenomenological—in an inseparably intertwined unity. Behaviorism, as a methodological position, and as operating within the context of a new understanding of behavior, is not limited exclusively to conduct as it is observable by others. Mead's "behaviorism" is pervaded by a phenomenological dimension in which the dynamics of experience are grasped from within. The phenomenological dimension of Mead's approach is elusive because he tends to view his examination of behavior from the perspective of psychology. Even his characterizations of behaviorism from the psychological perspective, however, are indicative of his implicit phenomenological approach, for as will be seen in the following progression, the language of psychology which he brings tends to both hide and house such an approach.

Mead holds that his position does not ignore "the inner experience of the individual—the inner phase of that process or activity. On the contrary, it is particularly concerned with the rise of such experience within the process as a whole."[13] Because of this focus on inner experience, Mead holds that introspection has a definite meaning even for behavioristic psychology. This meaning of introspection, however, is found in the fact that behavioristic science "looks within the experience of the individual for phenomena not dealt with in any other sciences—phenomena to which only the individual himself has experiential access."[14] He holds that the discussion of such so-called inner experience can be approached from the point of view of behaviorism if it is not too narrowly conceived, for he stresses that outwardly observable behavior finds expression within individuals, not in the sense of being in a subjective world, but in the sense of being within their organisms.[15] Something of this behavior appears in what Mead terms "attitudes," the beginnings of acts. And "if we come back to such attitudes we find them giving rise to all sorts of responses."[16] Or, as he further removes his position from that of introspection, "There are matters which are accessible only to the individual, but even these cannot be identified with consciousness as such because we find we are continually utilizing them as making up our world."[17]

Mead is in fact moving away from the concept of introspection toward the understanding of a field of consciousness in which a dynamic, active organism is intertwined with, and is partially constitutive of, the field. Consciousness as such refers to both the organism and its environment and cannot be located simply in either. The arguments for and against behaviorism have historically taken some form of the dualism-reductionism controversy, no matter how tenuous the link became. Mead's task is that of "restoring to nature the characters and qualities which a metaphysics of mind and a science of matter and motion had concurred in relegating to consciousness, and of finding such a place for mind in nature that nature could appear in experience."[18] With the emergence of mind, the environment becomes informed with meanings. Mind is an emergent within the context of observable behavior and is operative within a process of common meanings. Lower animals do not operate in light of common meanings or significant symbols, and thus their behavior is not indicative of the presence of mentality. Mind is not reducible to behavior, but as an emergent within the context of behavior is functionally related to it. As an emergent within a field of ongoing behavior, mind is not reducible to brain, nor can it be a container for, or confined within, subjective experience. Mead's position thus undercuts the dualism-reductionism controversy and avoids both mechanism and vitalism in that it undercuts the subject-object, mind-matter distinctions in favor of a field of activity, understood in terms of "the act as such . . . the organism as active."[19]

The difference between the physicist and the biologist, according to Mead, lies in the goals that their sciences contemplate, in the realities they are seeking. And their procedures answer to their goals.[20] Science starts with the experienced difference between the inanimate, life, and mind. Such distinctions are rooted in common experience of the everyday world. The understanding of the inanimate in terms of scientific matter, as well as the reduction of biological activity to the activity of matter, does not reach something more real than, or corrective of, our everyday experience, but rather grasps abstract orderings dependent throughout on a scientific enterprise rooted in the everyday world. A comprehensive, adequate understanding of behavior from "without" ultimately must accommodate an interpretive description or a phenomenological examination of the experiential features of behavior and perception as these reveal themselves in the world of everyday experience. The awareness of the qualitatively unique sets of structural relations that hold for the inanimate, for lower forms of life, and for the human, is rooted in everyday lived experience, and it is to this phenomenologically grasped difference that biology and psychology must be true if they are to be adequate. Mead's entire biological and/or psychological approach presupposes and attempts to be true to the phenomenological dimensions of the perceived world. Within this general context, the discussion which follows will turn to Merleau-Ponty's phenomenological focus on human behavior.

Merleau-Ponty begins in *The Structure of Behavior*[21] with the scientific treatments of behavior by physiology and experimental psychology in order to delve to their presupposed conditions and to derive an adequate grasp of behavior. In *The Structure of Behavior* he establishes the fact that these sciences distort behavior, that nature and consciousness reinterpreted can be understood in terms of one another instead of in opposition to one another, and that these scientific treatments of behavior demand a phenomenology of perception which, as such, can reawaken the experience of the world which, because it is overlooked in ordinary experience, needs to be rediscovered in reflection.[22] Merleau-Ponty deliberately begins within such reductionistic accounts in order to lead from within them to their own foundation and to a new philosophical solution that does justice to the problems engendered by them. These inadequate scientific treatments of meaningful experience, however, are not to be confused with the holistic sense in which Mead speaks of the biological aspect of behavior that was considered above.

Thus, in the general context of Mead's and Merleau-Ponty's treatments of behavior, three distinct attitudes toward behavior itself are evinced: first, one which understands it within a reductionistic science; second, a reflective attitude which understands behavior as observable by others and viewed from the outside, but not in any reductionistic sense; and third, an attitude that grasps behavior "first hand" in a reflection upon its pervasive and lived structure.[23] Merleau-Ponty, as Mead, opposes all reductionistic behaviorism from the start, upholding a holistic behaviorism which serves as a prolegomenon for a phenomenology of perception in its primary, foundational character. In addition, he explicitly expresses an openness to a holistic behaviorism in Mead's sense in stating that a return to the perceived world is not made in such a way as to "sacrifice objectivity to the interior life."[24] He accredits Gestalt psychology with showing that "structure, Gestalt, meaning are no less viable in objectively observable behavior than in the experiences of ourselves—provided, of course, that objectivity is not confused with what is measurable."[25] Here Merleau-Ponty preserves the possibility of the nonreductionist, biological approach in Mead's sense. Merleau-Ponty, however, devolves this holistic vision of the primordial level only after first entering the reductionistic sciences of behavior and showing their inadequacies to resolve the problems raised by their reductionism. After clarifying the distinctively human structure of behavior, he then opposes to the reductionistic view of those sciences a phenomenology of perception which they demand and which itself allows the possibility of Mead's approach. Thus, it can be affirmed that Merleau-Ponty's conclusions in *The Structure of Behavior* are quite compatible with Mead's view of the relation between organic activity and behavioral environment as a contemporary, nonreductionistic naturalism.

For Merleau-Ponty, "a truth of naturalism"[26] as a structure of behavior emerges as the result of phenomenology's attempt to deal with the relationship between nature and the human in nonreductionistic terms. In describing the structure at the root of human experience, he has evolved a unique position, both preserving the element of the empirical, naturalistic view as the natal bond between humans and nature on this basic human level of behavior, and, at once, preserving the constitutive aspect of experience prior to the level of conscious acts. This human level of structure, where the human body and nature are one, is a unique level, distinct from the lower physical and living levels. It is to Merleau-Ponty's engagement of the physiological and psychological sciences that the discussion will now briefly turn.

Entering the "natural attitude"[27] of the sciences of behavior and consciousness which assumes an ontology of reified scientific contents, Merleau-Ponty comes "to these questions by starting 'from below' and by an analysis of the notion of behavior." He takes up the term "behavior" because of its neutrality[28] with respect to both reductionistic empirical sciences of the mental and physical and to transcendental reflection with its pure consciousness, both of which he opposes. Merleau-Ponty thus begins with behavior, so understood, in order to introduce the consciousness-nature correlation as a structure, rather than as psychological reality or as a cause. Hence, the development in *The Structure of Behavior* involves the structure of behavior and the correlation between nature and consciousness in terms of structure or form in order to ensure a holism adequate to satisfy the demands of the sciences from within.

In opposition to all atomistic and decompositional approaches to behavior, Merleau-Ponty especially rejects the "constancy hypothesis"[29] according to which a one-to-one correlation obtains between stimulus and response, or "a point-by-point correspondence and constant connection between the stimulus and the elementary perception."[30] This hypothesis breaks down in the face of the evidence from the data of consciousness.[31] For example, the intensity of a sound can lower its pitch; two objectively equal figures appear unequal with the addition of auxiliary lines; a colored area appears to be the same color over the whole of its surfaces even though the chromatic thresholds of the different parts of the retina ought to make it red in one place, orange in another, and colorless in certain cases.

The breakdown of this hypothesis begins even in its most primitive level of stimulus-response, at which level it is seen that variation in the reaction cannot be solely attributed to variations in the elementary properties of the stimuli. The elements of a complex stimulus do not account for or allow prediction of their effects. The way in which the organism "accepts" the stimulus in part determines its spatial distribution. The behavior which results is "caused" by the organism's own behavior, which conditions the way in which the stimulus is received, as well as by the applied stimulus. Thus is established a circular rather than a linear relation. The effort toward subsidiary hypotheses by advocates of the constancy hypothesis is an attempt to account for these facts without changing the nature of the theory. The breakdown and failure of the constancy hypothesis in reflex theory, Gestalt theory, and Pavlovian reflexology demands a change in favor of a nonreductionistic holism, with the introduction of the notion of structure or form as a means of understanding behavior in terms other than mere causal processes of classical physics or any in-itself or element of a supposed totally independent real world. Thus the notion of structure or form as a "whole which has a meaning,"[32] or as a totality which is more than the sum of its parts, is the best means of understanding behavior as a phenome-non in a nonreductionistic way.[33]

It is not just the stimuli or the excitant, but also the organ-ism that contributes to the constitution of the structure or form. Quoting Weizsacker, Merleau-Ponty affirms: "The properties of the object and the intentions of the subject . . . are not only inter-mingled; they also constitute a new whole."[34] Hence the structure is created by both the organism itself and the excitant or stimuli "according to the proper nature of its receptors, the thresholds of its nerve centers and the movements of the organs"[35] which chooses the stimuli to which it will be sensitive. Thus, an ade-quate stimulus cannot be defined in itself independently of the organism, since it is neither a physical reality nor a physico-chemical agent; "it is a certain form of excitation of which the physico-chemical agent is the occasion rather than the cause. . . . [T]he excitation itself is already a response, not an effect imported from outside the organism; it is the first act of its proper functioning."[36] Due to the need to take account of the whole, in-cluding the organism and the stimuli, variations of the response in the presence of analogous stimuli are related to the meaning of the situations in which they appear, and differing situations can evoke analogous reactions.

In dealing with excitations in the above manner, Merleau-Ponty delves below the usual prejudice favoring the level of de-rived objectivity emerging from one interpretation of the contents of science. He indicates instead that the "real parts of the stimulus are not necessarily the real parts of the situation,"[37] revealing the relation of meaning between the situation and response, so that, rather than a derived objective presence, it is *for* the organism, *for* recognition.[38] He thus has emphatically rejected the alternative interpretations of behavior as either a thing of the scientifically objectified physical world or as a pure consciousness as the condi-tion of possibility of objectivity. The structure of behavior, involv-ing the situation as a whole and its meaning, reveals the fundamental reciprocity between the organism and its environ-ment that gives rise to things as phenomena of experience.[39]

It is precisely because the world of physics, of life, and of spirit are understood in terms of structure, and because each of

these orders consists in a qualitatively unique set of structural relations, that it is impossible to collapse one into the other. Aided
by the notion of structure or form, it can be concluded that "both
mechanism and finalism" should be rejected and that the "physical," and "vital," and the "mental" are each to be conceived as a
retaking and a "new" structuration of the preceding one.[40] Since
human life is more integrated than that of the animal, humans can
never be merely animal.[41] "Mind is not a specific difference which
would be added to vital or psychological being in order to constitute a man. Man is not a rational animal. The appearance of reason and mind does not leave a sphere of self-inclosed instincts in
man."[42] The emergence of higher orders eliminates the autonomy
of the lower orders and "give[s] a new signification to the steps
which constitute them."[43] This is what reveals the advent of human action and of human perception and shows that they are irreducible to lower forms of behavior.[44]

For Merleau-Ponty the notion of structure or form is a means
of understanding meaning in lived experience or phenomenal being in a way that overcomes the notion of the in-itself without
reverting to an idealism or to a phenomenalism.[45] The sciences,
even physics, do not demand philosophical realism. The world that
is determined scientifically, whether by physical sciences, life sciences, or the human sciences, is a derived world. Matter, life, and
mind, rather than merely three abstract scientific realities, are
three orders or "planes of signification"[46] within the perceived
world from which scientific significations emerge. Hence, it is
clear that the world of the sciences is neither one of things-
in-themselves nor a world of ideas the multiplicity of which is
unified in the epistemological subject. Further, the source of these
three orders is found neither in a world of things-in-themselves nor
in a world of mere appearances, but in the perceived world. Thus
it must be equally clear that for Merleau-Ponty, as well as Mead,
the scientifically determined world, rather than being the correction or revision of the naively perceived world, is, on the contrary,
founded and dependent upon it. Science begins with the difference
between the physical, the vital, and the human, a difference found
in naive experience. The attempt to understand behavior and
meaningful experience in an objective way ultimately leads back
to the naive experience used to characterize them, and demands a
descriptive, reflective account.

For Mead and Merleau-Ponty alike, then, the character of
meaningful experience is inseparable from the structure of human

behavior. And, for both Mead and Merleau-Ponty, any adequate articulation of the structure of human behavior must begin with, and elucidate the irreducible features of, its phenomenologically grasped dimensions.

From the above backdrop of the general behavioral and phenomenological dimensions of the positions of Mead and Merleau-Ponty, the following discussion will turn more specifically to Mead's understanding of "the act" as constitutive of the perceptual object, and then to Merleau-Ponty's own understanding of the role of activity. It will be seen that they each portray a field of ontologically "thick" or resisting objects whose manner of emergence undercuts the subject-object split and involves similar dimensions of human activity. Mead's understanding of the emergence of the field of objects in terms of the stages of the act will be seen to further deepen the implicit but pervasive phenomenological dimension to his pragmatism, while Merleau-Ponty's phenomenological account of the perceptual field in terms of the primacy of perception will be seen implicitly to contain elements of Mead's pragmatic understanding of the stages of the act. Thus each philosopher implicitly incorporates features of the other's position in a way that complements and enriches the understanding of both.

The perceptual object emerges within contours of what Mead calls "the act." Because of this, the content of perception is inseparably linked with activity, is partially constituted in action, and all forms of copy or representative theories of perception are repudiated. As he stresses, "The process of sensing is itself an activity."[47] Every act is an act of adjustment in which both the individual and its environment take on new characters or, with the emergence of minds, new meanings, and in which a durational spread of past, present, and future is incorporated. Mead distinguishes four stages or phases of the act in terms of the impulse or anticipatory attitude, perception (or distance perception), manipulation, and consummation. The perception of physical things already presupposes an ongoing act within which perception arises. The impulse toward some selective activity is the impetus for the entire act, for the selectivity of anticipatory attitudes determines the lines of further activity. And, the anticipated later process already aroused in the central nervous system controls the earlier. This constitutes "the teleological character of the act."[48]

The uniqueness of human activity, which distinguishes it from other organisms and which gives rise to the distinctively human awareness of a world of perceived objects, is founded in two interrelated conditions. First, between the impulse phase and the consummatory phase as the completion of the act and as the satisfaction of the demands of the first impulse phase, there lies, within human activity, the phase of perception and manipulation. In animal activity, contact experiences are not determined mainly by manipulation, but rather are immediately a part of the consummatory stage. What manipulation there may be functions directly and immediately to satisfy impulse demands. Thus, there is no opportunity for the emergence of things. By the time the consummatory stage of the act is reached, things must have already arisen in experience if they are to arise at all. As Mead succinctly states, "One eats things."[49] Secondly, the role of the human hand in manipulative activity freed from a direct link to impulse demand-fulfillment allows for a diversity of manipulative experiences as possible contact experiences. In the freeing of action from instinct and in the variety of manipulative experiences due to the function of the hand, there emerges the inhibition of action resulting from alternative and conflicting possible actions in passing from distance to contact experience. In contrast to most theories of perception, Mead claims that we are aware of a sensible object not primarily through visual experience but through contact experience. The manipulatory phase enters into and modifies the perceptual phase. The diversity of manipulative experiences due to the human hand is incorporated into perceptual awareness because of the inhibition of a process of movement in relation to a distant stimulus due to alternative possible completions of the act. Perception is thus a process of mediation within the act in which possible contact experience of the distance stimulation appears with that distant stimulation. In this way, "the percept is a collapsed act."[50]

Mead's understanding of the distinction between distance experience and contact experience as phases of the act is crucial in understanding the nature of the perceptual object. Distance experience can be found in the action of any sense, even touch. Tactile experience provokes actions that relate to contact experience. Contact experience is not the bare contact with the surface of the organism. Rather, it involves resistance, an "inside content." We do not feel or see the inside by taking apart the object, for this only yields more surfaces. The contact experience is not merely pressure, hardness or roughness, etc., but primarily resistance. The object of perception is always a distant object which invites us to action. Even the object of contact experience, "is such only in so far as it possesses an outline and position with reference to the whole environment which gives it the character of a distant object."[51] Any experienced object is an integral part of an environment which is brought to bear in the perception of the object.

In the reference of distance experience to contact experience, there is an abstraction from passage and the emergence of structures irrelevant to passage. Perceptual objects are simultaneous with the perceiver. As Mead notes:

> The theory of the subjectivity of secondary qualities exactly reverses the actual situation. The distance characters of stimuli are spatiotemporally away from the organism; but if the resistance of things, their inner matter, is to be dated simultaneously with the organism, this resistance must be excited in the organism, and thus wrench temporally distant stimuli characters out of the futurity.[52]

That which is spatiotemporally distant becomes transformed into objects which are spatially but not temporally distant. For lower animal forms there is no perceptual world of physical things, there is no experience of simultaneity, "no 'now' by which a perceptual object can be dated with the organism. The entire action is ahead and places the colors and sounds in the constantly emerging future."[53] There is no connection of distance perception and contact perception in terms of a stable core.[54]

Though the relation between distant and contact experience in the constitution of the physical object may at first seem to be the relation between the hand and the eye, there is more involved. In order to constitute the physical object as a center of resistance the individual must also make use of the ability to take the role of the other as developed in social interrelations.[55] The individual's act must call out an activity in objects that is similar in character to its own. "The necessary condition of this physical but cooperative 'other' getting into experience, so that the inside of things, their efficacy and force, is an actual part of the world, is that the individual in a premonitory fashion should take the attitude of acting as the physical thing will act, in getting the proper adjustment for his own ultimate response."[56] The ability of anticipatory role taking, developed in social interrelations, is applied in the emergence of nonsocial objects. Indeed, all objects are originally social objects. The physical object as inanimate is that kind of social object which can become depersonalized, leaving only the resistance, which is the stuff not only of inanimate physical objects, but the stuff of all perceptual things, including ourselves and others as objects of perception.[57]

In perceiving the object, the organism bestows upon it the active occupation of space which belongs to itself, thus giving the object an inside content which is irreducible to surfaces revealed to the eye or the hand. The organism identifies the resistance of the thing with its own active effort; it takes the role of the "other." In this identification, the hand again plays a crucial function. "What is essential to this social relation . . . is that the individual, in preparing to grasp the distant object, himself takes the attitude of resisting his own effort in grasping, and that the attained preparation of the manipulation is the result of this cooperation or conversation of attitudes. . . . I am prepared to seize this object, and then in the role of the thing I resist this grasp."[58] Further, since resistance belongs to the organism and its manipulatory area, "the 'what' of the object expresses a whole of which both environment and organism are essential parts."[59] The perception of organism and object as distinct emerges from a unified field of active resistance which undercuts the subject-object distinction. As Mead notes, "Each surface, that of the hand and that of the stone, is given as immediately as the other, and the resistance of the one is given as immediately as that of the other. . . . Out of the experience arise the physical thing and the organism. Neither is prior."[60] Organism and environment, behavior and perceived object, are unified in the holistic field of the "collapsed act." As Mead summarizes, "The act, then, must be antecedent to the appearance of things and of the organism as objects. It is illegitimate to place this original act within the organic individual as an object."[61]

Mead holds that the mechanism for such a field of resistance arises out of the action of different parts of the body against one another, primarily out of the hands.[62] Yet he stresses that there is a critical difference between the pressure of hand against hand and stone against hand, for in the former there is the sense of effort in each hand.[63] Once the self has emerged, it would seem that this forms the basis for the recognition of one's body as that which is both sensing and sensed. Further, the very constitution of the physical object through role taking, and the derivative nature of physical objects from social objects, explains why Mead can hold that inanimate objects can form parts of the social "other" in so far as an individual responds to those objects in social fashion.[64]

The ability to take the role of the other further allows humans to take many different perceptual viewpoints simultaneously and in this way reach a universal grasp of the object. The constitution of the physical object as embodying not only resistance but also a unified multiplicity of perspectives is possible only through the ability for role taking, an ability which arises in the context of social behavior and which gives rise to selfhood. The focus on social behavior and role taking in the development of selfhood will be postponed until chapter 4. But in light of this interrelation, it would seem that the distinction between instrumental action and communicative action can, within Mead's philosophy, be only a difference in emphasis rather than a difference in kind. The clarification of this point, however, involves the clarification of the term "instrumental," for it is too often taken exclusively as the active use of knowledge to change society or the environment; it is too often wrongly associated with the technological.

At a more fundamental level, operative throughout Mead's philosophy, "instrumental" indicates the manner in which one knows the world through the structures of the meanings one has created by one's responses to the environment. Here the focus on the instrumental is not a focus on what one should do with knowledge, but on what knowledge is, on human purposive activity as built into the very structure of meaningful awareness. In this appropriation, however, the instrumental or purposively guided transformational element between humans and their environment is incorporated in the very heart of the internal structure of meaning. Indeed, the "instrumental nature of the manipulatory experience,"[65] which is permeated by the impulse stage of anticipatory selectivity, is crucial in bringing the act to a pause in which it does not go through to its consummation at once, and the characteristics of the manipulative phase permeate and mediate the distance perception, thus giving rise to objects of perception. Purposive, instrumental activity, then, is incorporated within the very structure of meanings in general, and its character, as incorporated within these meanings, permeates and unifies them.

It was seen above that inanimate objects are derivative from social objects, since their constitution involves the social context of role taking ability which gives rise to selfhood. From the perspective of the present discussion, however, the full development of social objects and social interaction can be seen to be dependent upon the instrumental. For perception of resisting objects and one's organism arise together from an undifferentiated field, and, as indicated above, social objects are also resisting objects. As Mead states, social individuals or selves exist in their "efforts and tensions in social conduct.... They have besides these characters those of physical beings."[66] And, though it will be seen that awareness of meanings emerges only through the beginnings of communicative action, such action, involving as it does the resistance and efforts of organisms, is permeated with the instrumental activity that gives rise to the insides of objects as centers of resistance. Instrumental activity is thus pervasive for all meaningful experience, and communicative intent is permeated with the instrumental nature of meaningful awareness, while the instrumental nature of meaningful awareness is inherently social. For Mead, self, others, and things arise together in experience,[67] and instrumental and communicative action are inseparably intertwined in the structure of behavior which gives rise to them. Jürgen Habermas, espousing the popular distinction between these, separates communicative action and instrumental action in analyses that draw from Mead, and attempts to strengthen this position by noting the distinction between types of sentences that do and do not require communicative intent.[68] According to the present understanding of Mead, however, any sentence or any meaningful word incorporates both dimensions of activity by the very nature of the internal action-structure of meaning.

The purposive, instrumental character that pervades and unifies human awareness is precisely its binding intentional character as well. The teleological character of the act discussed above in relation to the impulse stage is at once the foundation for the intentional character and the instrumental character of human activity. All human activity, even at its most rudimentary level, is selective, creative activity guided by direction and noetically transformative of its environment. As such, it is instrumental or experimental, exemplifying the dynamics of scientific method. But, precisely as such, it is also intentional. The significance of the structure of human behavior developed above is that the dispositions, habits, or tendencies it incorporates are immediately experienced and pervade the very tone and structure of immediately grasped content. Thus, Mead's focus on behavior, far from excluding a descriptive analysis of lived or everyday experience, points directly toward such an endeavor. There is an inseparable relationship between the human biological organism bound to a natural environment, and the human agent who through meanings constitutes a perceived world.

There are two dimensions of the act as it develops in Mead's philosophy, for there is a twofold philosophical sense of "purposive activity" running throughout Mead's position, one biological, the other phenomenological, both of which undercut the level of the biological in terms of the contents of scientific analysis. The act, in its biological dimension, is understood as a process of adjustment of the organism to the conditions of the environment. In this sense Mead speaks of the adequacy of meanings in terms of the ongoing conduct of the biological organism immersed in a natural world.[69] The act, in its phenomenological dimension, is partially constitutive of its field of awareness and involves an intentional mind-object relationship as a field of meanings that can be phenomenologically studied from within. In this second sense Mead speaks of the adequacy of meanings in terms of the appearance of what is meant.[70]

From the context of organism-environment interaction, there emerge irreducible meanings which allow objects to come to conscious awareness. Such meanings are irreducible to physical causal conditions or to psychological acts and processes; yet they emerge from the biological, when the 'biological' is properly understood, for the content of human perception is inseparable from the structure of human behavior within its natural setting. The inseparable relationship between the human biological organism bound to a natural environment and the human agent whose noetic creativity is partially constitutive of the object of awareness, is concisely delineated in Mead's assertion that "when we reduce a thing to parts we have destroyed the thing that was there. . . . We refer to these differences as the meanings these things have in their relationship to the organism."[71] The focus on biological organism does not lead to causal analyses of human awareness and human knowledge in opposition to an irreducible field of meanings, but to a structure of behavior which, as purposive, instrumental, or experimental provides the activity out of which consciousness of a field of meanings emerges.

Mead concludes that his general analysis of the constitution of the physical object in terms of the act both accords with developed perceptual awareness[72] and does not require that we move from experience to a reality which lies outside an actual or possible perception.[73] These claims, indicative at once of both the biological and phenomenological dimensions of Mead's pragmatism, would indeed be, for Mead, the best evidence for the strength of his analysis, for any adequate articulation of the structure of human behavior must begin with, and elucidate the irreducible aspects of, the phenomenologically grasped features of experience. In light of the above analysis, the following discussion will show how Mead's phases of the act are implicitly entailed within Merleau-Ponty's phenomenological account of perceptual behavior, leading naturally to a field of perception similar in its features to those characterized by Mead.

Merleau-Ponty's phenomenology of perception, precisely as containing the thesis of "the primacy of perception," and not exclusive of the biological and behavioral dimensions emphasized by Mead, shows that perception emerges within an operative level of vital intentionality as an anticipatory orientation of the lived body.[74] Indeed, for Merleau-Ponty, human perception is inextricably linked to human action[75] which, as anticipatory in its receptivity of things perceived in the world, has the capacity "of orienting oneself in relation to the possible, to the mediate,"[76] thus distinguishing humans from animals in their limitation to their immediate milieu. The general aspects of human behavior brought together in this corporeally unified, vital intentionality are action, perception, and affectivity, each intertwined with the others, each reciprocally related to the others, and each revealing its aspects of original intentionality as essential features of existence. For Merleau-Ponty, then, the content of perception emerges within this basic and pervasive activity beneath the intentionality that posits objects and is constituted in action broadly considered. Thus all empiricist and intellectualist theories of perception are rendered false. It is within this context that Mead's four phases of the act are embryonically entailed. For Merleau-Ponty, perception, in its structure and process or passage and with its operative intentionality, contains an anticipatory attitude toward possible distance perception, a practical synthesis involving the pragma, a certain implicitly recognized manipulative aspect, and fulfillment or consummation. These can be explicated from his pervasive thesis of the primacy of perception at a level of operation or action below the split between subject and object as such.

This primacy of perception means that for Merleau-Ponty perception is irreducible in that it must be accounted for holistically as vital intentionality bringing to life a world of meanings within interactive experience rather than explained via reductionistic accounts. With this thesis Merleau-Ponty attempts to deal with the perceiving mind, reestablishing its roots in its body and in its world at the human level of behavior.[77] The perceived object as "present and living"[78] is the origin of objectivity and, as such, is not decomposable into a collection of sensations because "in it the whole is prior to its parts."[79] This whole is not an ideal whole, but rather occurs in an intentional "perceptual experience which gives us the passage from one moment to the next, which thus realizes the unity of time[80] and involves a "practical synthesis."[81] Merleau-Ponty states this thesis as follows: "that the experience of perception is our presence at the moment when things . . . are constituted for us; that perception is a nascent *Logos*; that it teaches us, outside all dogmatism, the true condition of objectivity itself, that it summons us to the task of knowledge and action."[82]

This task of action which pervades the primacy of perception leads to Mead's first phase of the act, for the impulse toward selective activity as the impetus for the whole act has its counterpart in Merleau-Ponty's phenomenology in the anticipatory dimension of perceptual experience mentioned above. This experience, as the attuned behavior aimed or directed toward a thing within an oriented focus, is already as such selective. Merleau-Ponty thus can be seen to interpret the anticipatory and sensory aspects of the structure of meaning to emerge within the context of prereflective, vital intentionality. It is not difficult to draw out the implication of this deepened sense of the structure of meaning and behavior.[83]

Although his context and style are different, Merleau-Ponty's treatment of distance in lived existence underlying scientific objectification converges with Mead's treatment of distance perception and of contact experience in the manipulatory stage of the act. For as with Mead's account, the perceptual stage in Merleau-Ponty's treatment can be seen to entail, within the very sense of vital intentionality, that process of mediation in which the possible contact experience appears with distance experience in the initial intentional projection. In Merleau-Ponty's account, perceived things can be seen to lead from what distant stimulation gives in terms of possibilities of fulfillment to what contact experience yields in terms of actual fulfillment.[84]

Further, a quasi-manipulative aspect is included within perceptual awareness, which is revealed first as "I can" rather than as "I think," manifesting motility (action) as basic intentionality. This practical synthesis and these phases of perception, entailed within the structure of behavior, are, as Merleau-Ponty constantly affirms against intellectualism, prior to that achieved by the understanding as such, so that the significance or structure of the thing perceived is not first and foremost a meaning for the understanding, but, rather, is a meaning in relation to this basic level of behavior. Emphasizing the practical, not as something to be done in the narrow sense, but, rather, as constitutive of human existence, Merleau-Ponty states: "We experience a perception and its horizon 'in action' (*pratiquement*) rather than by 'posing' them or explicitly 'knowing' them."[85] And again:

> In the action of the hand which is raised towards an object is contained a reference to the object, not as an object represented, but as that highly specific thing towards which we project ourselves, near which we are, in anticipation, and which we haunt. Consciousness is being-towards-the-thing through the intermediary of the body. A movement is learned when the body has understood, that is, when it has incorporated it into the 'world', and to move one's body is to aim at things through it; it is to allow oneself to respond to their call, which is made upon it independently of any representation.[86]

Hence, for Merleau-Ponty as for Mead, perceptual objects as simultaneous with the perceiver are constituted in action. When an object is seen at a distance, it is said to be already held, or still held. The object (e.g., the lamp) grasped at a distance is simultaneous with the perceiver, i.e., "distance is between simultaneous objects, and . . . this simultaneity is contained in the very meaning of perception."[87] The transitional-synthesis on this level is a synthesis not of disparate perspectives, but rather, one which brings about the passage from one perspective to the other, retaining, without mediation, a hold on one while anticipating others. Thus, distance cannot be understood by comparing various contents presented in an already constituted space, but, rather, in terms of this direct possession, and in terms of *"being in the distance* which links up with being where it appears."[88]

Though Merleau-Ponty's position, as represented above, includes action, it might at first seem that his emphasis on sight and vision contradicts Mead's emphasis on contact experience over that of sight. Merleau-Ponty's account of the inclusiveness of the perceptual object, however, actually confirms Mead's emphasis. For when Merleau-Ponty refers to the visual experience of an object, as for instance, seeing the lamp, he intends to include more than the detached or distant object seen. Rather, he aims explicitly to include the full ramifications of meaning structure, including the structure of the possible practical dimensions of the response. Thus, in his endeavor to account for the nonvisible sides of a perceptual object, revealing the synthesis as a practical one, he explicates the contact experience latent within the experience, noting that "I can touch the lamp, and not only the side turned toward me but also the other side; I have only to extend my hand to hold it."[89] Further, this analysis of perception yields precisely what is central to Mead's contact experience—a certain character of "resistance" of the perceived object which is evinced in Merleau-Ponty's view of the independence of the thing perceived.[90] Although the thing perceived is "for" the one perceiving, it is not given exhaustively, even though it is given as a whole, with its "unseen" or absent side present in the experience of the thing, but present precisely as "other" side. Hence, to some extent, Merleau-Ponty includes contact experience and a quasi-manipulative aspect in the primacy of perception within the fundamental structures of perceptual experience in existence. Further, it will now be seen that a certain commonness between the object perceived and the perceiver and the ability of the perceiver to take the role of the object makes perception possible.

If it were not for the common sensibility shared by both the body of the perceiver and the object perceived, there would be no perceived object.[91] It is in this context that the other objects, just as the other person, can be considered to allow the sentient organism to experience its own sensibility. For in attempting to draw a commonness between the perceiver and the perceived, between the seer and the seen, Merleau-Ponty is led to their common sensibility, the overlapping or intertwining of touching with touched, in the hand for instance, which, in touching, can be touched by the other hand, thus becoming the touching touched. It is clear, then, that in order to sense, it also must be sensible, and this sensibility is shared with the whole sensible realm. Hence, it can be said, enigmatically perhaps, that the tree which I see sees me[92] in the sense that I am visible from that standpoint as it is from mine; because we are both sensible, we are both made of the same stuff, the flesh of the world. This can be seen to involve a sense of role taking which is central to Merleau-Ponty's philosophy, which reveals a common interest shared with Mead, and which will, like Mead's understanding of role taking, be explicitly developed in relation to the self in chapter 4.[93] For there is a certain element of role taking in the attitude that the tree is looking back at me, as a role which I appropriate of something sensible viewing me as a sensible, showing the possibility of a perspective on me from the role of the perceived object, and possibly making me aware of the sensible within myself. Resistance, then, and other possible perspectives on an object are due to the shared sensibility of the perceiver and the perceived below the disjunction of subject and object, itself made possible and brought to awareness by a certain sense of role taking. It is precisely this latent sense of role taking, together with the phases of the act uncovered above, which rounds out the implicit dimensions of Mead's philosophy of the act in Merleau-Ponty's phenomenology of perception. It can be seen, then, that Merleau-Ponty's phenomenological descriptions implicitly entail not only Mead's stages of the act in a narrow sense, but also other pervasive features of activity which enter into the constitution of the object.

This chapter has attempted to show that though Mead's pragmatism and Merleau-Ponty's phenomenology may at first seem to represent two alien, even conflicting, approaches to the understanding of human behavior, they share a common view of the nonreductionistic, anticipatory activity or orientation of the lived body, as well as of the way in which the objects of awareness emerge within the context of a field of such activity. The implicit but pervasive phenomenological dimension of Mead's pragmatic approach becomes highlighted in the context of Merleau-Ponty's phenomenological focus, while Mead's stages of the act can be used to draw out implicit dimensions of Merleau-Ponty's phenomenological descriptions. This shared understanding of the emergence of perceptual objects within the context of holistic, anticipatory bodily activity represents their common rejection of a tradition of philosophy that begins with one of the several variations of the subject-object split, attempting then to deal with all the insurmountable problems such a beginning entails.

2. "SENSATION," OBJECT, AND WORLD: THE HOLISTIC VIEW

THE DISCUSSION OF the nonreductionistic and holistic interpretations of perception by both Mead and Merleau-Ponty can take two directions: that of a focus upon the involvement of the senses within perception, and that of a focus upon the world as the background for all perception. Both philosophers examine the field of perception to show its inextricable relation to the active role of the sensing body and to the world. Indeed, it is through the sensible body that the perceiver has a world, while it is from the backdrop of 'world' that its sensing takes shape. This chapter will turn first to the sensing dimension of experience and then more explicitly to the general backdrop of 'world' within which all sensing takes place.

For Mead, the perceived object is an extricable part of the environment, and as indicated in the previous chapter, this environment is brought to bear in the perception of the object.[1] Thus Mead stresses that perceptual unity is not a unity belonging to a single object, "but to the entire field, to the situation in which the object occurs,"[2] and approvingly details the import of James's concept of "the fringe."[3] While perception focuses the whole of the situational field in the object, the object focuses its whole in the "sensation." The stable core established by contact experience, which allows both for a permanent space and for the constancy of the object, "answers to varying experiences while it remains the same."[4] While the contact characters remain congruent with themselves,[5] any change of position varies the distance characters. Yet the constancy of the core or contact object roots the constancy of the distance qualities that vary with changing positions. Thus, we see the distant individuals as having the dimensions of those at close range.[6] Any sensing, then, takes place within a field and within the context of an act.[7] As Mead states, "In the end what we see, hear, feel, taste, and smell depends upon what we are doing, and not the reverse."[8]

The contextual nature of the sensing dimension of experience is brought into focus in Mead's discussion of "the much belabored penny,"[9] in which he shows that the correlation of the image on the retina and the visual object is a thoroughly misleading relationship.[10] One sees the penny as round though the contour present to the eye is an oval or a line. One actually sees the visual datum in the form in which one would see it in another situation. In this case, a favored perspective virtually substitutes for what is given in the so-called sense datum. This cannot be accounted for by the fusing of one content with another, for one cannot fuse an oval and a circle. It is not a substitution of the visual image of one retina for the image of the other, for one cannot recover the image that is rejected and hold as well the one that is selected. The so-called sense datum is not a mere visual content but rather is indicative of the experience of manipulation, and it is seen in terms of such activity. As Mead summarizes:

> From one position we see the penny as round even though it is an oval form that registers itself upon the retina, because its oval character is the stimulus to the movement which will bring it into what is the standard form for our conduct with reference to the penny. To see the penny in the character of integrating the movement to bring it into the normal position is to see it as round.[11]

Because of this, a shift in attitude can bring about a shift in the actual datum of experience. When the ellipticity of the penny serves as a stimulus to initiate the movement to bring it into the normal position, it serves in a mediate capacity, and the penny is seen as round. Changing the attitude toward the ellipticity can place the visual form of the penny in a final rather than a mediate capacity. Mead stresses that it is a mistake to assume that the ellipticity was there in that character in the earlier situation, in which it served a mediate function. Thus, the attitude "plays a most important part in determining the actual content that appears as the distance experience."[12] For this reason, the so-called illusory aspects of things are, in most cases, adequate cues for normal behavior, for characters which would be inconsistent within the same temporal phase of the act can consistently mediate the attitudes which represent the successive development of it.

Mead notes that in certain cases, as, for example, the bent stick in the water, it is not possible to so organize attitudes that the content of the perception answers univocally to an ultimate attitude. In this case, perceptual judgment rectifies the perceptual illusion. This point leads to two related issues: the status of these perceptual illusions and the relation between the immediate percept and the perceptual judgment. In illusory perceptual experience, the so-called illusory characters of things are "there" in the environment. "Nature in its relationship to the organism, is a perspective that is there."[13] To have common perceptual objects is to have the distinctively human ability to share perspectives; to share perspectives is to share attitudes. Such common or shared perspectives are not built up of individual perspectives, but rather individual perspectives emerge from the backdrop of the common perspective. Individual perspectives are not subjective, for all perspectives, common and individual, are there in nature; any perspective represents the relation between an organism and a part of its environment. The organism is in the perspective, not the perspective in the organism. "These perspectives of nature exist in nature, not in the consciousness of the organism as a stuff."[14] The usual distinction between objectivity and so-called subjectivity is in fact the distinction between the common and the individual perspective.[15]

Mead states that the contrast between the immediate percept and the perceptual judgment lies in the fact that in the judgment there is "the passage from some character to a consequence by way of an indicated meaning."[16] Yet this passage is already there in the percept. Because of past judgments, one can now "immediately perceive" the meaning of the characters of the percept, which are now fused into the "immediate perception." Thus the distinction between the percept and the perceptual judgment is a context-relative functional distinction. This shows that Mead has established a new understanding of *immediacy* within experience. Immediate experience is no longer the experience of pure immediacy, of raw data. Physical objects, as well as social objects, are immediately perceived.[17] All experience incorporates judgments of perception. These must be distinguished from reflective judgments or judgments of second level reflections such as those of science, but they are judgments nonetheless, though Mead recognizes that "the term 'judgment' in immediate experience is probably a misnomer."[18] Immediate experience incorporates judgments of perception in the sense that immediate experience is shot through with interpretive elements. It is not the experience of pure immediacy. The sense object is something the body can grasp, and its functional unity within experience is brought about by the vital intentionality or purposive activity of the body, which establishes the stable core, not by some abstract subjectivity or the association of brute data. There is not first an experience of separate senses which are synthesized, but rather a unity of sensory experience brought about by the activity of the lived body. Thus Mead states, "We see the object as hard."[19] As he elaborates such a position, "The objects about us are unitary objects, not simple sums of the parts into which analysis would resolve them. And they are what they are in relation to organisms whose environment they constitute."[20] The behaviorally founded meanings which provide such unity are themselves objective; they belong to the things.[21]

Before turning to an examination of Mead's understanding of *world*, the ensuing discussion will focus first on Merleau-Ponty's understanding of *sensation* and *immediacy*, and then on Mead's and Merleau-Ponty's respective understandings of the general structure of the meanings that inform the awareness of any content.

Sensation, through the body, is the living contact and existing encounter with things. "Sensations, 'sensible qualities,' are then far from being reducible to a certain indescribable state or *quale*; they present themselves with a motor physiognomy, and are enveloped in a living significance."[22] This focus on sensation will allow these living relations obtaining between the perceiver and the body, and the perceiver and the sensible and perceptual fields, to emerge, drawing out the findings of originary intentionality.[23]

This vital intentionality[24] on the level of sensibility is comparable to a communion in that sensation not only has a vital and motor significance, but is our openness upon the field. Our body is the place of this communion or coexistence.[25] By calling sensation communion or coexistence, Merleau-Ponty means "that it does not rest in itself as does a thing, but that it is directed and has significance beyond itself."[26] The thing from a certain particular place within the field does not cause a reaction, but has a significance, as seen in chapter 1, and is a being which is *acted* upon and seized by our body. Hence sensation is a coexistence in that it is a process toward that which elicits such a response, and in that each of the separate senses acts in a unity with, rather than in separation from, the others. Thus, the thing is presented through the unified senses and not through the operation of one isolated sense.[27]

Merleau-Ponty, attempting to clarify how the sensible and the sensing enter into the experience of sensation, tries to do justice to the truth of realism or empiricism and of intellectualism or idealism, but without subscribing to any of these. There is a certain independence to the thing perceived, while, at once, it comes to experience only as perceived and "for us." Neither acts while the other suffers the action, nor does one confer significance on the other. Unless the eye or the hand is synchronized with the sensible, the sensible is only a vague beckoning.[28] Thus one can see the blue of the sky or touch a hard surface only at the invitation of its sensible aspects. Further, even on so rudimentary a level as sensation, any particular sensation takes place within a field. Precisely because of this field of sensation, the eye, the hand, etc., guess the movement which will fix the perception.

This field character of sensation must not be misunderstood in any realist sense, but rather, in the context of Merleau-Ponty's intention to rectify the Husserlian notions of constituting and constituted by getting beneath them, to arrive at a primordial, lived level of our link to the perceptual field through sensation. Rather than interpret the forms and meanings to exist somehow "out there" in a world, or closed inside the mind, he clarifies the unity of reciprocity of sensible and sensing in sensation on a level prior to that of conscious acts, accounting for the independence of the object or thing, while, at the same time, doing justice to its full emergence as meaningful at a level prior to the distinction between subject and object.[29] Thus, in rejecting both intellectualism and empiricism, Merleau-Ponty has undercut the theory of the synthesis effected by a judgment which achieves the unity of the matter of discrete sense data. Below or prior to this level of understanding and its ideal signification taken in the narrow sense is the fundamental level of corporeal intentionality or the structure of behavior overlooked by empiricism and intellectualism.[30]

This fundamental and originary level of synthesis involves a meaning structure on the existential level.[31] Accordingly, the signification of the thing is not first and foremost a meaning for the understanding taken in a narrow sense, but a meaning in relation to this basic level of behavior, already unified before being taken up on the derived level. This corporeal intentionality is expressed in terms of existence in the following text: "Thus the thing is correlative to my body and, in more general terms, to my existence, of which my body is merely the stabilized structure. It is constituted in the hold which my body takes upon it; it is not first of all a meaning for the understanding, but a structure accessible to inspection by the body."[32]

At this level, a change in the notion of the "immediate" is required so that "the immediate is no longer the impression, the object which is one with the subject, but the meaning, the structure, the spontaneous arrangement of parts."[33] If the impression, instead of the meaning or structure, is mistaken for the immediate, it is because perception in experience is taken for granted in favor of the object perceived and hence is easily overlooked by reflection. Thus, correcting this tendency, he states: "The structure of the actual perception alone can teach us what perception is. The pure impression is, therefore, not only undiscoverable, but also imperceptible and so inconceivable as an instant of perception."[34]

The synthesis of our senses on this originary level, achieved by perception, is comparable to the synthesis of binocular vision. In binocular vision, when the gaze is fixed on something far away, retaining the focus on the far away, something near, such as a finger close to the eyes, gives rise to a double image. Each eye seems to some extent to have its images separately. If the person refocuses, then the object appears as it is, and is seen as one thing. This example shows that the two images do not merely become one image by means of a refocusing, but that the unity of the object is intentional. Furthermore, the unity is brought about by the body, not by an epistemological subject, as the intellectualist would have it. Since this synthesis is a corporeal and intentional synthesis and not a synthesis of some pure consciousness, it is experienced on the object itself in the world instead of in some thinking subject. The distinction between perceptual synthesis and intellectual synthesis is manifest in the fact that "I am aware of progressing toward the object itself and finally enjoying its concrete presence."[35] Thus, perception gives the thing from the first because the senses are not disconnected and autonomous, as though each were fixed only for one type of sense-data; our sensibility is a whole from the start, a synergy, so that what affects one organ is latently announced to all organs. And it is the body as a unified system of perceptual powers which unifies the sensible thing from its sensible aspects, the color, the form, the texture, the sound, the taste. Thus, it can truly be said that we see the softness or hardness or that we feel the color of an object.

For Merleau-Ponty, this intentional unity emerging from the unity of the body can be explicated by further comparing the synthesis of binocular vision with the perceptual synthesis:

> Let us apply it to the problem of the unity of the senses. It cannot be understood in terms of their subsumption under a primary consciousness, but of their never-ending integration into one knowing organism. The intersensory object is to the visual object what the visual object is to the monocular images of double vision, and the senses interact in perception as the two eyes collaborate in vision. The sight of sounds or the hearing of colors come about in the same way as the unity of the gaze through the two eyes: in so far as my body is, not a collection of adjacent organs, but a synergic system, all the functions of which are exercised and linked together in the general action of being in the world, in so far as it is the congealed face of existence.[36]

This corporeal unity of the intersensory object gives significance to both the natural object and to cultural objects. "In short, my body is not only an object among all other objects, a nexus of sensible qualities among others, but an object which is sensitive to all the rest, which reverberates to all sounds, vibrates to all colors, and provides words with their primordial significance through the way in which it receives them."[37] Merleau-Ponty's thesis of the primacy of perception involves the perceived realm of existential, corporeal intentionality as the context for the emergence of sensation. This existential focus on sensation gives rise to a deepening interpretation of sensation, as will now be seen.

In *The Visible and the Invisible*, Merleau-Ponty begins within the perceptual faith, which lives in the belief that what is perceived is the really real, and in which it is taken for granted that we have access to the things themselves. Reminding one of the treatment in *Phenomenology of Perception* of the thing and the natural world, Merleau-Ponty focuses in *Visible and Invisible* on the seen red in order to show the reflective character of sense.[38] This seen red, rather than an atomic datum, already requires a response of the seer in the focusing of the eye. As he says in "Eye and Mind," "Quality, light, color, depth, which are there before us, are there only because they awaken an echo in our body and because the body welcomes them."[39] For Merleau-Ponty, the seen red is not isolated from other colors or from other qualities, or from the depth of the thing revealed through this "surface appearance" of something which has depth and which is more than I see of it. And it is precisely this overlapping and intertwining which is the "chiasm."

Merleau-Ponty here develops a view of sensibility as a sort of concrete and corporeal reflection and integrates it with chiasm and flesh.[40] In this context flesh is a "general thing," a style or "element of being," and involves sensibility as embodying a sort of concrete and corporeal reflection. The flesh is a place where a "sort of reflection" takes place. This body as such is not the flesh, and the flesh of the body expresses the body as a reflexive generality, a "general thing midway between the spatio-temporal individual and the idea, a sort of incarnate principle that brings a style of being wherever there is a fragment of Being."[41] My body is to the greatest extent what everything is: "a dimensional this."[42]

In focusing on sensation from the direction of the primacy of perception in Merleau-Ponty's philosophy, one of the two possible directions of analysis[43] arising from perception has been pursued to explicate the ramifications of such a view for sensation, revealing that the past reductionistic interpretations of sensation are no longer viable. Thus, Merleau-Ponty, like Mead, has been seen to establish a new understanding of immediacy in experience, a new understanding which brings along with it a view of intersensory unity and constancy which is a function of both the stable core of the object and the holistic behavior of the lived body.

The above discussion has indicated that sensing is not the mere having of given data but rather involves the manner in which data are "taken." For Mead and Merleau-Ponty alike, the most rudimentary sensing is shot through with the meaningful experience of a field of objects. The ensuing discussion will turn to their respective understandings of the structure of the meanings which inform all sensing as well as all awareness in general.

For Mead, the "triadic relation holds between organism and nature,"[44] and this triadic relationship is incorporated within the very structure of meaning. Meaning, for Mead, is neither subjective nor psychological. It has an existence which can perhaps best be termed logical, for it arises out of a triadic relational matrix. Meaning is an emergent which arises out of a behavioral context and has a relational existence which is dependent upon this context but is not reducible to it.[45] And, it is this structure of meaning which allows for the emergence of universality in experience.

Mead notes that though an experience itself happens and is gone, never to be repeated, there is something recognized, a universal character given in the experience itself, which is capable of an indefinite number of repetitions. He states this character of the experience in terms of the response. In so far as the response is one that can take place with reference, for example, to the brick, the stone, or the hammer, there is a universal in the form of the response that answers to a whole set of particulars, and the particulars may be indefinite in number, provided only that they have certain characters in relation to the response. As Mead stresses, "The universality which we perceive in the individual cannot be mere similarity."[46] The universality, in a strict sense, lies not in the response or in the stimuli, but in the relationship between the response and an indefinite number of particular stimuli. He states that this "relationship of response to an indefinite number of stimuli is just the relationship that is represented in what we call recognition. When we use the term 'recognition' we may mean no more than that we pick out an object that serves this particular purpose."[47] This purpose of which Mead speaks must be characterized by consciousness of attitudes, of muscular tensions, or the feel or readiness to act in the presence of certain stimulations. In short, purpose or vital intentionality is an anticipatory habit or a disposition to act, and the phenomenological sense of its regulative, anticipatory functioning enters into the very tone and character of perceptual awareness, thus belying all forms of reductionistic understandings of perception. In this sense, the universal meaning determines the particulars that will be subsumed under it. Objects are not simply there to call out particular responses from which we abstract to obtain the universal response that answers to the particular stimuli of the particular objects, but rather the objects or stimuli which call out the particular responses have themselves been carved out of the experience continuum in accordance with our purposes or meanings in the form of dispositions to act. Thus Mead can claim that "the universals of a purely classificatory biology are really less than the particulars, while genuine universals are the source of them.[48]

To say that meaning *is* a disposition to act, however, is an oversimplification which obscures the relational nature of meanings. Mead states that "some sort of image with sensuous content . . . must accompany any concept, however abstract this may be."[49] Again, the image occurs "in varying degrees as the cognitive act is of the nature of sensuous recognition and conceptual interpretation."[50] Two points here become clear: sensuous recognition involves interpretive elements, and no concept, however abstract, is possible without some imagery. Sensuous recognition and conceptual interpretation do not represent two completely distinct cognitive acts, but rather, two ends of a continuum in which they are continually interwoven. Thus Mead stresses that "there can be no hard and fast line drawn between such perceptual consciousness and the more abstracted processes of so-called reasoning."[51]

Mead explicitly refuses to equate imagery and sensation, but he does hold that imagery always contains a core of sensuous content.[52] The basis of imagery is termed "sensuous" in that it must have reference to what is sensuously given in experience. Imagery, with its basic core of "sensuous content" must provide much of the criteria by which we are able to have sensuous recognition, for "it is most frequently the image which enables the individual to pick out the appropriate stimulus for the impulse which is seeking expression."[53] Thus, imagery, as having reference to what is sensuously given in experience, provides a criterion of recognition for the meaningful delineation of experience.

A clear example of this relation is given by Mead in speaking of the characteristics of the chair. He notes that "the lasting character of such an experience will not be found primarily in the so-called sensuous content of the stimulation but in the persistent attitude of the form toward it, though the persistent character of the attitude is mediated by this content."[54] The image or structure, which appears in the absence of the objects to which it refers, and which has a sensuous core which appears in the absence of the sensuous elements to which it refers, allows this logical relation between purpose and stimulus, or between response and object, to exist apart from the actual experiences which are denoted by the meaning. There are not merely two analytic factors involved but rather a triadic relationship.[55] While the sensuous core refers to the instigation of the act, the image refers to the completion of a set of relevant acts which in turn "fills in" the sensuous core. Thus, Mead states that in the physical object or percept the sensuous stimulation is merged with imagery from past experience of the result of acts which this stimulus sets going.[56]

If meaning is to emerge from a triadic relationship, however, there must be, in addition to the above three factors involved, that which makes them a triadic relationship or system rather than a mere collection. That binding element is the vital intentionality of habit as the living meaning which binds into a unity the various structural aspects of meaning. This does not imply, however, that there is a temporal priority of the three elements which in turn are unified by habit. Habit determines reaction, and furthermore, only as habit performs its function of unifying sensory core and reaction does imagery emerge at all. Though Mead presents a genetic approach in his discussion of meaning, his analysis of the structure of meaning is ultimately logical rather than either temporal or psychological. He speaks of the relationship of "particulars as stimuli that answer to the universals of our responses" as the "relation of implication."[57] Again, he speaks of the sensitivity of the organism determining its environment as a logical rather than a causal relationship and of "logical relations which pass into meanings."[58] The above discussion concerns precisely this passage of relations into the internal structure of meanings.

This relational structure existing within meaning between universal purpose and particular stimulus does not reintroduce particularity within meaning. Imagery, as having reference to the denoted objects of experience, without in fact being the objects, is part of the universality of meaning. The image—and thus also, it is to be supposed, the sensuous "core" of imagery—can never be a determinate singular. The meaning which arises out of this relational matrix held apart from actual denoted experiences cannot be reduced to the content of any particular experience, whether imagined or actual. What serves as the "particular stimulus" within the structure of meaning is itself a universal constituted at a more fundamental level. Meaning in all its relational aspects forms a principle or rule of interpretation as opposed to the manifold of particulars delineated or organized by it.

The image, as part of meaning, is required for the interpretation of experience, yet imagery is always memory imagery.[59] The role of memory in the establishment of imagery is built into Mead's analysis of imagery. Thus, it can arise only from our past interaction with the objects of experience. Yet without memory imagery there can be no objects of experience. This, however, does not imply a vicious circle of any sort, for two reasons. For Mead, there does not exist in experience such a thing as a "pure purpose" or "pure concept" on the one hand, and a "pure stimulus" or "pure sensory datum" on the other. The distinction is an analytic distinction, made for purposes of clarity, for in experience the two are found only in interaction. Secondly, a distinction must be made between the genetic origin of our meanings and the epistemic or phenomenological priority of these meanings. Genetically, meaning must have arisen from experience or interaction with an environment. Epistemically or logically, this meaning must be prior to any delineation or classification of what is presented in experience. Our purposes arise through interaction with an environment, but it is only through these purposes that we can inform the environment with meaning. This is a cumulative process based on the pragmatic interplay between meanings and experience. With the above analysis in mind, the discussion will turn to Merleau-Ponty's position which, though not as fully developed as Mead's, can yet be seen to embryonically contain the same general thrust.

Merleau-Ponty's emphasis upon the binding element of vital intentionality as an originary and anticipatory structure of behavior implicitly includes elements similar to Mead's view of disposition or habit and rule. The anticipatory structure is an orientation to receive, allowing for the senseful encounter with any entity given within experience, but regulated by this anticipatory structure.

Merleau-Ponty's understanding of the structure of meaning requires the altered view of immediacy discussed above. The immediate is not the impression, but rather the fundamental meaning in its structure and the object to which it gives access.[60] He avoids the modern prejudices of rationalism and empiricism with their split between subject and object by beginning, within the changed notion of immediacy, on the corporeal level of intentionality. The body has been seen to have a central role on the fundamental level of unity or of meaning in basic human rapport with the given. In this unique unity of perceived and perceiving is found the ground for all human behavior and meaning. Within this context it is not difficult to draw out the implication of this deepened sense of the structure of meaning.[61]

Merleau-Ponty deals with the perception of a thing as already given in that it is taken up in experience in so far as it is bound up with a field, "the basic structure of which we carry with us, and of which it is merely one of many possible concrete forms."[62] Although it is a part of our lived experience, it is not reducible to the here and now of our life because the human body has habits which constitute a human environment.[63] This sensible field has a certain foundational dimension in that all of the intersensory relations are anchored in it, and it is the "schema of intersensory relations."[64] For Merleau-Ponty, this is not a system of invariable relations or of changeless categories, or intellectual unities providing the possibility for knowledge.[65] The kind of corporeal understanding of which Merleau-Ponty speaks is unintelligible in terms of subsuming a sense-datum under an idea. For Merleau-Ponty, the general and anticipatory aspects of something emerge in terms of the experience of a bodily presence, and is not founded on the recognition of some law. To clarify how the experience of a thing through meaning is possible in terms of general characters, a brief account of habit is helpful.

For Merleau-Ponty the acquisition of a habit is a bodily grasping of a meaning entailing the motor grasp of a motor significance.[66] Every habit, however, is both motor and perceptual.[67] Merleau-Ponty employs the example of a blind man using a stick as an example of a motor habit, since the movements of the stick in hand mediate the objects and their field for him. This is equally an example of perceptual habit, since the blind man has extended his perception by using the stick as an extended limb. To show that such a habit consists neither in reflective knowing nor in conditioned reflex, and yet is motor and perceptual, the example of typing is employed. To know how to type is not to know the exact place of each letter among the keys, or to have acquired a conditioned reflex allowing the hitting of certain keys at certain specific signals from outside as causes. Rather, this habit is a "knowledge in the hands."[68] Thus, the phenomenon of habit requires a revision in our notions of understanding and body. Habit has its abode in the body as mediator of a field.[69] The bodily understanding which goes on in habit means that to understand is "to experience the harmony between what we aim at and what is given, between the intention and the performance."[70] It is the body which "gives to our life the form of generality, and develops our personal acts into stable dispositional tendencies."[71] And it is precisely the "form of generality" and "stable dispositional tendencies" which constitute the anticipatory structures of meaning on this corporeal level as entailing a concrete universal.

Thus, after rejecting the reductive interpretations of sense experience and the derivative sense of understanding, the descriptive account of sense and understanding within their essential connection to corporeal intentionality leads to the conclusion that the connective function is "spread over the whole intentional life."[72] This then requires the attempt to bring out the "instinctive substructure" and "the superstructure erected upon it by the exercise of intelligence."[73] Clearly then, such an amorphous spread or continuum includes both the anticipatory structure as an orientation to receive and the senseful element, but not spelled out as distinctive acts. On this level, any grasp of such a sensory element already contains an interpretive or general element and any concrete understanding contains the element of sense. Further, every conceptual element, no matter how derivative or abstract, must contain some reference to the sensory to be meaningful. Merleau-Ponty seems to agree with Mead that the sensory recognition and the intellectual interpretation are not totally distinct cognitive acts, but represent two ends of a continuum. Any grasp of the sensory already includes an intellectual interpretive element, and any concept, no matter how abstract, must have reference to the sensuous to be meaningful. It is within this relationship that universality emerges within experience through the unifying role of bodily habits.

For Mead and Merleau-Ponty alike, then, the inseparable linkage of the structure of human behavior and the content of human perception is incorporated within the very nature of the meanings which inform all human awareness. To round out the dimensions of the perceptual field, the following discussion will turn to their respective understandings of 'world.'

It has been seen that for Mead the object of perception is by its very nature a part of an environment which has bearing on the perception of the object. This is possible because of the anticipatory orientation of the lived body which gives rise to a perceived world. For Mead, "the world that is there" as the experiential horizon, as the encompassing frame of reference or field of interest of organism-environment interaction, provides the ultimate fundamental constancy which roots the constancy of the thing. Thus, while the thing grounds the constancy of qualities, the world grounds the constancy of the thing. Or, conversely, while experienced qualities are always qualities of the "thing," the "thing" is always a "thing in the world." The stable core, the resistance character of the object, thus opens in one direction toward the shaping of the sensing dimension of experience and in the other direction toward the horizons of world.

Meaning, for Mead, comes to be in human behaviorial rapport with that which gives itself in experience, but meaning is already "there" for conscious acts, because conscious acts emerge within a meaningful world. The world is the world of perception, the perceived world, the field of perception in which things emerge as meaningful within experience. Individuals live in a world of things of which they are not conscious, an experienced world in which noncognitive, prereflective acts take place and within which reflection arises. Such a world is the basic context of meaning for all perception, and therefore for all sensation. The relation of "sensation" and world within the structure of the perceived object is aptly captured in Mead's claim that

> It is palpably illegitimate to resolve all reality into such terms of individual experience, after the fashion of the phenomenalist or positivist, since the very definition and distinctive character of the individual's experience are dependent upon its peculiar relation to a world which may not be stated in such terms, which is not analyzed, but is simply there.[74]

The world that is there is both independent and constituted. Though it is indeed "there" as the context of meanings within which reflective acts take place, it is what it is partially through its relatedness to an organism. As Mead states of the unquestioned perceptual world within which reflective experience arises,

> It is the world that is there in independence of the self, though the reference to the self as point of reference is always implied. That is, the distinction between here and there, between now and then, which has meaning only with reference to the organism, is involved in all conduct however unreflective. We live, then, in a world that is independent of us, except in so far as we determine its perspective, but within this world lies a field of so-called consciousness in which appear the character and meanings of things.[75]

Mead concisely captures these two dimensions in his assertion that "In a sense there exists an absolute universe of events, but . . . . There is no absolute world of things."[76] Or, as he also describes the world that is there, it is at once a "slab of nature" yet also dependent on "the teleological determination of the individual."[77] Mead can hold, then, that although we can conceive of a nature that would not be uniform, we cannot so conceive of a world. The experienced world must exhibit uniformity because it is partially constituted by anticipatory, selective human activity.[78]

The inherent relatedness of world to the lived body is evinced in Mead's claim that "the world about us is a set of ends to be reached or avoided."[79] Indeed, "The perceptual world is made up of ends and means."[80] The purposive activity or vital intentionality of the human organism thus provides the behavioral "schema" of the fundamental horizons of world. In this way Mead can hold that, the "perceptual world . . . is itself a perspective."[81] The universe, as it enters the horizons of human experience, is a meaningful world which is what it is in part because of its relation to the organism. For Mead, world, things, and the individual are mutually determinative. He holds that the world functions as the "conditions of the act," yet the act allows for the emergence of world, things, and self.[82] "The world, things, and the individual are what they are"[83] through the situations into which they enter, situations which "are not those of appearances or phenomena which inadequately reflect an absolute reality. These situations are the reality."[84] Precisely this very nature of Mead's world that is there as requiring the interwoven dimensions of the independent and the constituted is unrecognized in Natanson's claim that Mead holds an implicit dualism between the world as given and as constituted, a dualism which he claims is rooted in the irreconcilable conflict between Mead the pragmatist and Mead the phenomenologist.[85]

The world that is there has the dimensions not only of being both constituted and independent, but also of being both shared or common, and individually unique. The common world is the precondition for the individual perspective, yet the world exists uniquely for each individual. The common world that is there and which lends its character to the character of an individual experience is what it is through its relatedness to the vital intentionality constitutive of prereflective behavior. And, though the individual perspective, the unique, emerges within the context of the common world, the individual perspective can in turn change that common world. This dynamic can best be understood by anticipating the next chapter and turning very briefly to the temporal nature of the world that is there.

Mead holds that the world that is there is "continually ceasing to be as it passes into the world of the following moment."[86] The world that is there changes with time in part because it incorporates the results of previous reflection, reflection which arises in the experience of the individual in the form of novel hypotheses. As he states,

> The common world is continually breaking down. Problems arise in it and demand solution. They appear as the exceptions . . . in the experience of individuals and while they have the form of common experiences they run counter to the structure of the common world. The experience of the individual is precious because it preserves these exceptions. But the individual preserves them in such form that others can experience them, that they may become common experience. . . . If they have been put in the form of common experiences, the task appears of reconstructing the common world so that they may have their place and become instances instead of exceptions.[87]

Mead holds that the seemingly unchanging character of the world results from the generally fixed conditions which provide the contexts for the problematic situations which undergo directed change through the creation of hypotheses initiated by individuals in order to resolve problems. The possibility of calling into question any content, whatever it may be, means always that there is left a field of unquestioned, stable reality.[88]

Experience, then, is first had in a world about which there is neither doubt nor conscious belief.[89] Such a world is the precondition for the emergence of doubt and conscious belief, for questioning cannot occur without the world as the context within which the doubt and questioning make sense. Thus, the very dynamics of human experience as manifesting experimental or scientific method require the backdrop of world for all that takes place in perception. The doubtful arises within the context of the world, and within the doubtful situation, data, abstracted in terms of the problem situation, gain their meaning. In one sense it can be said that the world that was there, and out of which problems arise, becomes a different world because of new sharable meanings that emerge in the resolution of a problem. Yet, in its deepest sense, the doubting and questioning which changed the world that was there could only occur within a context which did not change but lent the preflective constancy of its meaning to the meaningfulness of both the problem and its resolution. Thus, in a sense we restructure the world. Yet, in another sense, we restructure only within the world.

It is within this context that Mead's doctrine of truth can best be understood. As he himself is quick to point out, "The crux of such a doctrine, of course, lies in the common world."[90] This in turn, is interwoven for Mead with his understanding of the nature of experience as experimental. As was seen in chapter 1, experience is experimental for Mead in that the very nature of human activity involves selective, creative activity guided by direction and noetically transformative of its environment. Truth is the missing facet of this previous description of scientific method. Truth emerges in the process of experimental activity within a common world when problematic situations are resolved by restructuring a part of the world that is there in ways which work, which allow ongoing conduct, that had been stopped by a conflict of meanings, to continue.[91] In this sense, "truth is synonymous with the solution of the problem."[92] These points incorporate what Mead sees as the two phases of pragmatic doctrine as pertains to truth: "the testing of a hypothesis by its working" and an approach which "brings the process of knowing inside of conduct."[93]

Mead's position is a thoroughgoing rejection of both correspondence and coherence theories of truth. The concept of correspondence makes no sense within the structure of Mead's position, for there is no fixed, structured reality to provide one pole of the correspondence relationship. It has been seen that neither the world within which knowledge emerges, nor the data abstracted to resolve its conflicts, are independent of the structurings of human activity. Thus he states that "when the hypothesis works it ceases to be a hypothesis; it is reality, not eternal, indefeasible reality, but the only reality with which we are acquainted, which we fear or hope will break down or be again reconstructed."[94] Mead realizes that such a claim may seem to "sweep us into the current of Idealism," and its coherence theory of truth,[95] but he aptly notes that though any relational complex must be coherent if it is to be used in an adequate fashion, "coherency is not truth. It is not the coherence of doctrine but its cogency that implicates truth, and cogency resides ever in the field of activity."[96] Additionally, according to Mead, idealism with its coherence theory of truth ultimately involves, like the correspondence theory, the concepts of copying or resembling.[97]

Mead further criticizes both coherence and correspondence because they allow for—at times demand—the wholesale questioning of experience itself. This criticism again brings out the two "phases" of the pragmatic theory of truth, for "if the pragmatic doctrine is a logical generalization of scientific method, it cannot merge the problem that engages thought with a larger problem which denies validity to the conditions that are the necessary tests of the solution which thought is seeking."[98] Any questioning must take place within a context of experience, or world that is there, which is not brought into question, but which allows the questioning and reconstruction to take place within it. "The only test that can be offered of the truth of the reconstruction lies in the fitting in of the hypothesis into the common world insofar as it is not affected by the problem, which appeared in the exception."[99] In this way, this relation of the old and new is understood not in terms of the relation between a subjective world and an objective universe, but as a process of logical reconstruction by which out of exceptions or problems a new law or interpretation arises to replace a meaning structure that has become inadequate.[100] And, in this way, the relation which constitutes truth can best be understood as neither coherence nor correspondence but rather as "agreement" or "fitting."[101]

In light of the above discussion, two possible misconceptions should be anticipated. First, it should be reemphasized here that the focus on scientific method in relation to truth does not make knowing only for the sake of doing.[102] Mead clearly recognizes the importance of knowledge for its own sake, stressing that, in determining the possibilities which changing conditions bring, "our world of reality thus becomes independent of any special ends or purposes and we reach an entirely disinterested knowledge.... Knowledge for its own sake ... alone makes possible the continual reconstruction and enlargement" of situations.[103]

Secondly, his focus does not relegate truth to the level of linguistic assertions, but rather, just the opposite, brings truth down to its foundations, in existence. A proposition is a "presentation in symbolic form of the copula stage of the judgment,"[104] while "truth expresses a relationship between the judgment and reality."[105] And, as this translates in his "formula," "the relationship lies between the reconstruction, which enables conduct to continue, and the reality within which conduct advances."[106]

Truth then, arises within the process of experience, within the world that is there, through the dynamics of experimental inquiry. The adequacy of the application of any hypothesis, of any bestowing of meaning within experience, from the most abstract articulations of science to the most prereflective behavioral grasp of things in the world, lies in the ongoing conduct of the biological organism immersed in the natural world. In this way, "when we act in such or such a fashion," what we expect to happen does in fact do so. To achieve this is the function of scientific method.[106] Or to express this situation in terms of the phenomenological dimension of Mead's pragmatism, through the functioning of scientific method we are able to correctly anticipate the appearance of what is meant.[108] This characterization leads us to Merleau-Ponty's understanding of the world and the emergence of truth within it.

Since the perceiver has a world through the sensible body in its sensing, the analysis of sensation throws into focus the vital relation of the perceiver to his body and to his world.[109] This body, as part of the world, reveals the world through sensation as the living contact and existing encounter with things. Thus the basic context of all sensation and of all perception is the world lived prereflectively as the horizon and field of all experience, the existential foundation of all derived activities.

Merleau-Ponty avoids reductionistic and idealistic interpretations of sensation and of perception which overlook the lived world in favor of a distorted view of world, as has already been seen. The lived world springing from the uniquely human level of signification, once explicitly grasped in reflection, requires the rejection of interpretations of perception as "decompositional"[110] since "the perceived world is not a sum of objects."[111] Rather, in perception the whole, and not an ideal whole, is prior to the parts, as seen in chapter 1. Thus, perception is not built up, as the building block model would have it, from impressions or qualities, nor is the world something we come to see as an "idea" from on high unifying all sense experience, nor is it that which is "out there," presupposed as a cause of the empiricist's impressions. An understanding of the lived world, however, requires a phenomenological change of focus which prescinds from the presuppositions of second level attitudes and which delves to the originary level grounding reflection. This primary level reveals the natural, human, and social worlds[112] unravelled as structural dimensions of concrete existence in the effort to "rediscover" phenomena.[113] This return to the phenomenal field avoids reading into it the assumptions of a whole truncated tradition. It is to the "already there" aspect of the world that the discussion will briefly turn before analyzing the latter in terms of constancies.

For Merleau-Ponty, as for Mead, experience and consciousness emerge within the world that is "already there," yet these are the very conditions making a world possible. This world is "already there" in the sense that it is the presupposed foundation for all intentional acts as their backdrop, context, and horizon, as an operative level of intentionality more basic and originary than specific acts of intention, and which underlies such acts as its presupposed and necessary foundation; further, the world "already there" captures that independent dimension of world which, as such, is not constituted by human activity since it pre-exists such activity as the horizon and context for all possible experience.[114] Finally, for Merleau-Ponty, the world that is there refutes the possibility of an absolute beginning as does the interpretation of Mead.[115] For Merleau-Ponty the world is "there" as a context of meanings within which perception takes place. It is this constancy of context in relation to things and qualities which must be further elaborated.

The world, as the horizon of all our experiences, provides the primordial constancy in which the constancy of the thing is grounded, and the thing in turn provides that constancy in which the constancy of qualities is grounded. In this way the true significance of perceptual constancies are evident, for as Merleau-Ponty says: *"the constancy of color is only an abstract component of the constancy of things, which in turn is grounded in the primordial constancy of the world as the horizon of all our experiences."*[116] The perceptual object, already unified on the corporeal level of perceptual experience, reveals both the constancy or unity of the thing and the corporeal synthesis as well. The body on this originary level reveals, at once, the significance of and relation between the natural and human worlds, the analysis of which further clarifies the world as "already there" while yet a structure of corporeal existence; the correlation between the unity of the world and the unity of the body; other selves, the common world, and coexistence. Thus, this central role of the human body in the world of perception must be further discussed, for it is in the discussion of the body that the perceived world is further illuminated.

"The body is our anchorage in the world,"[117] and at once is a "mediator of the world."[118] The human body has a movement toward a world, with its habits which weave around it a human environment. Differing from animal behavior aiming at an animal setting (*Umwelt*), human life "understands" an infinite number of possible environments and understands itself because it is thrown into a natural world.[119] The human body affords the "possession of a universal setting, a schema of all types of perceptual unfolding and of all those inter-sensory correspondences which lie beyond the segment of the world which we are actually perceiving."[120] A thing given in perception is actually taken up, reconstituted, and experienced in so far as it is "bound up with a world, the basic structure of which we carry with us, and of which it is merely one of many concrete forms."[121] As intimated above, the body has a world as an "incomplete individual," and the world gives rise to the body:

> I *have* the world as an incomplete individual, through the agency of my body as the potentiality of this world, and I have the positing of objects through that of my body, or conversely the positing of my body through that of objects, not in any kind of logical implication, as we determine an unknown size through its objective relations to given sizes, but in a real implication, and because my body as a movement towards the world, and the world my body's point of support.[122]

The body emerges as central in the phenomenal field,[123] for as Merleau-Ponty says, "Our own body is in the world as the heart is in the organism: it keeps the visible spectacle constantly alive, it breathes life into it and sustains it inwardly, and with it forms a system."[124] Further, as the unity and synthesis of the object are correlative to the unity and synthesis of the body, so too those of the world and prereflective consciousness are correlative and exist only with one another. On this level, consciousness crosses over or transcends to world; as Merleau-Ponty indicates, "my experience breaks forth into things and transcends itself in them.[125] World is the correlate of prereflective consciousness without which it could not exist or have meaning. Thus, consciousness of world is not based on self-consciousness, because they occur together. "There is a world for me because I am not unaware of myself; and I am not concealed from myself because I have a world."[126]

The inherence of consciousness is experienced in its body and in its world. Thus consciousness discovers in itself, along with sensory fields entailed within the world as the field of all fields, the opacity of a primal past, and then "perception of other people and the plurality of consciousnesses no longer present any difficulty."[127] The other as thus experienced completes the system I-other-world.[128] The communication between consciousnesses is possible because they share or "co-exist through a common world,"[129] and are brought together in a single world in which all participate, a participation made possible because existence is carried by the body.[130]

Merleau-Ponty attempts to overcome two extremes in his treatment of the body, the natural world, and the human world, viz., that they cannot be considered first as objects given as such outside us, nor can they be treated as objects inside, i.e., arising from the constituting consciousness of transcendental idealism, as has already been mentioned. The world and the body are first lived before their derived and objectified modes come onto the scene and are meaningful. Thus, it is not surprising that Merleau-Ponty's treatment of the human world is found to be intrinsically interwoven with the natural world. The problems involved with each, and with the relation between them, quickly reveal the body as the focal point for a solution, manifesting the lived interrelation among body, world, and others on the originary level. And on that existential level, the natural, the social, and the corporeal intersect as essential aspects of lived, corporeal, human existence. It is first to the natural aspect of world that the discussion will turn.

Nature is not first and foremost objectively outside or inside, but rather, is at the "core of my personal life"[130] and at the center of lived existence. And, human life understands "itself because it is thrown into a natural world."[131] Natural perception lives with things and is the "primary faith" binding us to a world "as to our native land."[133] Thus, habits or behavior patterns settle into that nature at the core of one's existence, so that nature in human existence is the host of the cultural world. "Not only have I a physical world, not only do I live in the midst of earth, air, and water, I have around me roads, plantations, villages, streets, churches, implements, a bell, a spoon, a pipe. Each of these objects is molded to the human action which it serves."[134]

The natural world and the social world are mediated through the cultural world, the first object of which (i.e., cultural object) is the body of the other person.[135] And for Merleau-Ponty the social world is a permanent field or dimension of existence. Thus, he says:

> We must therefore rediscover, after the natural world, the social world, not as an object or sum of objects, but as a permanent field or dimension of existence: I may well turn away from it, but not cease to be situated relatively to it. Our relationship to the social is, like our relationship to the world, deeper then any express perception or any judgment. It is as

false to place ourselves in society as an object among other objects, as it is to place society within ourselves as an object of thought, and in both cases the mistake lies in treating the social as an object. We must return to the social with which we are in contact by the mere fact of existing, and which we carry about inseparably with us before any objectification.[136]

This social world shares the same fundamental dimension of human life and existence as do the body and the natural world, for they exist only to the extent that I take them up and live them. As Merleau-Ponty observes, "We have discovered, with the natural and social world . . . that ambiguous life in which the forms of transcendence have their *Ursprung.*"[137] Since this holds for both the natural and social worlds, they are both put on the same fundamental level. Thus the thing emerges in the context of the natural world and its constancy; other selves in the context of the human and social world—all of which must be discovered on the basic level of existential and ambiguous life. Both dimensions of world are forms of transcendence within the structure of life. It is to the emergence of truth within this conception of the world that the discussion will now turn.

Within the context of the perceived world as a field of presence, truth arises.[138] Even the most abstract truths, such as those of geometry, find their ultimate base in perceptual experience and in the situatedness of human existence.[139] In thus bringing truth back to earth in lived experience, Merleau-Ponty does not embrace relativism, but rather denies any absolute status to truth and any "ideal of an absolute spectator" in knowledge.[140] These general contours about truth are witnessed in the following brief text: "But there is also nothing that we can actually and effectively think without relating it to our field of presence, to the actual existence of the perceived object—and in this sense the field of presence contains everything. There is no truth that can be conceived[141] only outside the field of presence, outside the limits of some situation or some structure."[142] And this is what the "primacy of perception" means.

Truth is already latently entailed in the anticipatory structure of the initial dimension of perception which already calls for fulfillment involving the practical dimension as essential to the initial intentional orientation. Further, the "primacy of perception" means to be present at the birth of truth and to be instructed on "the true conditions of objectivity itself."[143] It is precisely the context of this primacy of perception which reveals truth, for truth is rooted in the very rudimentary experience which gives things to us and us to things within the world. Indeed, it is the realm of perception and the perceived object which accomplish "the actual truth of what is understood."[144] Thus, for example, the other side of the lamp is not deduced in an abstract process to be there, as true in the geometrician's sense, nor is it within an objective world outside us which we come to and experience in a sensory event. Rather, it is the whole lamp which is behaviorially experienced and present in perception through the body and in the world. The other side of an object is given and present as "other side" and as "able to be touched."

Thus, Merleau-Ponty's understanding of truth is not alien to Mead's view that truth entails meanings which work in the interaction with things in the world. For Merleau-Ponty, it is in the domain of experience that all truth transpires, and here that meaning gets fulfilled and sedimented as deposits in experience to be tapped for future use. And it is within the world as the field of presence that this takes place.[145]

Merleau-Ponty's later attempts to situate the phenomenology of his early considerations within an ontology rounds out rather than cancels out the phenomenology. In this process, the system of world, self, other selves, the role of the body, the view of truth, and the role of sensibility[146] are given a more enriched treatment. Thus, the transcendence of human existence to world reveals explicitly the positive ontological dimensions of the world latent in the lived and perceived world undergirding the objective world of science.[147]

It is clear, then, that for both Mead and Merleau-Ponty, the world that is there emerges within the context of the primordial vital intentionality constitutive of organism-environment interaction. In its emergence, the world grounds all levels of experience and knowledge, at the same time giving meaningful access to the independent reality of the natural universe.

The above various analyses have attempted to show that there are striking similarities in the way Mead and Merleau-Ponty portray the perceptual field as it arises in the context of human activity. They each portray it as an ontologically thick field of objects which are essentially related to the horizon of world and which allow for the very structure of the sensing which gives access to them. In this way they both reject all attempts to begin with the presence within experience of something unaffected by human activity or with any sort of atomic elements as the building blocks of knowledge, thus belying all epistemic forms of reductionism, phenomenalism, and foundationalism, and at the same time undercutting the alternatives of rationalism or traditional empiricism. From this common setting the ensuing chapters can further relate, interpret, and expand, as well as begin to critique, the respective positions of Mead and Merleau-Ponty through the clarifying light each offers the other.

3. APPROACHES TO THE NATURE OF TIME

MEAD AND MERLEAU-PONTY, within their essentially differing philosophical orientations and positions, each independently work toward lived time as basic and as the source of all derived senses of time. Such an approach is intended to reintegrate humans and nature, rescuing them both from various forms of scientism which have denied the significance of the temporal structure of lived experience in favor of derived senses of time. In so doing, they each oppose the realist view of an objective time structure independent of perspectives, as well as a subjectivist structuring of an inner stream over against a fixed objectivity. Rather, they each reach a level of the constitution of temporal experience which undercuts the subject-object split and which provides the foundations for all derived understandings of time. And, for each, the constitution of time is rooted in a present which is not a knife-edged moment, a series of now points, but rather a durational spread which contains in its temporal span both past and future. This focus can best be reached by turning to their respective analyses of the issues of the prevailing physical science of their time, relativity theory, as these relate to the philosophical understanding of time. In working toward lived time from the problems presented by relativity theory, their criticisms take them to diverse lines of agreement with, and criticism of, both relativity theory and Bergson's attempt to handle the problems of science. Yet, these diverse lines themselves stem from different interpretations of what is to be found in relativity theory and in Bergson's position, not in any differences concerning the problems to be avoided and the solutions to be reached.[1] The following discussion will turn to their respective understandings of the problems of the philosophical interpretations of relativity theory and to Bergson's own focus on temporality.

Merleau-Ponty's account of lived time takes the lead from Henri Bergson in coming to grips with the implicit philosophical issues involved in relativity theory. Both Merleau-Ponty and Bergson address critically the latent philosophical paradox of Einstein's position, a paradox which Bergson attempted to help Einstein overcome. Though Merleau-Ponty considers Bergson's attempt to need redirection, as shall be seen later in this chapter, they both agree that it is lived time which relativity theory and its philosophical interpretations overlook. The scientific critique of the forms of space and time which emerge from non-Euclidean geometry and relativity physics demand the rediscovery of the observer's situation and thus of lived space and time, bringing the derived space and time to their proper origin and providing their context and horizon. The critique of absolute simultaneity by relativity theory does not necessarily lead "to the paradoxes of the radical plurality of times,"[2] a plight which Einstein's interpretation of relativity physics engenders.

Further, according to Merleau-Ponty, Einstein's accounts of reality and of the speculative interpretation of the physicist support two essentially irreconcilable points. He attempts to maintain "classical physics' ideal of knowledge," i.e., "that the world is rational"[3] and contains a truth: "I believe in a world in itself, a world governed by laws I try to apprehend." Yet he attempts to uphold his own "wildly speculative," revolutionary way of creative construction. The paradox emerges from Einstein's attempt to uphold both the intensely creative, "wildly speculative" constructs and, at once, the world in itself as rational, independently out there, and governed by laws. Thus, Merleau-Ponty points out that in retaining the classical scientific ideal of knowledge as a direct notation of reality, he condemns himself as a philosopher "to the paradox that he never sought as a physicist or a man."[4] Henri Bergson, addressing this same paradox, suggested to Einstein the distinction between the derived time of the physicist and the lived time which grounds it, but Einstein insisted on retaining the priority of the physicist's claim to truth.[5] He claims, as Merleau-Ponty put it, that "it is to science alone that we must go for the truth about time and everything else. And the experience of the perceived world with its obvious facts is no more than a stutter which precedes the clear speech of science."[6] Einstein, then, persisted in reverting to the derived realm of the physicist as the absolute court of appeal for truth and rationality, thus not agreeing "to recognize any reason but the physicist's." Merleau-Ponty goes on to affirm that "this physicist's reason, invested in this way with a philosophical dignity, abounds in paradoxes and destroys itself, as it does for example when it teaches that my present is simultaneous with the future of a different observer sufficiently distant from me, and thereby destroys the very meaning of the future."[7] Hence, according to Merleau-Ponty, Einstein understands lived time to be limited to the merely subjective, not allowing the possibility of "extending our intuitive idea of simultaneity to the whole world."[8] In contrast, for Bergson, it is upon prescientific evidence of a single world, instead of upon the "divine right of a dogmatic science,"[9] that rational science and all universal formulations have their origin. He, like Merleau-Ponty, wants to return to and regain the concrete world of perception with its horizons in whch the derived constructions of physics can be situated, allowing physics to "develop its paradoxes" without recourse to what is contrary to the demands of reason.[10]

Merleau-Ponty notes that certain physicists reproached Bergson for introducing the concrete observer into relativity physics.[11] According to those physicists, time is relative to the system of references or of measuring instruments. For Bergson, however, precisely what needs to be explicated is the relation of that derived level to the overlooked lived experiential time of such an observer and the philosophical implications involving the experience or perceptual role of the observer. For Bergson and Merleau-Ponty alike, only perceived things of such experience participate in the "same line of present,"[12] so that there is "without any measurement, simply perceived simultaneity" of two events in the same field or even between all perceptual fields, all observers, and all durations. Thus there is no simultaneity among things in themselves. On this perceptual level, however, the presupposed lived world and its lived time come into focus and are rediscovered, instead of clouded over by a derived time which assumes a quasi-absolute status. It is in this way that the simultaneity and plurality of time for physics can be properly grounded in a lived, unified, real time: "The multiplicity of times I obtain in this way does not impede the unity of real time; it rather presupposes it."[13] Within the perceptual field there are simultaneous events, where we can also see different observers whose fields transgress upon our own, and by extension our ideas of simultaneity include events which are as distant from each other as can be and which do not depend on any one observer, thus revealing "one single time for everyone, one single universal time,"[14] "a pre-objective temporality which is universal in its own way,"[15] which the physicist's calculations presuppose. Further, Merleau-Ponty explicitly agrees with Bergson in affirming that when perceivers perceive one another, when their "perceptual fields cut across and envelop one another and they see one another in the process of perceiving the same world," there is a "restitution of all duration to a unified whole. . . . In its own order perception posits a universal duration; and the formulas which enable us to pass from one system of reference to another are, like physics as a whole, secondary objectifications which cannot make a determination about what is meaningful in our experience as incarnate subject, or about being as a whole."[16] Bergson, in a way which Merleau-Ponty makes thematic in his early writings, outlines a philosophy that would make the "universal rest upon the mystery of perception" and would take up the task, as Merleau-Ponty quotes Bergson, of "penetrating into perception" instead of "sweeping over" it.[17]

Thus Merleau-Ponty's criticism of Einstein, like Bergson's, is an objection to absolutizing the abstract reflections of relativity theory, derived from and oblivious to the temporal nature of the lived experience which grounds those very reflections. Merleau-Ponty wants to correct Bergson's tendency to have recourse to space instead of to the essential character of time in his attempt to deal adequately with time. Merleau-Ponty explains:

> Space, motion and time cannot be elucidated by discovering an 'inner' layer of experience in which their multiplicity is erased and *really* abolished. For if this happens, neither space, nor movement, nor time remains. . . . If, in virtue of the principle of continuity, the past still belongs to the present and the present already to the past, there is no longer any past or present. If consciousness snowballs upon itself, it is, like the snowball and everything else, wholly in the present.[18]

According to Merleau-Ponty, the weakness in Bergson's view of time is that it does not sufficiently deal with the passing of the present into the past from the future, with the present crossing over or stretching out to the past and to the future.[19] Thus

Merleau-Ponty objects to the fact that Bergson does not consider time to be the structure or sense of human life or existence. Bergson's view of time, then, as well as his view of the body,[20] leaves it alienated from lived experience, as Merleau-Ponty remarks: "But the body remains for him what we have called the objective body: consciousness remains knowledge; time remains a successive 'now', whether it 'snowballs upon itself' or is spread in spatialized time. Bergson can therefore only compress or expand the series of 'present moments'; he never reaches the unique movement whereby the three dimensions of time are constituted, and one cannot see why duration is squeezed into a present, or why consciousness becomes involved in a body and world."[21]

Merleau-Ponty's phenomenological attempt at a rediscovery and recovery of lived time and space explicates precisely that layer from which any scientific abstraction, including the Newtonian timeless space, is derived. On this lived level, the space-time and the here-now are not separated as in second level, derived scientific treatments, nor is distance alien to simultaneity. A distant object, not only in space, but in time as well, is simultaneous with the perceiver, i.e., "distance is between simultaneous objects . . . and this simultaneity is contained in the very meaning of perception."[22] Merleau-Ponty thus brings together these two existential characteristics of human being, space and time, as is clear in the following text:[23]

> But co-existence, which in fact defines space, is not alien to time, but is the fact of two phenomena belonging to the same temporal wave. As for the relationship of the perceived object to my perception, it does not unite them in space and outside time: they are *contemporary*. The 'order of co-existents' is inseparable from the 'order of sequences', or rather time is not only the consciousness of a sequence. Perception provides me with a 'field of presence,'[24] in the broad sense, extending in two dimensions: the here-there dimensions and the past-present-future dimensions. The second elucidates the first. I 'hold', I 'have' the distant object without any explicit positing of the spatial perspective (apparent size and shape) as I still 'have in hand' the immediate past without any distortion and without any interposed 'recollection'.

Distance, then, is understood in terms of this direct possession, and in terms of "a being in the distance which links up with being where it appears."[25] Further, it is the body which inhabits, belongs to, and includes space and time, and exists necessarily here and now,[26] and bodily movements are in a space which is already within a relation to time.

Thus, though Merleau-Ponty ultimately departs from Bergson, they both, in emphasizing the observer's situation and the priority of the lived perceptual realm, endeavor to redirect philosophical attention to the lived time underlying any derived time of physics, and to provide its full context. The scientific abstractions of both Newtonian physics and relativity theory lose the richness of lived simultaneity and "polymorphous" time.[27] From this backdrop the discussion will now turn to Mead's more explicit attempt to come to grips with and further elucidate these fundamental problems of time emerging from physics.

Mead approaches the character of lived time from the interpretive issues involved in the time of relativity theory, critiquing, in the process, the philosophical implications of relativity theory as developed in the positions of Minkowski and Whitehead and, indirectly, in the position of Bergson. Mead focuses on the fact that the theory of relativity introduced the view that simultaneity could not be understood, as in the Newtonian worldview, in terms of objective movements in points of time independently of the perspectives of observers. And, like Bergson and Merleau-Ponty, Mead holds that the significance of the role of the observer cannot be adequately understood in terms of derivative measuring instruments alone. Rather, the measurement of simultaneity within relativity theory requires ultimately that account be taken of the perspective of the concrete human observer engaged in practical activity. And, precisely the philosophical implications of this relativity to the observer for the importance of lived experiential time had not been adequately taken into account. What relativity led to was Minkowski's concept of a four-dimensional space-time continuum of events. According to Minkowski's view, past, present, and future events are laid out in a unalterable space-time continuum and the relation of each event to every other is fixed. There is an absolute order of events, and alternative space-time systems are merely subjective manifestations. Mead critically notes that this view leaves nature closed to human perspectives and "reduces the present to a negligible element that approaches the world at an instant."[28]

Mead's interest in Whitehead[29] lies in the fact that Whitehead, with his concept of the event, tried to retain motion and change in a relativisitic universe, and to have the different time systems as perspectives in nature rather than as merely subjective. To accomplish this, Whitehead made a metaphysical distinction between the events and their substantive attributes. These latter were relegated to a realm of "eternal objects" which ingress into events, thus giving rise to alternative orders. Mead critically points out that Whitehead portrays a universe still "closed to mind"; that he does not avoid the rigidity of the geometry of the four-dimensional space-time continuum;[30] and that his ingression of eternal objects into events is an attempt to get contingency from a space-time rigidity that does not adequately allow for contingency and emergence.[31] As he summarizes Whitehead's problem, "The geometry of space-time denies emergence unless it is brought in by way of Whitehead's metaphysics; and if I am not mistaken such a view must surrender the ordered geometry of space-time that Whitehead retains."[32]

In addition to the inadequacy of its solution, Mead objects in principle to Whitehead's use of eternal objects as an illicit metaphysical hypostatization of an abstraction. Extensive abstraction "as a method of analysis and integration . . . asks for no other justification than its success. But Whitehead uses it as a method of metaphysical abstraction. . . . This seems to me to be an improper use of abstraction, since it leads to a metaphysical separation of what is abstracted from the concrete reality from which the abstraction is made, instead of leaving it as a tool in the intellectual control of that reality."[33] Mead's own analysis of temporality is intended as the basis for understanding novelty, emergence, and perspectives as objectively real in nature, and for understanding the primordial lived constitution of time as the basis from which any intellectual abstractions are made. Mead's criticisms of Minkowski and Whitehead, like Merleau-Ponty's criticisms of Einstein himself, are objections to absolutizing, in some form, the abstract reflections of relativity theory, losing in the process the temporal nature of the lived experience which grounds such reflections.

Mead's position can be further elucidated by turning to his significant correction of Bergson, in which he stresses that the temporal flow of experience is at once the experience of a temporally constituted world of perceived objects:

> The specious present is not only a passing experience in a permanent world; the specious present does actually answer to something that is itself taking place. . . . The object that is

there in experience is an object that is essentially going on. . . . If we get that object as continuous in the world as well as in our experience, we can get the world as continuous. Then we do actually have experience of that which answers to the laws of cause and effect. The reality of immediate experience is an experience of that which is taking place and the dependence of that which is taking place on the temporal structure that belongs to it.[34]

And, as he further criticizes Bergson:

He fails to see that the flow, the freedom, the novelty, the interpenetration, the creativity, upon which he sets such store, are not necessarily limited to the interpenetration of experiences in the inner flow of consciousness. They may also be gotten in an objective statement just as soon as we see that the objects of experience have the same type of interpenetration, the same essential spread, as that which Bergson discovers in our inner experience; as soon as we see that the ideas which we get in reflection, the objects that we get in science, and against which Bergson is particularly vehement, are the result of analysis and are not presumed to be reports of the nature of the objects themselves.[35]

Mead's criticism of Bergson here, though different in fashion than Merleau-Ponty's, basically makes the same point. The perceived world is a temporal world, and our perception of an identical thing in a common space and time is itself the result of the temporal spread of lived experience which is constitutive of these features.[36] Bergson ultimately went astray, according to Mead, because he failed, in the last analysis, to recognize the derivative nature of the objects of science as opposed to the temporal nature of the perceived world. He substituted physical time as the time which is thought according to the model of space for the real temporal features of the perceived world, and thus according to Bergson, time could be adequately grasped only by a passive sympathetic subjective attunement with the flux, a grasp which could not be apprehended rationally. Thus Mead, from his own direction, is led to agreement with Merleau-Ponty's claim that for Bergson, time and body remain alienated from the lived, for the subjective grasp of flux is not the lived, and the lived body is not the body of science. Rather, lived experience involves the temporal body embedded within a temporally founded perceived world.

Mead, then, understands "the objects that we get in science" within the context of a general theory of the temporal constitution of human experience through praxis. If we abstract from the temporal distances of objects, we obtain a Newtonian timeless space in which all objects can simultaneously exist and have the common properties of the manipulatory stage of the act. While distance qualities tend to vary from observer to observer as well as within various stages of the act, the manipulatory properties tend to yield general agreement. Because of this, the manipulatory or contact properties of the object have a special value in characterizing the physical objects of science, and the distance characters are then relegated to the mind. Thus Mead states, "For the purposes of scientific method, the importance of contact experience does not lie in the greater reality of tactual or resistance experience over that of color or of sound, but in the fact that observation and experiment do come back to the distance experience which must be itself directly or indirectly referred to what we can actually or conceivably get our hands upon."[37] The Newtonian distinction of absolute space and time, as well as its support of the distinction between primary and secondary qualities, is thus a functional distinction accounted for in behavioral terms and in terms of the temporal constitution of the object. As Mead emphasizes, "The real is qualitative, and you cannot get quality at an instant. It occurs over a period, whether it be color, melody, or the ionization of an atom."[38] Metaphysical dualisms of various kinds result from the illicit reifications of these functional distinctions rooted in the temporally constituted phases of the act.

While the Newtonian world results from the translation of things into common manipulatory characters, relativity translates between distance qualities. The theory of relativity finds the translation formulas which allow distance qualities of one perspective to be predicted for another perspective. Relativity theory involves a transformation between the distance experiences of different perspectives:

> Now relativity, with the electro-magnetic theory out of which it has so largely arisen, has not only vastly complicated the spatio-temporal theory of measurement, but it has also reversed what I may call the reality-reference. Instead of saying that the reality of the perspectives of our distance ex-

perience is to be found in that contact experience which is firmly bedded in a geometry of a Eucliden space and the even flow of a uniform time, we must say that it is only as we can read over this seemingly Euclidean space of our contact world into perspectives dependent upon the motion of distance objects and discover transformation formulae between these that we can reach the reality of what we perceive.[39]

Or, as he compares relativity theory and Newtonian physics, "There is as close a parallelism between an electro-magnetic universe and the world of distance experience, that of visions, as between the world of mass mechanics and our contact experience."[40] Again, "The universe of relativity is entirely visual, fashioned by the mechanism of light signals."[41] This does not, however, rule out the importance of contact experience or the importance of the relation between distance experience and contact experience as constituted by the act. Rather, in relativity theory the distance experience is in a peculiar way independent of contact experience. The distance experience of the measurement of an object in a reference system moving relative to the reference system in which one is at rest is very different from the measurement of the same object through contact experience when one is in the system in which that object is at rest. The calculation of the relation between distance experience and contact experience can be accomplished only through the Lorentz transformation equations.

Two points should be noted here. First, the emphasis on distance experience in relativity theory as opposed to contact experience in Newtonian physics indicates that what is involved is not two competing metaphysical realms, but diverse types of functional distinctions emerging from the context of human action. Secondly, in both, the relation between distance and contact experience, as constitutive of the act, is crucial in one way or another. Relativity, however, further requires the taking of the perspective of the other as developed in Mead's general theory of role taking.[42] Thus Mead states, "Newtonian relativity *permitted* the observer to transfer himself from one system to another. . . . But electro-magnetic relativity exhibits results within our system which *compel* us to have recourse to the other system with its space-time structure in order to account for them."[43]

The focus on relativity theory by Mead and Merleau-Ponty leads each to highlight different aspects of the relation of lived temporality and relativity theory. Merleau-Ponty objects to the "paradoxes of relativity theory," with its diverse time perspectives, and wants to root this in the temporal constitution of primordial lived common time. But, the temporal constitution of lived experience requires the ability to "take the role of the other," to place oneself in diverse perspectives, incorporating this diversity into the very constitution of one's awareness. He indicates this qualification obliquely in his statement of prescientific temporality which is universal *in its own way.*[44] In his concern with the perceived simultaneity of a common time, Merleau-Ponty perhaps does not adequately note the importance of taking the role of the other, and the diversity of perspectives this involves, in the very constitution of simultaneity—a point highlighted by relativity theory. Mead, on the other hand, views relativity as an ideal model for indicating the feature of the diversity of temporal perspectives and taking the role of the other in the temporal constitution of a common perceptual world. But, with this emphasis on the clarifying aspects of relativity theory, he perhaps does not adequately stress that relativity theory, with its abstract diversity of temporal perspectives, is itself made possible through a commonly shared, everyday temporal perspective incorporating the intuitive, common sense idea of simultaneity, though this is implicit throughout his discussion.

For both Mead and Merleau-Ponty, the constitution of the shared temporal perspective of everyday experience is what allows for the derived objects of scientific reflection, be they the objects of relativity theory or of Newtonian physics. Only by recognizing the emergence of the scientific world from the temporally constituted common world of lived experience can the potential paradoxes presented by science be avoided. For both Mead and Merleau-Ponty, then, the examination of the philosophic interpretations of relativity theory leads downward to the constitution of lived temporality. Correlative to what has been seen in the previous chapters on the perceived world, and as will be further seen in the next chapter on self, this constitution of lived temporality involves both the individual temporal perspective as the dimension of uniqueness and the shared temporal perspective as the dimension of commonality. Further, the constitution of temporal perspectives is at once the temporal constitution of the perceived world, and these perspectives are "there" in the world.

After clearly rejecting the conceptions of time as a succession of nows, as the realist view of an objective time structure independent of perspectives, and as a subjectivist structuring of an inner stream over against a fixed objectivity, each of which, in some way, fails to adequately grasp the derived nature of the time of science, Mead and Merleau-Ponty alike recognize a privileged role of the present as a durational spread out of which the subject is open onto past and future. Thus, an examination of their respective understandings of temporality will focus on their understandings of the nature of the present in the general context of the basic constitution of time in lived experience, first in the philosophy of Merleau-Ponty, and then in that of Mead.

In opposing the realist's interpretation of time as "out there" in an objective world-in-itself which contains the subject, and the rationalist's interpretation of time as a product of intellectual synthesizing activity of the subject outside of time, Merleau-Ponty emphasizes the positive contribution of both views in relation to lived time. Realism situates the subject in the present—"time exists for me because I have a present"[45]—while rationalism, in Merleau-Ponty's account, recognizes that the subject must be open to the past and to the future in a primordial way in its lived dimensions instead of merely by mediation or abstaction.[46] In order to emphasize these positive dimensions, Merleau-Ponty takes up the metaphor of the flowing river often used to account for time.

The usual account of the river metaphor interprets the present to emerge from the past and the future to emerge from the present, similar to the flow of the river from the melting snow on the mountain above, down the stream as from the past to the present, and then further down to the future. But Merleau-Ponty holds that such comparison involves a derived time—an actual succession of nows that is recorded—and then "surreptitiously putting into the river a witness of its course,"[47] who sees the melting of the snow and its flowing downstream. Rather, what is past or future to this witness, to the subject in being-in-the-world, is structurally related to the present, setting up an appropriation of the constitution of time in relation to human existence. It is precisely human existence which is the pre-existence of future and survival of past in relation to the field of presence of the present. This presence, as will be seen below, is not an immediacy of intuition, but rather involves both a crossing over to world within a passage and a crossing over of time to its next moment. From this perspective of the lived world, time "arises from *my* relation to things."[48] Time is destroyed if the derived and objectified world is separated, as an in-itself, from the lived finite perspectives which open onto it.[49] These issues will be further clarified by turning to the present in the lived experience of time.

Merleau-Ponty's treatment of time focuses upon the priority and "thickness of the pre-objective present"[50] in relation to presence and to a new notion of existential sense. This sense is a structure of existence which both makes possible and is confirmed by his analysis of time. Further, time as the sense of human existence underlies any meaning for understanding,[51] entailing the sensory fields and the perceptual fields, thus involving "a schema of all possible being, a universal setting in relation to the world. At the heart of the subject himself we discovered, then, the presence of the world"[52] which, as presence, is his sense of transcendence. This notion of transcendence in relation to the present and to time needs further clarification, showing its radical separation from any vestiges of Husserl's transcendental.

Two senses of *transcendence* permeate Merleau-Ponty's view of lived time: first, transcendence as the presence or weddedness or crossing over to the world, the quasi-organic relation or natal bond between the preceiving subject and the perceived world; and, second, transcendence as the passing of the present into the past from the future, so that the present is seen as crossing over or stretching out to the past and to the future. Since time is the sense or tenor or structure of human life and, like world, is accessible only to the person from within, it must be deemed the basic structural dimension of human existence within which being in the world takes place. Thus, presence means openness to world, reflecting the intermeshing of world and human life, the mutual interdependence, the springing of one from the other, as seen above in chapter 2. And the living present is where presence at the heart of existence takes place. It is within this context that the "living present" is the focal point for the analysis of time. This concrete present is rooted in presence which is rooted in time as the sense of existence. The integration of presence and the network of intentionality reveals the deeper implications of the rootedness of presence in the structure of time, involving distinguishing the "fresh present"[53] from the present in its "wide sense."[54]

Merleau-Ponty rejects any notion of time ordered in a one-dimensional linear succession in favor of time as "a network of intentionalities."[55] Here it should again be stressed that although Merleau-Ponty borrows terms and insights from Husserl's treatment of internal time consciousness, he has unequivocally rejected any so-called Husserlian transcendental consciousness. Precisely Merleau-Ponty's existential and corporeal interpretation of intentionality, which includes the practical and affective dimensions of environment-organism interaction, links his understanding of temporal experience with that of Mead. This network of corporeal intentionalities is connected to the present out of which the subject is open onto past and future, revealing the genuine character of this network itself and its connection with presence to world and presence to self. The present in its "wide sense," inclusive of its horizons of primary past and future, enjoys a privilege because "it is the zone in which being and consciousness coincide." "My present outruns itself in the direction of an immediate future and an immediate past and impinges upon them where they actually are, namely in the past and in the future themselves."[56]

This consciousness, "by taking up a situation,"[57] is the action of temporalization. Time is lived from the present as an incomplete whole,[58] so that the "fresh present"[59] does not collide with past and future or stack them up against one another. Merleau-Ponty refers to the "fresh present" in order to clarify the existential sense of retentions and protentions of the network of intentionalities.[60] Since time is neither discrete nor linear, it cannot be adequately understood as the sense of existence if represented as "an instantaneous cross-section of time."[61] Thus rather than the heaping up or snowballing of present, "the fresh present *is* the passage of future to present, and of former present to past, and when time begins to move, it moves throughout its whole length."[62] Thus, the "fresh present" is as such in process or passage to past from future which involves the present in the broad sense, the whole of futures anticipated and pasts sedimented or retained. "This amounts to saying that each present reasserts the presence of the whole past which it supplants, and anticipates that of all that is to come." It further means that "by definition the present is not shut up within itself, but transcends itself towards a future and a past."[63] There is not one present, then another present, nor a present with its vistas, then another with its vistas needing synthesis . . . , but rather, "there is one single time which is self-confirmatory, which can bring nothing into existence unless it has already laid that thing's foundations as present and eventual past, and which establishes itself at a stroke."[64] Humans actually effect the passage of one present to the next, rather than merely see it as onlookers or grasp it conceptually, and are already at their impending present as a gesture is already at its goal. I am myself time, a time which 'abides'."[65] I do not, however, initiate the process of temporalization, as Merleau-Ponty says: "I am not the initiator of time any more than of my heart-beats. . . . yet once I am born, time flows through me, whatever I do."[66] The present is a presence of a subject that is present to the world, that *is* only in its transcendence to the world bespeaking a characteristic of human existence as such. This presence, then, is a unique structure,[67] of which subject and object are two abstract moments, as mentioned above. It is precisely the relation between this network of intentionalities and the "field of presence" which needs further clarification.

The "field of presence" contains the immediate and remote past and future as horizons of retentions and protentions, "intentionalities which anchor me to an environment,"[68] and run from my perceptual field which draws along in its wake its own horizon of retention, and bites into the future with its protentions. This aspect of the field of presence and its depth renders impossible the linear view of time as passing through a series of instances of nows placed end to end. Rather,

> with the arrival of every moment, its predecessor undergoes a change: I still have it in hand and it is still there, but already it is sinking away below the level of presents; in order to retain it, I need to reach through a thin layer of time. It is still the preceding moment, and I have the power to rejoin it as it was just now; I am not cut off from it, but still it would not belong to the past unless something had altered, unless it were beginning to outline itself against, or project itself upon, my present, whereas a moment ago it *was* my present. When a third moment arrives, the second undergoes a new modification; from being a retention it becomes the retention of a retention, and the layer of time between it and me thickens.[69]

Thus, time consciousness, as already unified, does not need to be synthesized, and as already containing lived depth, is neither unidimensional nor discrete. This lived depth and thickness is accounted for by the fact that the prior moment is retained in the present precisely as immediate past and so on to more and more remote past moments and their retentions, and equally by the fact that the upcoming moment is involved in the lived thickness and presence of the present as protentions or anticipations. Thus, as mentioned "time is not a line, but a network of intentionalities,"[70] a passage involving present, past and future as a whole, but as an incompletely constituted whole. "Since in time being and passing are synonymous, by becoming past, the event does not cease to be."[71] This passage of one moment to the next, with the first retained beneath the surface of the next moment, involves, beneath the level of a thetic consciousness of objects by the intentionality of acts, an operative intentionality which makes the former possible. This operative level of intentionality, effecting a self transcendence precisely as crossing over to the world in being-in-the-world, entails the network of intentionalities of retentions and protentions constitutive of human existence.

This network of intentionalities originates from the perceptual field and the human organism anchored to its environment at a task, thus reflecting and intimating the practical and purposive dimensions of this operative intentionality. Human existence is present to the world as familiar with it, as at or in the world in action. In a primary way, the relationship of active transcendence between this human organism and the world finds its own root in lived time.[72] Such decentering of the 'I' of consciousness toward the whole of the concrete human existent as source of the network of intentionalities holds true for the unity of time, already there on that level and not requiring the synthesizing activity of a unifying 'I'.[73] This corporeal and existential intentionality, including the structure of the concrete situation of the concrete individual in such a way as to subtend all derived activity, performs or effects the passage of one present to the next, so that there is "no need for a synthesis externally binding together the *tempora* into one single time, because each one of the *tempora* was already inclusive, beyond itself, of the whole open series of other *tempora* being in internal communication with them, and because the 'cohesion of a life' is given with its *ex-stase*."[74] This is precisely the point at which Merleau-Ponty objects to Bergson's account of memory. For his understanding of time as a "preserved present," or as involving the stacking up of presents snowballing upon themselves, does not adequately reach or do justice to lived time,[75] nor does his understanding grasp time as the essential structure and therefore as the sense of human existence. It is this latter point which needs further clarification here, though it will be taken up again in the next chapter.

That time is the sense of human existence and not merely an external attribute means that time is an essential characteristic of human existence and a "dimension of our being."[76] Merleau-Ponty indicates this identity between time and human existence in saying that "we must understand time as the subject and the subject as time."[77] The essence of this temporal individual is bound up

with "that of the body and that of the world . . . because my existence . . . is merely one with my existence as body and with the
existence of the world,"[78] and because I am, when taken con-
cretely, inseparable from this body and this world found ontologically at the core of the human organism, which hence is
essentially a temporal and corporeal being in the world.[79] Thus, it
is not surprising that the chapter on temporality in the *Phenomenology of Perception* incorporates the earlier exhaustive treatments of body and world bringing them in that chapter to a final
stage of depth.[80] And since human being is essentially temporal,
bespeaking the "much more intimate relationship"[81] between
time and human existence, then transcendence, corporeality, and
reflexivity must be central not only to such human existence, but
also to time, as seen above. For the two senses of *transcendence*
are essential structures of temporal human being. Further, the corporeal dimensions of existence, and the relation between consciousness and body, have been seen to pervade the most essential
dimension of existence according to Merleau-Ponty, i.e., time.
Time essentially entails both spontaneity and acquisition or sedimentation.[82] And the reflexive dimension of consciousness and of
the body permeate time since the subject is essentially temporal.
Merleau-Ponty contends that "it is of the essence of time to be not
only actual time, or time which flows, but also time which is
aware of itself, for the explosion or dehiscence of the present towards a future is the archetype of the *relationship of self to self.*"[83]

This intimate relation between time and the human existent
is further highlighted in Merleau-Ponty's later account of sensibility, where he develops a view of sensibility as a concrete and corporeal reflection, deepening the treatment of the early works,
and integrating it with newly introduced terms, "chaism" and
"flesh."[84] It is within this context that he understands time as
chiasm, so that the past and present are intertwining (*Ineinander*);
"each enveloping-enveloped—and that itself is the flesh."[85] From
this backdrop, the ensuing discussion will now turn to Mead's understanding of lived time and the centrality of the present.

Mead's understanding of the present must be placed, ultimately, in the broad cosmic context of a general metaphysics of
sociality, and the discussion of the present from which human experience opens onto past and future could perhaps best be presented in terms of its location within such a cosmic context.
Because Merleau-Ponty remains limited to the lived time of the

concrete subject, however, the ensuing discussion will turn first to those features of Mead's position which can best relate to Merleau-Ponty's focus.

In claiming that the locus of reality is the present, Mead holds that "a reality that transcends the present must exhibit itself in the present."[86] A present contains past, present, and future within itself. Further, the present is the locus of reality in that through its emergence, which exhibits both past and future, it alters them. Thus, "We are neither creatures of the necessity of an irrevocable past, nor of any vision given on the Mount."[87] The concept of the present involves both Mead's understanding of the event and of a process. Any present involves an event, a becoming, a happening in experience. An event does not occur in an instant of time, but requires a temporal span. The event is what becomes, and in its relation to other events it gives structure to time. The event, as the locus of the present, "is not a piece cut out anywhere from the temporal dimension of uniformly passing reality."[88] Rather, the happening is an emergent, an occurrence of something which is more than the processes that have led up to it and which adds a content to later passages that they would not otherwise have had.[89] What is involved in a process is neither a mere continuity nor a mere duration, for a process is more than the extending of one event over another event. Any process involves a situation in which the past both conditions and adjusts to what is taking place in a present, and in which what is taking place adjusts to the future as the oncoming event.[90] In this way, both past and future "find their reality in the concretion of what is taking place in an actual present,"[91] and each new present brings about a new past oriented toward a new future. And in this way, while past and future emanate from a present, each temporal dimension of a process is in a sense spread through every other. The human being is understood as a process through which occurs the praxis-oriented constitution of time through acts of adjustment. Its present, as the locus of reality, is understood in terms of the act, which incorporates past and future in its process of adjustment. As Mead states, in stressing the temporal nature of existence, "The unit of existence is the act, not the moment,"[92]

This process of adjustment, which characterizes the present, Mead calls "sociality," and the emergent happening which gives direction to time is "an expression of sociality."[93] Sociality, as "the capacity for being several things at once,"[94] is the stage of transition or phase of adjustment between the arising of the novel within the old and the reorganization which gives rise to the new, and in that transitional span the emergent is in both the old and the new at once. Sociality thus exhibits the temporal nature of the adjustments which constitute the present. It is "the stage betwixt and between the old system and the new that I am referring to. If emergence is a feature of reality, this phase of adjustment, which comes between the ordered universe before the emergent has arisen and that after it has come to terms with the newcomer, must be a feature also of reality."[95] Mead's understanding of the constitution of time incorporates his understanding of emergence or novelty within experience and the reorganization of experience to adjust to the emergent. And, as Mead is careful to point out concerning the significance of time in relation to continuity, "one present slipping into another"[96]—does not constitute the flow of time, but rather as one present slips into the next there must be some break, not of continuity, but within continuity.[97] The continuity is the condition for the novelty, while the novelty reveals the continuity through the oncoming adjustment which accommodates the novel, rendering it continuous with what came before. This relation of novelty and continuity is built into the very fiber of temporal experience: "there is a tang of novelty in each moment of experience."[98]

In light of the above brief and deliberately limited overview, the ensuing discussion will turn to Mead's understanding of the distinction between the specious present[99] and the wider functional present, both of which are defined in terms of the act, and which relate to Merleau-Ponty's understanding of the "fresh present" and "the present in a wider sense." Mead holds that "the functional boundaries of the present are those of its undertaking— of what we are doing. The pasts and futures indicated by such activity belong to the present. They arise out of it and are criticized and tested by it.[100] Further, any functional present is contextually located within, and continuous with, a more encompassing functional present, with larger activities, and thus "we do not tend to have a sense of isolated presents."[101] Any functional present is extended by incorporation of pasts and futures relevant to the activity which marks out a present. These margins or horizons are extended both spatially and temporally through ideation, or the process of reflective awareness. Our functional presents "have ideational margins of varying depth, and within these we are continually occupied in the testing and organizing process of thought."[102] The pasts and futures are crucial to the activity which is constitutive of a functional present and are drawn into our experience of the functional present in the form of memory and expectation.

Whatever the span of the functional present, it is always wider than the specious present, for the functional present is constituted in terms of the ongoing act, while the specious present emerges for awareness when the act is disrupted in some way. Mead states of the specious present that "while it is an actual duration and not a knife-edged present, its duration is not that of the completion of the act within which the object is there"; rather, the characters of things are "related to the individual."[103] As he elaborates,

> The specious present is, then, that within which are present not only the immediate abstracted sense data but also the imagery of past and future experiences taken out of their place in the acts which they imply. It is a real duration, but this duration has no relation to the completion of these acts. These experiences belong to the reconstruction to which a later response will take place. They belong to the beginning of a later act. As such they are in a present.
>
> They do, however, lie within acts which we call those of thought or reflection.[104]

This claim concerning the relation between the functional and specious present is reflected in his following characterization: In a certain sense one's present takes in an entire undertaking through the use of symbolic imagery, and "since the undertaking is a whole that stretches beyond the immediate specious presents, these slip into each other without any edges."[105] But, for example, a loud noise behind an individual may mark out a specious present. "Its lack of relevance to what is going on leaves it nothing but the moment in which the sound vibrated within our ears."[106]

Mead exemplifies the specious present in his analysis of the flight of a bird.

> Thus there is not only the flight of a bird before the individual but also the marking to the individual of the separate positions of the bird within his so-called apperceptive grasp. Such a set of indications to himself, which marked the limits of the immediate change in his experience, is the so-called specious present. It defines the limits of the span within

which temporal passage does not transcend existence for this individual's experience. The limits of this span are uncertain because it so connects with the coming experience that there is no break in the temporal continuity, and because the passing experience goes over into memory imagery so imperceptibly that with difficulty he draws the line between them.[107]

What these examples of the specious present exemplify is twofold. First, the specious present represents the reconstructive phase in the breakdown of the act rather than the act's process toward completion, the moment of the loss of the objectivity which characterizes the ongoing act in the functional present. This point will be put aside until the discussion of self in the next chapter. Second, and more relevant for the present context, though also important for the next chapter, the experience of the specious present involves the direct experience of change. Change itself requires the feature of sociality, for "change involves departure from a condition that must continue in some sense to fulfill the sense of change from that condition."[108] And, Mead is careful to note that the specious present or the "immediacy of the now is never lost," but rather, this experience of the specious present provides the basis for diverse constructions of the past and projections of the future.[109] The direct sense of change given in the specious present is never lost and is the starting point for the constitution of a functional present temporally structured through praxis. The immediacy of the now, with its direct sense of change, is absorbed into the functional present in the ongoing act, though it can come to the fore in the disruption of the act. And thus, "There is an unalterable temporal direction in what is taking place. . . . There is a certain temporal process in experience. What has taken place issues in what is taking place, and in this passage what has occurred determines spatio-temporally what is passing into the future."[110] The change that occurs in the process of adjustment is directly experienced in the specious present and forms the starting point for the constitution, through praxis, of the structure of the functional present. Thus Mead does not hold that memory and anticipation create the sense of temporal flow, but rather build on it at each end. To get beyond the specious present, to the constitution of the functional present, involves both memory and ideation. Memory is reconstructive. The function of memory imagery is the filling out of our present perceptions. The reconstruction of the past lies in a present oriented toward a future. Thus Mead takes issue with Bergson's understanding of memory in a way similar to Merleau-Ponty's criticism of Bergson on this point. As Mead states,

> The picture which Bergson gives of it seems to me to belie both its character in experience and its functional character—the picture of an enormous incessantly accreting accumulation of "images" against which our nervous systems defend us by their selective mechanisms. The present does not carry any such burden with it. It passes into another present with the effects of the past in its textures, not with the burden of its events upon its back.[111]

It can be seen from the discussion thus far that there are striking similarities between Mead and Merleau-Ponty in their respective treatments of time. Both reject any absolutizing of the derived time of science in favor of the priority of lived time in which such derivations are rooted, and in the process reject various philosophical understandings of time that in one sense or another result from an inadequate understanding of the derivative nature of the time of physics. For both, lived temporality entails the human praxis which gives rise to a perceived world, and incorporates a temporally extended present within which experience opens onto past and future and to which past and future adjust. Because of this, time, for both, moves as a whole, and does so with depth. Both look at the priority of the present in a strict and in a broad sense, and explicate the sense of a depth of the present. They offer a view of time which is constitutive for the very sense of human existence.[112] As indicated earlier, however, while Merleau-Ponty remains rooted in the lived time of the concrete subject, Mead's understanding of time must ultimately be placed in the broad cosmic context of a metaphysics of sociality, and it is to this context that the discussion will turn.

Joas holds that in light of Mead's criticism of Whitehead's metaphysical hypostatization of an abstraction in his world of Platonic 'eternal' objects, Mead himself could not "seek fulfillment of his own task" concerning temporality "in a speculative philosophy of nature."[113] As Joas continues, "Mead does not believe it necessary to take recourse to a Minkowskian four-dimensional unexperiencable world, but rather to introduce a concept of the 'common world', into which the human individuals who are linked with one another through signals have in fact always entered."[114] Mead, however, does have a temporalist speculative philosophy of nature, though one which does not either move to an unexperiencable reality or reify abstracted aspects of experience, but which rather attempts to provide an understanding of the concreteness of experienced reality as the foundation for any abstraction. Mead's approach to a speculative philosophy of nature is not via metaphysical hypostatization of abstractions but via the implications of the concrete experience from which abstractions are made.

Mead avoids recourse to a Minkowskian world or any metaphysically reified scientific world in two different ways, both of which relate to his location of the method and concepts of science within the context of a general theory of the temporal constitution of human experience. First, as noted by Joas, the common world provides the context of lived experience from which scientific abstactions are made and to which they ultimately refer back, thus avoiding the reification of scientific contents. And, second, because of his recognition of the functional status of the objects of scientific reflection, his own temporalist metaphysics will not be a metaphysics of events as understood in the context of science but of events in the context of a metaphysics of sociality which provides the indefinitely rich concrete basis for the common "world that is there" as well as for the second-level abstractions of science.

Mead holds that sociality runs throughout nature in so far as the emergence of novelty requires that objects be at once both in the old system and in that which arises with the new. Because, for Mead, sociality runs throughout nature, and because relativity is "an extreme example of sociality,"[115] Mead at times speaks as if relativity theory itself provided the cosmic context within and from which human activity emerges. However, Mead holds not only that "the Minkowski space time is as much an hypothesis as the de Broglie wave constitution of matter,"[116] but also that relativity theory itself carries only "the logical finality of any consistent deduction. . . . The scientist himself expects this doctrine to be reconstructed just as other scientific doctrines have been reconstructed."[117] The real significance of relativity theory for Mead is that relativity theory points out more sharply than ever before the dependence of scientific theory upon the perceived world.[118] This is not an attempt to absolutize relativity theory in any way, but rather to show that relativity itself helps reveal the *method* by which any scientific content is achieved. Further, relativity theory, as exemplifying both the broad concept of emergent environments in relation to organic activity as well as the distinctively human ability to take the role of the other, is uniquely suited for highlighting some key features of everyday temporal experience. This examination of the temporal constitution of lived experience in turn shows not only that the Minkowski universe is inadequate because it does not fit with experience, but also that no scientific explanation, with its derivative content, yields the concreteness of the reality of lived experience.

Mead claims to have "endeavoured to present the world which is an implication of the scientific method of discovery with entire abstraction from any epistemological or metaphysical presuppositions or complications."[119] Yet, his objection here to metaphysics is an objection to the move to an unchanging reality, to understanding science as a method of knowing the unchangeable rather than as a method of determining the form of change.[120] For Mead, the understanding of scientific endeavor as a method of determining the form of change, combined with his understanding of the temporal constitution of the perceived world, leads toward a speculative metaphysical vision of a universe engaged in the ongoing temporal activity of the adjustments of sociality. This accounts for Mead's continual tendency to illustrate the temporal dimension of both the organic and the inorganic universe in terms of examples drawn from relativity theory. For Mead, not only does relativity theory, properly interpreted, point toward the priority of lived temporal experience and help highlight certain of its key features, but it also helps highlight and reflects the dynamics of a temporal, evolutionary universe which provides the cosmic context for the temporal constitution of the perceived world as well as for the second-level derivative abstractions of science.

Though Mead's metaphysics of sociality is drawn from the features of everyday experience, his metaphysics is not an anthropomorphizing of the universe but rather an attempt to understand, by speculative analogy, the features of a universe within which the human is at home and with which the emergent activities of the human are at once continuous and unique. Mead's metaphysics is an extension of his focus on human experience as radically temporal. From the character of experience he projects the character of a universe in which such experience can come to be and in which science can develop its various contents. Mead is not seeking a comprehensive scientific view of the universe in any sense[121] but, rather, is seeking to understand the conditons by which any scientific view can emerge. Here it must be noted that while Mead's general theory of sociality is often held to be an extension of his social psychology, Mead's social psychology has been seen to incorporate a strong phenomenological strain. Thus, his general theory of sociality can be read also as an extension of his phenomenological examination of concrete human existence. His social psychology is indeed more than a specific application of his general theory of sociality because his phenomenological examination of concrete human existence is not a specific application of the general theory of sociality but rather the concrete ground for it, though the general theory in turn accounts for a universe that allows for such an experience of concrete human existence as described by Mead, and this general theory gains its verification in the textures of concrete human existence. Mead's metaphsycial claims, like all claims according to his pragmatic philosophy, conform to the dynamics of experimental method, a method which itself has been seen to include a phenomenological dimension.[122]

Mead's concern with the sense of nature, not as a Minkowskian universe or any scientifically described universe, nor as the world that is there through human time constitution, but rather as that natural order within which the human emerges, is caputred in his concern with nature as that which we never totally encompass in our perception or theories, "which is independent of all the worlds of perception and scientific theory, that would explain all of them and yet would not transcend them in the sense of being of a nature which could not appear in perception or scientific theory, and would be independent of observation and perception and thought, and would itself include these."[123] Mead backs away from such a conception, for as frequently happens when he comes close to focusing on reality apart from life, he seems to find in this focus a danger of absolutizing the contents of science, confounding his own drive toward a speculative temporalist metaphysics of sociality with the illicit reification of the eventful world of science.

The strength of this metaphysical drive, combined with the implicit but misplaced concern over its ultimate reification of scientific contents, sheds light on Mead's ambivalence in his writings concerning the scope of application of several of his key concepts relating to temporality.[124] A process, as involving ordered time as opposed to mere continuity or mere duration seems, on the one hand, to be limited to life processes. Mead states that "I know of no process that is not that of a living form."[125] And again, he says of perspectives to which processes give rise, that "the conception of the world without any organisms is one that is without perspectives."[126] Yet, he applies the principle of sociality, which implies and is implied by processes and their emergent characters, to inorganic situations. Mead wanted explicitly "to emphasize the fact that the appearance of mind is only the culmination of that sociality which is found throughout the universe, its culmination lying in the fact that the organism, by occupying the attitudes of others, can occupy its own attitude in the role of the other."[127] As he exemplifies, "Emergent life changes the character of the world just as emergent velocities change the characters of masses."[128] In a similar vein he refers to "the increase in mass of a moving object as an extreme example of sociality. That is, if we keep this increase in mass within the field of possible experience, we have to treat the moving body as in two different systems, for the moving object has its own time and space and mass due to its motion, which time, space and mass are different from those of the system relative to which it is moving."[129] Thus Mead holds that even for the atom, "the present is as much weighted with the future as it is for more specifically organic structures."[130]

The role of process in lower levels of organic forms is unambiguous, and is well exemplified in Mead's example of the plant. "In the twisting of a plant toward the light, the later effect of the light reached by the twisting controls the process."[131] And the temporal dynamics of sociality, even at this level, involve the stratification of nature by perspectives, at least in rudimentary form, for organic activity lower than the human brings about an ordering of spatiotemporal events via selection and acts of adjustment. The perspectives of nonhuman organic forms, however, are nonsharable, neither time nor space are experienced by these organisms, and, concomitantly, no enduring physical objects emerge. Lower animals experience a universe which contains no space-time reference systems, a Minkowskian universe of events in which there is mere passage. Thus he states:

> In living forms lower than the human, the distant perspective may through sensitivity exist in the experience of the form and the grasping of this in the adjustments of conduct answers to the formation of the stratification of nature, but the reconstruction of the pattern within which the life of the organism lies does not fall with the experience of the organism. . . . The maintenance of a temporal structure, i.e., of a

process, still stratifies nature, and gives rise to spaces and times, but neither they nor the entities that occupy them enter as experiential facts into the process of the organisms.[132]

Here it is important to note that for Mead such lower forms *experience* the universe as one of a Minkowskian universe of mere passage, a claim quite different from the assertion that the universe in which such organisms act is in fact a Minkowskian universe of mere passage, for Mead's understanding of the sociality of the present that runs throughout nature rules out the latter claim. As Mead stresses, "Now what we are accustomed to call social is only a so-called consciousness of such a process, but the process is not identical with the consciousness of it, for that is an awareness of the situation."[133] Nature, for Mead, is radically temporal and radically historical, though his discussions are frequently ambiguous concerning the scope of the temporal features most fully displayed in human experience.

An emergent novelty cannot be known in advance, for though what emerges is continuous with what came before, this is not so until after it has emerged, with the accompanying readjustment it involves. Thus, it could not be predicted from what came before. Mead's tendency to speak in terms of the inability to predict or deduce the novel emergent from what has gone before can again well hide the full cosmic significance of his claim, for not only is the novel not epistemically predictable or deducible from its conditions, but it is not ontologically reducible to them. Mead's claim here is not about our knowledge only, but also about the ontological status of novelty. Further, with the emergence of the event, its relations to antecedent processes become conditions or causes, for the becoming marks out and "in a sense selects" what has made possible its unique occurrence.[134] Causality, like temporality and novelty, is ultimately not limited to the level of human experience, though it enters uniquely into the conscious experience of the human. And, at no level can the operation of causality be identified with determinism.

Mead's ambivalence concerning the cosmic extension of certain concepts is very much in evidence in his discussion of the past, though from a slightly different focus. In Mead's central doctrine of the nature of the past, he is concerned to show that it is not only our viewpoint or interpretation of the past that has altered, but rather that the past itself has changed, for the past "in itself" is not a past at all. If we could recapture the past in its total concreteness, simply as it occurred, it would not be a past for any present, but would be simply a recaptured present, a present that once was. Its relation to the present is the very ground of its pastness.[135] As he summarizes, "One present slipping into another does not connote what is meant by a past."[136] Yet this turns out, within Mead's focus, to be explicitly directed not toward the relation between past and future in an independent ontological reality, but toward the reality of the perspective of the interpreter, who elicits the meaningful structure of the past from the perspective of the present.

As Mead states, in one of his few clear distinctions, "The long and short of it is that the past (or *the meaningful structure of the past*) is as hypothetical as the future."[137] Yet this clarification can itself be quite misleading, hiding the radically temporalist nature of his understanding of the past, especially when combined with his further claim that in the sense that certain events have occurred, the past is obdurate, finished, final. In this sense " 'the past' in passage is irrecoverable as well as irrevocable. It is producing all the reality that there is."[138] The above two statements by Mead may at first seem to clearly distinguish a fixed past as independent of human knowing from the meaningful structure of the past as changing in relation to present interpretations. This reference to the finality of the past, however, is in fact a reference only to one dimension of the past in its independence of human interpretation. For the past as a past to the present, even independently of our present interpretation of the past, is a different past because of its relation to the present.

The present possibilities and potentialities of what is past relate to the present as the conditioning factor of its pastness. The potentialities and possibilities of a past present are gone, but the past, as the past to the emerging future, exists now as the potentialities and possibilities within the present. And as any present to which it relates changes, so its changes, no matter how slight this change may be, for the potentialities and possibilities that make it what it is in its concreteness change. As long as there is a present actualizing possibilities that can be actualized but need not be, there is a changing past, for with every emergent present, certain possibilities that were in the past real possibilities are no longer possibilities for future emergent presents, while possibilities that were once not there come to be.

As Mead emphasizes, the organism's holding together of future and past as possibilities "is but an instance of what takes place in nature, if nature is an evolution, i.e. if it proceeds by re-construction in the presence of conflicts, and if, therefore, possibil-ities of different reconstructions are present, reconstructing its pasts as well as its futures. It is the relativity of time, that is, an indefinite number of possible orders of events, that introduces possibility in nature."[139] This point is manifest more fully in the following:

> The past is there conditioning the present and its passage into the future, but in the organization of tendencies embod-ied in one individual there may be an emergent which gives to these tendencies a structure which belongs only to the sit-uation of that individual. The tendencies coming from past passage, and from the conditioning that is inherent in pas-sage, become different influences when they have taken on this organized structure of tendencies. *This would be as true of the balance of processes of disruption and of agglomera-tion in a star* as in the adjustment to each other of a living form and its environment. . . .
>
> This emergent character, being responsible for a rela-tionship of passing processes, *sets up a given past* that is, so to speak, a perspective of the object within which this char-acter appears. . . .
>
> This amounts to saying that where being is existence but not becoming there is no past, and that the determina-tion involved in passage is a condition of a past but not its realization.[140]

Within Mead's radically temporalist philosophy, neither the past independent of our interpretations nor the past as interpreted is a past that is 'just there' independently of what is taking place in the present. There is no past except in relation to a present, for the relation of the past to the present is the ground of its pastness. This claim holds both for the metaphysical concreteness of the past independent of human historical awareness and for the past in relation to our knowledge of it. Mead often fails to make clear pre-cisely this distinction, thus leading his dicussions to a not infre-quent ambiguous slipping between these two dimensions, an ambiguity connected with his ambivalent attitude toward specula-tive metaphysics, and manifest in his ambiguities concerning the scope of sociality and its related temporal features.

As indicated above, past, present, and future are analytic parts of the ongoing process of adjustment that is made by the emergent, the novel, in the context of sociality. In this sense, time, sociality, emergence, and perspectives pervade all of nature, and there are diverse levels of sociality, temporality, and perspectives emergent within nature, as well as diverse levels of emergence itself. As Mead illustrates, while there is a continuity among the inorganic, the organic, and the mental, there is also "a great contrast between application of the principle of sociality in these different fields."[141] Any emergent novelty affects an environment, and different levels of sociality or adjustment give rise to different kinds of environments. Both the process and the environment which it effects are objectively there in nature. And, once an emergent has arisen, it enters into the conditions for the emergence of further novelties.

Sociality and its related temporal featues all become specialized in human activity. Thus, in its most developed sense, time emerges only with the emergence of the spatial features of the perceived world, for time "is a passage that is a whole which is broken up into parts and abstracted from those dimensions that persist when action is inhibited. It is out of this abstraction that these dimensions appear as space."[142] Time, in this sense of human experience, involves the constitution of the consciousness of time in the context of the intersubjective praxis which gives rise to a perceived world. And, once intelligence, which is itself a creative process, has emerged, it enters into the conditions for the emergence of new orders of events by selecting and acting upon novel hypotheses which in turn stratify nature in novel ways. The human is uniquely temporal in that the constitution of time consciousness is essential to the distinctively human level of functioning. The existence of a past is not memory of a past, and the existence of a future is not anticipation of a future. The consciousness of time is inextricably connected with the emergence of the spatial features of the perceived world through the functioning of memory and anticipation. The constitution of time consciousness is inherently intersubjective, for such constitution involves the intersubjective praxis which gives rise to a perceived world.[143] Human temporality, like the being of the human in general, is continuous with the rest of nature yet unique. Indeed, Mead finds such a conciliation between continuity and novelty itself possible through the evolutionary, temporal nature of the universe: "Ancient metaphysics divorced the two inseparable components of passage—the continuous and the emergent. The doctrine of evolution has obliterated the scandal from the union out of which arise all objects in experience."[144]

Mead's discussion of time from the cosmic perspective can be seen, then, to reveal the same situation reached through his analysis of the human constitution of time consciousness. It was seen that neither the durational spread of the specious present nor the actively constituted functional present are subjective experiences set over against a static world. What the cosmic approach further points out is that the temporal features of the perceived world, and the constitution of time consciousness which gives rise to these features, are possible because experience throws one outward onto a universe exhibiting the temporal dynamics of sociality. The consciously temporal, historical nature of human experience is an emergent level of functioning continuous with the temporal, historical nature of the independent reality within which the world of human experience emerges and within which it is embedded. Thus Mead stesses that "what calls for emphasis is that the independent reality carries with it no implication of finality."[145] Mead's metaphysics of sociality in fact characterizes an independent reality with no implication of finality. As he aptly summarizes, "Creative intelligence is an instance of the creative advance of nature."[146]

It has been seen above that Mead's metaphysics of sociality moves beyond the confines of Merleau-Ponty's phenomenological focus, which remains within the context of the temporal dimensions of human existence. Mead, however, does not, in the process of expanding these temporal dimensions, fall into the trap of reifying the objects of scientific reflection, though he draws heavily upon relativity theory as a model both for understanding lived temporality and for expanding such an understanding to a radically temporalist metaphysics. Although Mead avoids such a pitfall, the very concept of sociality, as extended beyond the human constitution of time consciousness, requires a cautionary note highlighted by Merleau-Ponty's more limited phenomenological focus. Mead defines sociality as the capacity for being in two systems at once: "There is sociality in nature in so far as the emergence of novelty requires that objects be at once both in the old system and in that which arises with the new."[147] Yet it has been seen that simultaneity is a product of the praxis-oriented constitution of time consciousness and the correlative development of a perceived world. By the term "at once" here, Mead must be taken to intend not simultaneity in a literal sense but rather transition. The being in two systems at once represents the passing nature of the present, the present in its process of reconstruction or adjustment to the novel, that gives rise to a new past and a new future. In brief, it cannot be understood in terms of a measurement of time, such as simultaneity, but as the activity which allows time to be, because it is the activity which is constitutive of the present as a present.

Even in speaking in this way, however, the warning contained in Merleau-Ponty's refusal to follow such a speculative path maintains a certain validity, which is implicitly recognized by Mead:

> A present marks out and in a sense selects what has made its peculiarity possible. It creates with its uniqueness a past and a future. As soon as we view it, it becomes a history and a prophecy. . . . If we ask what may be the temporal spread of the uniqueness which is responsible for a present, the answer must be, in Whitehead's terms, that it is a period long enough to enable the object to be what it is. *But the question is ambiguous, for the term 'temporal spread' implies a measure of time.* The past as it appears with the present and future, is the relation of the emergent event to the situation out of which it arose, and it is the event that defines that situation. The continuance or disappearance of that which arises is the present passing into the future. Past, present, and future belong to a passage which attains temporal structure through the event, and they may be considered long or short as they are compared with other such passages. But as existing in nature, *so far as such a statement has significance,* the past and the future are the boundries of what we term the present, and are determined by the conditioning relationships of the event to its situation.[148]

Thus, Mead's ambivalence concerning the extension of temporal concepts to include a full-blown speculative metaphysics of nature can, in the last analysis, be seen to involve a fear not only of reifying the events of scientific theory, but also of extending his phenomenologically founded claims beyond the confines of human experience. But, "turning the tables," so to speak, while Merleau-Ponty's existential approach can offer a cautionary note to Mead, Mead's own extension of temporality to a metaphysics of sociality can provide an expanded context for Merleau-Ponty's insights into the lived experience of temporality, offering the opportunity, perhaps, for a more complete philosophical stance.

This chapter has shown that the respective analyses of temporality by Mead and Merleau-Ponty reflect the diverse but complementary frameworks of their respective pragmatic and phenomenological orientations. Though the cosmic scope of their respective examinations differ, yet for both the human is uniquely temporal, and its action-oriented time consciousness is interwoven into the very fabric of the content of awareness. Perceiver and perceived are thus bound into an inseparable temporal unity in a way that at once undercuts the claims of both realism and idealism, rationalism and traditional empiricism, and renders illicit all attempts to reify the contents of science or to substitute derivative time for the lived experience of temporality that grounds these abstractions. This lived experience of temporality reveals the depth and movement of temporal passage, as well as the privileged role of the present from which the subject opens onto past and future. What remains to be examined is the manner in which the intersubjective constitution of time is inseparably interconnected with the intersubjective constitution of the self, such that the temporally founded unity of perceiver and perceived is ultimately the unity of self and world, made possible through the radically temporal nature of the self. This leads directly to the focus of the next chapter.

4. DIMENSIONS OF
   THE DECENTERED SELF

THE RESPECTIVE VIEWS of the self found in the positions of Mead and Merleau-Ponty include a common focus on the nature of the self as social or intersubjective and on the importance of a type of role taking in the development of the self which involves the mutual interrelation of the emergence of self-awareness and the awareness of the other. Thus, they both reject any trace of a view of the awareness of other selves as derived by analogy with one's own self-experience, or of one's own self-experience as derived by imitation of the other. Further, they both reject any vestiges of an underlying, atemporal, intuited thinking substance, yet without dissolving the self into the content of introspective awareness or a psychical awareness accompanying experience. While Mead has an explicit doctrine of the self and its emergence, however, that of Merleau-Ponty, although central to his philosophy, is only latent, and can be drawn out in terms of Mead's position. And, while Mead explicitly focuses upon the self as the cognitive and reflective dimension of the biological organism, Merleau-Ponty's focus on the lived body points toward the direction for a fuller development of Mead's concept of the self, a development which is to some extent already latent in Mead's philosophy.[1]

The following discussion will turn to the intersubjective nature of the self and to the function of role taking in the development of the personal level of intersubjectivity out of a primordial, pre-personal sociality or corporeal intersubjectivity of the lived body, first in Mead's, then in Merleau-Ponty's philosophy. For Mead, the significant symbol, consciousness of meanings, mind, and self, all arise in interrelated fashion. Although there can be societies without minds or selves, the reverse does not hold, for mind and self are generated in the social context. Mead explains this in the biosocial terms of an ongoing social process[2] of interacting biological organisms. He defines the social conduct of any individual "as that conduct arising out of impulses whose specific stimuli are found in other individuals belonging to the same biologic group."[3] Any society, to be a society even on a minimal level, must be made up of biological organisms participating in a social act, using the early stages of each other's actions as guides to the completion of the act. In this way a "conversation of gestures" takes place. A gesture represents a tendency or attitude of an organism, and a "conversation of gestures" consists in the continued readjustment of one individual to another. Nonsignificant gestures have meanings and are signs in that they mean the later stages of the act, but their function does not include an awareness or consciousness of their meanings. In the process of becoming aware of meanings, the biological organism is transformed into the minded organism and the self; nonsignificant gestures become significant symbols, meanings "in mind," ingredients in conscious communications; the conversation of gestures becomes the conversation of meanings.

This transformation to significant symbols requires a particular kind of society and particular physiological capacities in organisms. Significant symbols emerge when individuals can call out in themselves the responses their gestures call out in the other, using the responses of the other to control their own ongoing activity. This function is not that of imitation. As Mead stresses,

> The likeness of the actions is of minimal importance compared with the fact that the actions of one form have the implicit meaning of a certain response to another form. The probable beginning of human communication was in cooperation, not in imitation, where conduct differed and yet where the act of the one answered to and called out the act of the other. . . . Here we have the matter and the form of the social

object, and here we have also the medium of communication and reflection..[4]

Indeed, for Mead, "Social consciousness is the presupposition of imitation."[5]

This social consciousness at the pre-personal level of the human organism is evinced in Mead's discussion of the effective adjustment of the infant "to the little society upon which it has so long to depend." As he explains, "The child is for a long time dependent upon moods and emotional attitudes. How quickly he adjusts himself to this is a continual surprise. He responds to facial expressions earlier than to most stimuli and answers with appropriate expressions of his own, before he makes responses that we consider significant."[6] This pre-personal coexistence is the social foundation for role taking. It is the "being with" which underlies the taking of roles. Such intercorporeality underlies the very ability to take roles, for taking the role of the other presupposes "being with" the other.

Though meaning emerges in the interplay of gestures, consciousness of meaning emerges, not when meanings are habitualized, but precisely when conflicts in action lead to an intensification of the discrimination of stimuli. Meaning, however, cannot be understood in terms of the experiential association of, or accumulation of, stimuli, for "the association of one content with another content is not the symbolism of meaning."[7] Rather, only in the interaction among actors can such an intensification lead to the awareness of one's own responses that constitutes the awareness of meaning, for only in this situation must one pay reflective attention to one's own attitude in order to anticipate the response of the other, which then becomes the occasion for a further anticipatory attitude of one's own. As Mead summarizes,

> A man's reaction toward weather conditions has no influence upon the weather itself. It is of importance for the success of his conduct that he should be conscious not of his own attitudes, of his own habits of response, but of the signs of rain or fair weather. Successful social conduct brings one into a field within which a consciousness of one's own attitudes helps toward the control of the conduct of others.[8]

In this way individuals take the role of the other in the development of their conduct, and in this way there develops the common content which provides community of meaning. The emergence of mind involves this ability to be aware of meanings, and this awareness relates, strictly speaking, not to the actual reaction of the other, or even to an awareness of one's own attitude, but rather to the *relation between* one's own actions and the anticipated possible responses of others to them. And, in this way there emerges not just consciousness but self-consciousness. These human capabilities all require the ability to go beyond the limitation to the present, to be aware of the future possible phase of the social act.

Within this process of taking the role of the other, minds and selves arise through the internalization of the conversation of gestures in the form of the vocal gesture. The basis of the significant symbol is the vocal gesture which, more than any other gesture, affects the individual as it affects others. As Mead exemplifies, "When a man calls out 'Fire!' he is not only exciting other people but himself in the same fashion. He knows what he is about. That, you see, constitutes biologically what we refer to as a 'universe of discourse'."[9] It is a common meaning which is communicated to everyone at the same time it is communicated to the self. With the presence in behavior of significant symbols, mind has emerged. Mind is precisely this symbolic structure of behavior. Meanings are not subjective or private or mental. Rather they are "there" in the social context and are thus objective.

Mead denies that the self can be identified with "what is commonly called consciousness, that is with the private and subjective thereness of the character of objects,"[10] and distinguishes between consciousness and self-consciousness. *Consciousness* as frequently used refers to the field of experience. "A man alone has, fortunately or unfortunately, access to his own toothache, but that is not what we mean by self-consciousness."[11] Rather, "the essence of the self . . . is cognitive: it lies in the internalized conversation of gestures which constitutes thinking, or in terms of which thought or reflection proceeds. And hence the origin and foundations of the self, like those of thinking, are social."[12]

Through taking the role of the other, and specifically through the role taking involved in language, individuals can respond to themselves from the perspective of the other, thus becoming objects to themselves. The self is that which can be an object to itself, a characteristic "that distinguishes it from other objects as well as from the body. . . . The body does not experience itself as a whole, in the sense in which the self in some way enters into the experience of the self."[13] The self is not awareness of the body, for one may experience and be conscious of one's body, with its feelings and sensations, as a part of the environment rather than as one's own. Only when the self or self-consciousness has arisen can these experiences be identified with, or appropriated by, the self.[14]

Mead holds that after a self has arisen, we can in a certain sense conceive of it as existing alone, since it can in a certain sense provide for itself its social experiences. But, it is impossible to conceive of a self arising outside of social experience.[15] Not only can selves exist only in relationship to other selves, but no absolute line can be drawn between our own selves and the selves of others, since our own selves are there for and in our experience only insofar as the selves of others exist and enter into our experience. Thus Mead presents the very process of thought as a "play of gesture between selves, even when those selves are a part of our inner self-consciousness."[16] The significance of Mead's understanding of the genesis of the self in terms of intersubjectivity is well summarized in his emphasis that

> the appearance of the self is antedated by the tendencies to take the attitudes of the others, so that the existence of others is not a reflection of his self-experiences into other individuals. The others are not relative to his self, but his self and the others are relative to the perspective of his social organism. . . . The individual, the other, and the environment are selectively determinitive of each other.[17]

Within this context, the other is not grasped by analogy with one's own interiority but rather other selves exist in their corporeal conduct and are grasped by direct access in perception. As Mead states, "Persons, or selves, are things in our immediate experience, and the individual in that social environment of things is himself a person, or, better, a self. . . . This amounts to saying that social objects, or persons, are immediately present in our experience, or, in customary psychological language, are perceived."[18]

Mead emphasizes the import of his interactional view in his claim that "The attempt to proceed otherwise leads to an impossible solipsism or to an equally impossible determinism."[19] The organism, as social or intercorporeal or intersubjective, is the source of the intersubjective nature of selfhood and of the self as cognitive, of the "ability to be the other at the same time that he is himself."[20] This ability to be the other, as indicated earlier, is developed through Mead's concept of role taking.

Mead distinguishes two phases in the genesis of the self through role taking, as illustrated respectively in play and in games.[21] In play the child takes different roles, passing from one role to another according to whim. The child plays at being a parent, a teacher, etc.[22] "You cannot count on the child; you cannot assume that all the things he does are going to determine what he will do at any moment. He is not organized into a whole. The child has no definite character, no definite personality."[23] The child is taking the role of the other, for "the child says something in one character and responds in another character, and then his responding in another character is a stimulus to himself in the first character, and so the conversation goes on."[24] In this stage, however, the self is constituted merely by an organization of the particular attitudes of other individuals toward oneself and toward one another in individual social acts.[25]

In the second stage the self reaches its full development by organizing the individual attitudes of others into the organized social or group attitudes. In this way the self becomes "an individual reflection of the general systematic pattern of social or group behavior in which it and the others are all involved—a pattern which enters as a whole into the individual's experience in terms of these organized group attitudes which . . . he takes toward himself, just as he takes the individual attitudes of others."[26] This organized community or social group which gives to the individual the unity of self Mead calls "the generalized other." The generalized other varies in scope, and while Mead refers to the generalized other in terms of a community or society, there are many types of groups or subgroups which exemplify a generalized other.[27]

An organized game, as opposed to mere play, involves this incorporation by the individual of a generalized other. In an organized game, the child who plays must be ready to take the attitude of everyone else involved in the game, and these different roles must have a definite relationship to each other. Thus, using Mead's example of a baseball team as an instance of a social group, a participant must assume the attitudes of the other players as an organized unity, and this organization controls the response of the individual participant. Each one of the participants' own acts is set by "his being everyone else on the team," in so far as the organization of the various attitudes controls his own response. "The team is the generalized other in so far as it enters—as an organized process or social activity—into the experience of any one of the individual members of it."[28] The generalized other of whatever type of group consists in the organization of the roles of individual participants in the social act. As Mead summarizes the import of the process of role taking, "this process of relating one's own organism to the others in the interactions that are going on, in so far as it is imported into the conduct of the individual within the conversation of the 'I' and the 'me', constitutes the self."[29] Before turning to a somewhat detailed examination of the 'I' and the 'me' in Mead's understanding of the cognitive or reflective or dialogical nature of the self, the ensuing discussion will turn first to Merleau-Ponty's understanding of the existential self, for his more limited focus on the self can both help set the stage for, and itself gain added significance from, a detailed analysis of the "I-me" dynamics of the self in Mead's position.

Merleau-Ponty's latent view of an existential self, immersed in his well-known doctrine of the lived body and the lived world[30] in the *Phenomonology of Perception*, has its ground prepared in the account of the emergence of the human level of behavior in relation to levels of behavior that precede it, dealt with in *The Structure of Behavior*. There, he, like Mead, emphasizes that the higher, human or symbolic level of signification emerges from the lower level, but is not reducible to or explainable only in terms of it.[31] This parallels, in part, Mead's account of the transformation from nonsignificant gestures in animals to significant gestures on the human level. Further, in distinguishing the vital and human levels of behavior, Merleau-Ponty recognizes the ability of animals to relate to signs as signals in contrast to the response of humans to signs as symbols. That in "animal behavior signs always remain signals and never become symbols"[32] is evinced by the fact that if an animal is trained to jump from one chair to another, it will not be able to jump from another object which it does not recognize as a chair.[33] In contrast, the human level of behavior, as essentially symbolic, and as entailing the comprehension of possibilities latent within its situation, is incarnated in the lived body.

This notion of the lived body (*le corps propre*) indicates the body which is owned and proper to an individual, with its prepersonal and personal dimensions and with its individual and general levels. The concrete subject's generality and individuality are "two stages of a unique structure"[34] between which there is a certain reciprocity of receiving and giving. The general stage, as the pre-personal dimension of the lived body prior to the personal level, is that to which the personal is receptive, and that which constitutes the world with a pregiven meaning in relation to personal constitution. Hence the pre-personal dimension of the lived body also mediates the personal aspect of the other, since on that level there is already a corporeal unity in a common world.

For Merleau-Ponty the "primordial generality" of the lived body, like a general function, plays a central role in the system of self-others-world. On this level, the body expresses meaning and entails a oneness with a unified field or world as well as a oneness with others at a fundamental level of quasi-indifferentiation from others.[35] As Merleau-Ponty states the inadequate alternative to this, "The other is never quite a personal being, if I myself am totally one, and if I grasp myself as apodictically self-evident."[36] This pre-personal dimension of the lived body is comprised of my body and that of the other at an anonymous level of unity from which the personal level is derived. It is through this lived body and its gesture that the other (self) is grasped as a subject of perceptual consciousness, as "manifestations of behavior"[37] coexisting in a common world and as existence or being-in-the-world. Hence, for Merleau-Ponty the lived body of the other, its conduct and gestures, its corporeal intentions and significances, are experienced by direct access through the perception of the lived body, and thus he overcomes opposed views, which presuppose this dimension of experience.

The primordial level of the lived body is presupposed by scientific objective thought, for which "the existence of other people is a difficulty."[38] Similarly, the view that it is by analogy with our own interiority that we understand others is overcome by this account of the lived body. According to this latter view, others are grasped as exterior so that "the actions of others are . . . always understood through my own; the 'one' through the 'I'."[39] For Merleau-Ponty, these two rejected accounts of access to the lived body through explanation in terms of the objectified body and through correlation with one's own interiority presuppose what they are trying to explain, the intentions and conduct of the lived body already grasped on the lived level. This conduct is directly accessible through a basic level of affinity central to the lived body and human existence precisely as primordial generality, as intersubjective, and as pre-personal.

The above two inadequate theories presuppose the significance of intentions in the other's body which are immediately grasped as one with the intentions of my own body and as "the prolongations of my own intentions, . . . a familiar way of dealing with the world. Henceforth, as the parts of my body together comprise a system, so my body and the other's are one whole, two sides of one and the same phenomenon." In a sense, then, there is a commonness between my body and the bodies of others, which are constituted as an internal relation, so that corporeal intentions exist at this level prior to any explicit distinction between individual bodies.[40] Because these are internal relations between my consciousness and my body, and between my lived body and that of others, one cannot be complete or adequately understood without the other. Thus, there is a certain completion achieved in the system in the interrelation among the self and others on this level of the lived body, as Merleau-Ponty explicitly indicates: "Between my consciousness and my body as I experience it, between this phenomenal body of mine and that of another as I see it from the outside, there exists an internal relation which causes the other to appear as the completion of the system."[41] Hence, corporeal intentions expressed in the lived body are grasped as such in a whole which precedes this experience. For Merleau-Ponty, it is this dimension of inherence of self in the lived body accessible from within and from without on which movies both depend and which they reveal. "This is why the movies can be so gripping in their presentation of man: they do not give us his thoughts . . . but his conduct or behavior. They directly present to us that special way of being in the world, of dealing with things and other people, which we can see in the sign language of gesture and gaze and which clearly defines each person we know."[42]

It is precisely this lived body and its intentions, as directly accessible, that are exemplified by the fifteen-month-old baby who opens its mouth when its fingers are playfully taken between the teeth with a pretense of biting them, showing how such intentions are already intersubjective in the immediate grasp of their significance. For the baby, its mouth experienced from the inside is for the same purpose as my mouth experienced from the outside, both capable of the same intentions, made possible by the corporeal intersubjectivity. " 'Biting' has immediately, for it, an intersubjective significance. It perceives its intentions in its body, and my body with its own, and thereby my intentions in its own body."[43] Further, it is only in the context of the intentions grasped in others that the awareness of awareness is constituted. For on the prepersonal level, precisely as lived, entailing the lived world and the lived body, there is a oneness with others and with the world more basic even than the personal level.

It is clear, then, that for Merleau-Ponty as for Mead, solipsism is a fallacy and a misconception. For, that others and my body are engendered together means that there is no level prior to this intersubjective carnal life, that there is "neither individualtion nor numerical distinction" prior to this general level. As long as solipsism conceives the other person in terms of whom one's self is alone, it is not solipsism, for that is to situate the ego in relation to a "phantom of the other person." True solitude results only if the other is not even conceivable, in which case there would be neither a self nor self-awareness. Being alone in this sense requires lack of awareness of being alone. Thus, it is an anonymous life of primordial, pre-personal coexistence, rather than solitude, which is basic.

This anonymity must not be overextended at the expense of differentiation from others, for, even prior to an explicit development of a reflective personal level, this anonymity of the lived body already contains the principle of differentiation from others. Thus, it is both one with and bound to others and, at once, differentiated from them. Once the personal dimension has emerged, it appropriates the whole of the lived body as its own, encompassing in its sweep even that primordial level in its concrete existence, finding therein the foundation for the differentiation between individuals. Yet, in another sense, my primordial perception as corporeal self-awareness is not "my" perception, since I am conscious only on the basis of my natural, cultural, already *acquired* "pre-personal" body, the originary operating intentions of which constitute the horizons of my perceptual field, even prior to the emergence of the personal level.[44]

This view of the general and pre-personal dimension of the lived body and of self-consciousness not only opposes solipsism, but equally demands the rejection of the Cartesian body which Merleau-Ponty refers to as "Descartes' dummy," as that which Cartesian philosophy allows humans to see of their own bodies upon looking in the mirror. For, with the separation resulting from dualism and the body as a part of the mechanism of nature according to the reductionism of the body in the Cartesian view, conduct, structure of behavior, consciousness, or mind are not grasped in the apprehension of the body as it is according to Merleau-Ponty.

A Cartesian does not see *himself* in the mirror; he sees a dummy, an 'outside,' which, he has every reason to believe, other people see in the very same way but which, no more for himself than for theirs, is not a body in the flesh. His 'image' in the mirror is an effect of the mechanics of things. If he recognizes himself in it, if he thinks it 'looks like him,' it is his thought that weaves this connection. The mirror image is nothing that belongs to him.[45]

Thus, it is clear that Merleau-Ponty, like Mead, has overcome solipsism, has rejected dualism involving body and mind, and, in the process, has developed a view of the essentially intersubjective or social nature of the self. It is now to the genesis of the self in terms of role playing and the appropriation of the personal pronouns in Merleau-Ponty's philosophy, which presuppose the corporeal intersubjective level, that the discussion will turn.

The uniquely personal level of behavior, as involving that which precedes it within the broader development of the self, is evinced in the child's acquisition of language. Further, it is precisely the original level of intentionality which must be understood and presupposed as the backdrop for Merleau-Ponty's investigations, in a different context, of the development of the child and of the child's acquisiton of language. The child's immersion in and identification with its situation reveals the stage prior to that of the differentiation from others and prior to the explicit emergence of personality and self. The roles assumed in the development of the use of the personal pronoun reveal embryonic phases in the development of the personal level.

Merleau-Ponty considers the acquisition of language to involve a "kind of habituation" similar to the acquisition of any habitual modes of behavior, and to evince role playing, with the acquisition of the personal network of references presupposed by and expressed in the use of personal pronouns.[46] The employment of language is founded upon the "child's assimilation of the linguistic system of his environment in a way that is comparable to the acquisition of any habit whatever: the learning of a structure of conduct."[47] This habitation involves the social environment, for to acquire a habit of employing such an open system of mediating expression involves the appropriation of the roles expressed or mediated in the use of the language in which the child learns to live and move. Thus, it is indeed a learning of a structure of behavior. "To learn to speak is to learn to play a series of *roles*, to assume a series of conducts or linguistic gestures."[48] This account by Merleau-Ponty is not necessarily restricted to role taking in the learning of the use of personal pronouns in language, nor need it be limited to language. For such role taking resides in the experiences underlying the language to which it gives rise. As such, this acquisition of language is what Merleau-Ponty calls "a phenomenon of identification," meaning the lack of differentiation between projection and assimilation, or between his own experiences and those of another, or between himself and various roles assumed or appropriated one after the other.[49] In a case of a newborn brother into a family, Merleau-Ponty shows the emergence of imperfect and future tenses in the child's use of language.[50] More significantly, the employment of some future verbs reveals an active stand in terms of what is to come.

The immersion in and identification with the situation account for the child's makeup as a composite of these roles in his situation. Only later, when the personal and individual dimension emerges by means of further interaction with others, does the self of reflection arise—a fact which Merleau-Ponty portrays through the account of the acquisition of the use of personal pronouns. He thus brings together the pre-personal and general conditions with the development of the child into a personal and individual self. Such interaction with others and appropriation of numerous and various roles enters into the reflective activity once the self has emerged onto the scene as an integration of the personal and general dimensions, and, indeed, leads to that activity. For with the acquisition of personal differentiation and identity the child has developed a personality that evinces the appropriation of that stage of undifferentiation into a new type of activity. The acquisition of the use of personal pronouns shows this development.

This use of the personal pronouns comes to the child later than the use of the proper name.[51] The child learns to use the proper name, even the child's own proper name, before learning the use of the personal pronoun. And the child learns the full meaning of the personal pronoun or its use as such, not to designate its own person or for himself and no one else, but rather when he understands that each person is an "I" for himself and a "you" for others. "In order for it to have been a real acquisition, he must have grasped the relations between the different pronouns and the passage from one of their designata to the others."[52] This use of personal pronouns occurs regularly at about the end of the second year, when the child grasps that the same pronoun can serve to designate different persons, whereas a person has only one proper name. The use of even his own name does not indicate a consciousness of his privileged perspective. This acquisition of the use of personal pronouns marks the child's development toward his differentiation from his sitution and from others.

Since at around three years children begin to cease confusing themselves with their situation or role, they understand that they are individuals over and above particular situations and roles. This does not happen, however, without the children's explicit awareness of themselves as seen by the other. "The ego, the I, cannot truly emerge at the age of three years without doubling itself with an *ego in the eyes of the other.*"[53] Now the child invokes the relation of "me-and-other" resulting in the differentiation between the child and the other and the child and his situation. In this phase of their development (of the self) children depend upon the reactions which they bring out in others, for it is through interacting with others, through role playing in relation to the other, that children begin to constitute for themselves a private interiority of experiences that have public names, even though, in a sense, the referents will never be publicly observable. This social interaction forms the child in the image of the other, developmentally marking the passage from the pre-personal to the personal.

Thus is constituted the form of inherently social subjectivity which, as non ego-logical, is decentered in the interacting and intertwining of self and others achieved through the central role of the lived body. As a consequence of this view of the self as a whole, including the general and personal aspects, Merleau-Ponty adamantly rejects classical psychology's interpretation of the psyche as a closed interiority radically inaccessible to another person from the outside[54] and in need of being decoded from effects behind which "I project, so to speak, what I myself feel of my own body."[55] Merleau-Ponty, denouncing the psychologist's view of the psyche as a series of states of consciousness closed in on itself, considers consciousness expressed in the lived body to be related to the world as "conduct," as action with a meaning found in things in the world and as "themes of possible activity for my body."[56] He thus reinterprets the sense of the psyche to be a conduct and that of the body to be "lived body." If the lived body is thus to appropriate the conducts of the other and make them its own, it must itself be given to me not as a mass of utterly private interiority, but instead by what has been called a "postural" or "corporeal scheme."[57] He says: "I can perceive, . . . that the other is an organism, that the organism is inhabited by a 'psyche,' . . . because the other is interpreted through the mediation of my own lived body and thus is grasped as the visible envelopment of another 'corporeal schema'."[58] This perceived other is a system of behavior or a conduct that aims at the world and thus is offered to my motor intentions transgressing to the world. Merleau-Ponty employs the "phenomenon of coupling" to account for the perception of others as a quasi-coupling or pairing of bodies (*action a deux*). Communication is possible because there is initially a "state of pre-communication . . . wherein the other's intentions somehow play across my body while my intentions play across his," a phase of an anonymous collectivity, an "undifferentiated group life (*vie a plusieur*),"[59] seen above as the general and anonymous dimension of the concrete subject. Consequently, the origin of consciousness cannot be treated as though it were explicitly conscious of itself "nor as though it were completely closed on itself."[60]

In a similar way Merleau-Ponty rejects all traces of a Cartesian *cogito*, even the *tacit cogito* of his early works,[61] as a secret immanence of self or as a prereflective self-presence. Such a self-presence prior to the unity and bond of world and lived body is forfeited. "The acts of the I are of such a nature that they outstrip themselves leaving no interiority of consciousness."[62] Consciousness reaches world and things in the world and is constituted by that transgression of itself beyond itself to the world, and only as such reaches self-awareness.[63] With this rejection of the *tacit cogito* in deference to originary transgression to the world, Merleau-Ponty deepens his reflections on the lived body as the corporeal emergence of originary meaning prior to the personal level and thus as an original level of intentionality which grounds all human behivor and all meaning.

This existential view of the self, opposed to any *tacit cogito*, includes the reflective dimension, which itself is central to the temporal structure of human existence.[64] And, in turn, this temporal dimension, as in a sense reflective, is the "archetype of the relation of self to self"[65] in the unfolding of the present to the future in the sense that "time . . . is aware of itself."[66] Further, reflection is a character of existence as both epistemic and ontological. These two perspectives on existence account for the essentially reflective character of the self, with its manifold dimensions. Thus it can be seen that Merleau-Ponty's focus on the existential self includes the beginnings of what Mead considers to be the cognitive self. Before turning to Mead's view, however, Merleau-Ponty's existential self must be given a fuller account through a focus on the various dimensions of sedimentation.

Since human existence is essentially temporal, as seen in the last chapter, and the self rooted in it likewise is essentially temporal, self and time share the same characteristics, one of which is the sedimentation constituting lived time of the concrete subject below derived time.[67] The centrality of sedimentation stems from its emergence from lived time pervading the lived world, lived body, language, freedom, etc. This sedimentation involved in human existence, including the individual or personal and the general or pre-personal dimensions of self, constitutes the relation between the present and the past in the process of passage. Thus, as seen above in other terms, with the arrival of every new present moment the one prior changes by sinking away below the level of the present, and with the continuity of passage, any prior moment recedes or sediments deeper with deepening retentions. Thus, each "fresh" present "reasserts the presence of the whole past which it supplants, and anticipates that of all that is to come,"[68] so that passage must be understood in terms of the sedimentation of an originary level of retention of prior presents which are still present in sedimentation. Further, in passage, time moves throughout its whole length and the sedimented depth is present as constitutive of the depth of existence which itself entails the lived body.

Likewise, the embodying organism as the essentially corporeal self involves primal sedimentation or acquisition. Primal acquisition refers to the past because, in order for something to be established or stabilized with reference to a subject, it must have passed through the present into the past: "It is by coming into the present that a moment of time acquires that indestructible individuality, that 'once and for all' quality which subsequently enables it to make its way through time and produce in us the illusion of eternity."[69] This sedimentation as primal acquisition provides the foundation for personal acts, requiring, first, that the past which gets established be carried over into the present at a level beneath that of personal acts. It is precisely the structure of retention by which the past is retained in the present. "What is true, however, is that our open and personal existence rests on an initial foundation of acquired and stabilized existence. But it could not be otherwise, if we *are* temporality, since the dialectic of acquisition and future is what constitutes time."[70]

Further, it is equally true that activity on the personal level becomes sedimented, so that acts springing from explicit and reflected choices of thematized possibilities may subsequently become automatic. For instance, a gesture such as raising the eyebrow, a chosen thematized possibility sometimes learned by children only with difficulty, or the gestures involved in driving a car, can become automatic.[71] This accounts for the fact that a normal subject may perform habitual acts with ease and with lack of reflective deliberation. Further, sedimentation gives an account of such phenomena as conditioned reflex, habituation, and the like.

Thus, for Merleau-Ponty the sedimentation involved on the pre-personal level of generality, relating both to the world and to the lived body, and emerging from time, involves as well the derived and founded personal level of individuality, and hence includes both of the two stages of the unique structure of the concrete subject as an existential self. Further, the "world-structure, with its two stages of sedimentation and spontaneity, is at the core of consciousness,"[72] so that sedimentation is always an accompanying dimension within the context of which all acquired and creative dimensions of world take place. And, sedimentation involved in world structure and its space can take place both on the personal level and on the pre-personal level which, as prior to the personal level, is thus prior to explicit reflection, as, for instance, in the emergence of the child's world. For the child builds up world which has its stage of sedimentation prior to the emergence of the personal level or explicit reflection. Hence, world constitution precedes self and involves an initial stage of spontaneity or creativity at a level before which the personal creativity emerges and to which it is passive. Thus, each stage of the structure of the concrete subject involves its own type of sedimentation, for at the general stage sedimentation is involved in the manner in which the present creative meaning structuring gets retained in the flow of lived experience as a prior moment retained in the present flux, not as past, but, rather as a past retained in a present now. Thus, the present contains depth with retention and protention, constitutive of the lived experience of the lived body in the lived world. And a further stage of sedimentation is that of the personal level of activity. For the personal level spontaneously reconstitutes new elements into its already sedimented world, and creatively reconstitutes itself in its responses, which, in turn, become sedimented in the next present of the flow. Thus, the sedimentations of this personal level overflow into the pre-personal.

The first 'me', which is latent, virtual, and implicit, is undifferentiated and not explicitly distinguished from that of the other, as mentioned above. Consciousness of oneself as a unique individual, whose place cannot be taken by anyone else, is derived and not primitive, thus coming after the pre-personal and general dimension or stage of the concrete subject.[73] For this indistinction between me and the other on this primitive level of "confusion" at the core of a situation common to both of us, Merleau-Ponty invokes the term "syncretic sociability." The origin of consciousness, then, rather than explicitly conscious of itself, is not closed in on itself.

Thus Merleau-Ponty, in questioning back to the originary dimensions of the lived body or concrete subject, uncovers various levels of sedimentation: the sedimentation of time, the pre-personal sedimentation of world and concrete subject, and the sedimentation resulting from personal activity of this concrete subject. And once the personal level of the unique individual has developed, it then appropriates the whole lived body as its own, including even its pre-personal dimension; thus both the personal and pre-personal sedimentations enter into the self-reflection of the concrete subject, giving rise to the possibility of a unique and authentic self in terms of which we are individuated in a specific lived body. When the personal 'I' appropriates its acquisitions, as the child can do with the whole of language, including the level of the personal pronouns, making all acquisitions its own and thus personal in a sense, then the personal 'I' seems to become the focal point of the whole, even of what goes on beneath at the level of the general and pre-personal, which both subtends and sustains the personal level. All such sedimentations, essential to temporal existence, become incorporated into the personal and individuated self, but not in such a way as to centralize the ego in the sense of deleting the pre-personal dimension of existence.

This view of lived, unifying time moving in the fresh present as a whole and as the sense of life, and of the lived body giving rise to individuation, is, in a sense, true to the flux and at once to the unity of experience and of the self. And Merleau-Ponty's later treatments of the flesh, chaism, and a sort of sensible reflection[74] do not preclude this dynamic self, but rather, incorporate it into an expanded and deepened context.

In the later development of the ontology of the flesh, the self is not as such eclipsed, but rather, is put more explicitly in its ontological context. For the self dwells within the folds of the flesh in which the flesh of the body, with its concrete sensible reflexivity, is contained within the flux. Within the priority of the sensible sensing, the self dwells, though decentered, yet still alive in

time as chiasm of the flesh. This deepening both confirms and fulfills the earlier version of lived time.[75]

The view of self latently contained in Merleau-Ponty's writing has been seen to emerge from the lived body as central, to be
correlated with the lived world, and to be grounded in temporality.
In explicating Merleau-Ponty's position in light of Mead's own general considerations seen in the first part of this chapter, affinities
have been revealed with Mead's general context for a self as inherently intersubjective and as constituted through role taking. Further, Merleau-Ponty's focus on the existential self can be
considered to provide the groundwork for an I-me self-reflective,
cognitive relation, which for Mead constitutes the essential nature
of selfhood. From the context of Merleau-Ponty's existential focus,
the ensuing discussion will turn to Mead's understanding of the
self as essentially cognitive in a way which, it is hoped, will cast it
in a somewhat new and fruitful light.

For Mead, the 'I' and the 'me' aspects of the self are neither
metaphysically nor numerically distinct but rather are functional
distinctions which, in their inseparable interrelation, constitute
the self. The 'I' is the functional pole or functional dimension of
the self as the immediacy of the present, spontaneity, creativity,
the individual perspective, the subject pole. The 'me' is the functional dimension of the self which represents the constraints of
the past, of tradition, of culture and institutionalized practices, of
the shaping of the self by the other, the community perspective,
the object pole. The discussion of these two dimensions of the self
can best proceed by way of Mead's rejection of traditional notions
of psychical immediacy, which parallels Merleau-Ponty's rejection,
and his own unique understanding of the functional status of "psychical immediacy." And fundamental to understanding this rejection is the backdrop of that which is so pervasive and essential to
Mead's view of the self that it is at times perhaps not given the
needed explicit emphasis: that is, Mead's understanding of the biological dimension of the self, a dimension whose significance can
be brought to the fore when approached in light of Merleau-Ponty's
intense focus on the lived body.

Mead, in referring to the rise of the 'me' as prior to the 'I',
notes that the child, as an object to itself, is at first the reflection
of the attitudes of others toward it.

The child in this early period often refers to his own self in
the third person. He is a composite of all the individuals he

addresses when he takes the roles of those about him. It is only gradually that this takes clear enough form to become identified with the biological individual and endow him with a clear-cut personality that we call self-consciousness.[76]

The social aspect of the self, the 'me', the incorporation of the generalized other, arises before the 'I' aspect can emerge. One has an 'I' only over against or in relation to the 'me'. The 'I' pole emerges subsequent to the 'me' pole as its correlate, and the internal conversation between the 'I', and the 'me' as the voice of the other, becomes possible. As Mead carefully points out, however, "though the voice is the voice of another, the source of it all is one's self—the organized group of impulses which I have called the biologic individual."[77] As he states, "I have termed it 'biologic' because the term lays emphasis on the living reality which may be distinguished from reflection."[78] And, as he characterizes the biologic individual, "this self adjusted to its social environment, and through this to the world at large, is the object.[79]

The term "biologic individual" then, as used by Mead in the above context, is the self in its primordial biological dimension, the concrete, decentered subject in its living reality as the source of reflective awareness and hence of the I-me poles of internal dialogue. It is prior to and the source of the cognitive I-me distinction, prior to its appropriation of itself as an object of reflection, as both knower and known. It is, as Merleau-Ponty stresses, the lived body as intentional and social, the concrete subject which is prior to reflection but which, once reflection has arisen, is appropriated as a 'me' by an 'I'. Mead's reference to the *source of* the cognitive relation as in any sense a self may appear somewhat strange, for in his view the self is essentially cognitive,[80] consisting of the nature of a dialogue between the 'I' and the 'me'. Yet, this label is in another sense most appropriate, for the functioning of the concrete subject which gives rise to the I-me cognitive dynamics of the self is not discarded when the reflective self arises in experience. It is never discarded but subtends such dynamics; it is not just genetically prior to the cognitive self but logically prior in its ongoing dynamics. Thus, the concrete subject, as that which underlies the I-me distinction, is a dimension of the self, the "living reality" which pervades reflection. When the cognitive self breaks down, the concrete subject with its constructive or constitutive intentional activity remains, and, as will be seen, it is the functioning of this concrete subject—the lived body—which Mead intends in his discussions of subjectivity. Within this context, the ensuing discussion will turn to Mead's understanding of the psychical in experience.

Both the importance and neglect of Mead's essay, "The Definition of the Psychical," has been well noted by Hans Joas.[81] According to Joas, however, this early phase of Mead's thought, which claims the self is directly accessible to reflection, contradicts his later view concerning the intersubjectively constituted character of the predicates used for self-interpretation.[82] Joas further holds that a similar contradiction appears between Mead's theory of the social genesis of the self, "regarded approvingly even in 'The Definition of the Psychical', and Mead's claim that the self is directly accessible to reflection."[83] In contrast, the following analysis will attempt to show that far from indicating a contradiction between the early and later stages of Mead's thought, this early view provides a focus for grasping, in a unified way, the full dimensions of self-awareness latent in Mead's writings.

Mead rejects physiological reductionism, but objects strongly to the views of psychology as a science based on inner experience, either as effects of, or as in some sense running parallel to, things in the world. Psychical awareness must be understood in terms of its function, which Mead finds to lie in its reconstructive character. The psychical is not a permanent phase or aspect of consciousness, but a phase which has a functional role within the process of cognition. Its congnitive value lies in its reconstructive activity in the breakdown of a situation. Mead states his agreement here with Dewey's position that in the psychical phase of consciousness the object is gone, and the psychical character of the situation lies in the process of disintegration and reconstruction.[84] In this reconstructive phase there emerges, in varying degrees, a direct experience, but this can be called neither a direct experience of the 'I' nor an experience of the cognitive self with the I-me dimensions, but rather an experience of subjectivity in which the objectivity of both self and other has broken down.[85] This subjectivity, though here representing the creative 'I' dimension, cannot be considered an 'I', because the 'I' indicates "the subject end of the polarized process of cognitive experience,"[86] and it is precisely this cognitive experience which has disintegrated; the reflective self and its object world have broken down. In this situation, the biological dimension of the self is not directly accessible to reflection but is directly experienced in its vital functioning as the creative source of reflective activity. The 'I' as knower cannot, through self-reflection, be caught as a psychical awareness which parallels on-going acts within an objective situation of self and world. This is the point of Mead's arguments in "The Definition of the Psychi-cal" and it is the point of his arguments in his focus on the 'me' which always is what is caught when the 'I' attempts to reflect on itself. The subjectivity experienced in the breakdown of a situa-tion is not the 'I' pole in the bipolar dynamics of self-reflection, but rather it is that "living reality" of the human biologic organ-ism out of whose creative intentional directedness emerges the I-me, subject-object distinction in its reflective relation to itself. The 'I' and the 'me' are functional relations, not metaphysical dis-tinctions, because they represent two ways in which the lived body, the decentered subject, functions. Thus Mead states that what is immediately experienced is the "original subjectivity out of whose 'projection' . . . arise not only the others' selves, but reactively our own."[87] The 'I' is the elusive pole of the I-me reflec-tive, cognitive, relationship, but subjectivity is the living reality of the concrete or decentered subject in its organic or vital inten-tional activity.

Here it must be remembered that the emergence of mentality is not something added on to the vital, but rather the higher level transforms the lower level. The diversity of impulses is trans-formed into creativity guided by intelligence, the vital drives of organic activity are transformed into vital intentionality. In the re-turn to subjectivity as the living reality of the concrete subject, one is returning to the direct sense of the felt, intentional creativ-ity which is a dimension of the functioning of the lived human body. This return to subjectivity as the intentional creativity of the lived body is not to be confused with subjectivism, for it is precisely subjectivism in any of its forms which this focus on the intentional creativity of the lived body as the source of the subject-object distinction avoids, for Mead as for Merleau-Ponty. This subjectivity, it has been seen, is not an object of awareness, nor is it a subject set over against an object, since objectivity has broken down. Rather it is "an immediate and direct experience," "the point of immediacy that must exist within a mediate process."[88] As indicated above, the return to the immediacy of subjectivity in the disintegration of the objective situation is the return to the immediacy of the vital intentionality of constitutive activity which permeates the human organism. It is the immedi-ate experience of the "process of attention and apperception, of choice, of consciously directed conduct."[89] It is, according to

Mead, the experience of functioning creativity which in its immediacy continually eludes the objective grasp of self-reflection, but which, as grasped as an object by reflection, is converted into aspects of the 'me'.

Here it is important to distinguish between ambiguous uses in Mead's writings of "the body" and of "immediacy" or "immediate experience." Mead holds, as was noted earlier in more brief fashion, that "we can distinguish very definitely between the self and the body. . . . It is perfectly true that the eye can see the foot, but it does not see the body as a whole. . . . The parts of the body are quite distinguishable from the self. . . . The body does not experience itself as a whole, in the sense in which the self in some way enters into the experience of the self."[90] The phenomenological sense of the lived body, however, is not something partially grasped by sight, the body as something that I have. Rather it is something which is a lived unity grasped as a whole in experience, the body that I am, the body that is an expression of selfhood, the lived body of Merleau-Ponty. It is this which Mead intends when he stresses that the self "must be related to the entire body."[91] Mead's focus on the body in these two different ways leads to his diverse treatments of the body in relation to the self, and it is the latter focus which leads to his most important, though often brief, indications of the biological dimensions of the self.

Mead also uses "immediate experience" in two distinct senses. Immediate experience in its "thick" sense is for Mead the everyday world of structured objectivities 'there' for one's experience. As already seen, common sense objects as well as other selves within the lived world are immediately 'there'. They are not inferred from data of consciousness but immediately experienced. In this sense the 'me' and the objects within its objective world are immediately given. Such immediate experience is not the experience of pure immediacy, however, but is shot through with or mediated by the intentional structurings which give rise to experienced objectivities of any sort. There is also the "relatively pure" immediacy which is experienced as a moment in the constitutive process when workability breaks down and objectivity is lost. This is the immediacy of subjectivity, of creative vital intentionality functioning in the restructuring of its world.

I cannot know this immediacy of creative functioning, for to know is to interpret, to bring meaning. But though I cannot know it in its immediacy, I can have a "sense" of this functioning. It is "felt" rather than known.[92] The objectivity of the situation breaks down as a segment of a meaning system fails to work, and in the span of time before the new objective situation begins to emerge, there is, in Mead's terms, a "feel" or "sense" of the immediacy of subjectivity functioning as a creative system of possibilities. In this span of time, as a meaningful context disintegrates, and before a new one begins to emerge, there is a return to the elusive but real sense of the immediacy of creative functioning of corporeal subjectivity, which in cognition or self-reflection is represented by the 'I' pole and grasped as a 'me'. Mead illustrates the return to subjectivity and relatively pure immediacy through the following example:

> An illustration of these characteristics can be found in social experiences in which we are forced to reconstruct our ideas of the character of our acquaintances. . . . The whole social environment would be more or less definitely organized as the background and the sustaining whole of the individual or individuals who were the immediate stimuli of our conduct. If we assume now that some experience should run quite counter to the nature of an acquaintance as we have known him, the immediate result would be that we would be nonplussed and quite unable to act with reference to him for the time being. The immediate result would be a state of consciousness within which would appear mutually contradictory attitudes toward the acquaintance which would inevitably formulate themselves in a problem as to what the real nature of the man was. . . . The contradictory attitudes . . . include in their sweep not only the man in question, but also ourselves insofar as mutual interrelationship has helped to form our selves over against his. . . . Insofar the subject and object relation, the ego and alter, would have disappeared temporarily within this field. The situation may be of such hopeless perplexity that consciousness in this regard could be well called protoplasmic; or at least would be of the same nature as the original subjectivity.[93]

The return to the immediacy of the functioning of subjectivity is one of degree, for "the subject and predicate . . . may be reduced as contents to zero in the equation and be present only as felt functions. In this case we have the limit of subjectivity. Or we may have definite conditions and a working hypothesis, and then the state approaches objectivity."[94] The sense of the functioning of corporeal subjectivity emerges in the reconstructive phase "when the consciousness is more or less incoherent or, in other terms, the distinction between subject and predicate cannot be made."[95] In this phase of subjectivity, "i.e., in the construction of the hypothesis of the new world," the individual "qua individual has his functional expression or rather is that function."[96] The logical correspondent of this psychical process, Mead notes, "can be no other than the copula phase of the judgment: that in which subject and predicate determine each other in their mutual interaction."[97]

It has been seen that this felt immediacy is not accessible in its immediacy to reflection. It is mutatis mutandis not accessible in its immediacy to the reflections of the psychologist. However, a science of the psychical as functional can avoid the false understandings of it by past psychologies and focus on reconstructive activity. It would deal with "that phase of experience within which we are immediately conscious of conflicting impulses which rob the object of its character as object-stimulus, leaving us insofar in an attitude of subjectivity; but during which a new object-stimulus appears due to the reconstructive activity which is identified with the subject 'I' as distinct from the object 'me'."[98] In this reconstructive phase the contents of awareness are nonobjective and are "functionally psychical" as the materials of reconstructive activity. Such contents are never brute uninterpreted data, however, for as seen earlier, data are abstractions from things in the world, and gain their structure from the problematic context within which they emerge.[99]

The assumption that there are sensations or psychical contents in ongoing coordinated experience which refer to, parallel, or accompany coordinated processes, even though we cannot detect them, is, according to Mead, the real psychologist's fallacy, the attempt to interject a psychical state into a process which is not psychical, to introduce it where none exists.[100] Mead's statement of this fallacy is detailed in the following:

> The psychical contents which belong to these phases of disintegration and reconstitution, if referred to physical or logical objects that belong to other phases of consciousness, can be only representative, can be only sensations *of* something. They inevitably lose their immediacy. . . . We carry over as an element a content whose peculiar quality depends upon its functional value in one phase of consciousness into another, and insist that it exists there as the subjectivity of this sec-

ond phase. Under these circumstances it is reduced to the position of standing for something, and this so-called subjective consciousness is made of nothing but sensations of registrations.[101]

Mead stresses the 'me' and the elusiveness of the 'I' throughout his writings precisely to avoid this psychological and philosophical fallacy of introducing a supposed experience of sensations representing an objective reality as well as the fallacy of a supposed reflective or cognitive grasp of the immediacy of an 'I'.

The 'I' as subject, it has been seen, can never exist as an object for consciousness. The 'I' by its very *function* can never be an object of reflection, because in being reflected upon, it becomes a 'me'. Mead admits that there is, as a "more or less constant feature of our consciousness," a "running current of awareness of what we do," which has often led to the assumption of a self which is conscious of both subject and object, a subject of action toward an object world and at the same time directly conscious of this subject as subject. Mead's response here is that the observer of our self-conscious conduct is not the 'I' but the rapidly changing series of 'me's' which occur in experience.[102] In a related but slightly different vein, Mead recognizes that there is a way of observing oneself in which both the observer and the observed do appear. For example, a person remembers asking himself about something, scolding himself for his actions, congratulating himself for his achievements, etc. Though one finds both a subject and an object, however, "it is a subject that is now an object of observation and has the same nature as the object itself."[103] In brief, it is not a true 'I', but a 'me'. No reflection can ever yield a true 'I', for reflection can only yield an *object of* reflection.[104] Only in memory is the 'I' constantly present in experience according to Mead.

> The 'I' of this moment is present in the 'me' of the next moment. There again I cannot turn around quick enough to catch myself. I become a 'me', in so far as I remember what I said. . . . The 'I' in memory is there as the spokesman of the self of the second, or minute or day ago. As given, it is a 'me', but it is a 'me' which was the 'I' at the earlier time.[105]

As Mead stresses, "When the self becomes an object, it appears in memory, and the attitude which it implies has already been taken."[106] Thus, the 'I' enters one's experience as a historical figure. "It is what you were a second ago that is the 'I' of the 'me'. It is another me that has to take that role. You cannot get the immediate response of the 'I' in the process. . . . It is not directly given in experience."[107] Again, Mead claims that a 'me' is inconceivable without an 'I', and thus such an 'I' must be a presupposition, though it is never 'there' as a presentation of conscious experience.[108]

Mead concludes that "the very conversational character of our inner experience, the very process of replying to one's own talk, implies an 'I' behind the scenes who answers to the gestures, the symbols that arise in consciousness."[109] As behind the scenes, this 'I' is like "the transcendental self of Kant, the soul that James conceived behind the scene holding on to the skirts of an idea to give it an added increment of emphasis."[110] Thus Mead claims, in extreme form, that the 'I' is "fictitious" in that it is always out of sight of itself.[111]

Yet, the creative activity of the concrete subject as represented by the 'I' pole, is not really "behind the scene" but "within the scene." Mead points toward this in various ways, but seems to back off, afraid always, it would seem, of the reappearance of that running current of psychical awareness paralleling activity—either as an intuited 'I' or as representative contents, to which he so strongly objects. Perhaps it is this concern which explains to some extent his failure to adequately explore the implications of his own analysis of temporality for the nature of self-awareness. Indeed, his discussions of the self seem at times to contradict this very analysis.

The ensuing discussion will turn more closely to Mead's understanding of temporality in connection with "one of the problems of most of our conscious experience," that is, the getting into experience of the 'I' with which we do, in a certain sense, identify ourselves.[112] Mead holds that one cannot get the immediate response of the 'I' in this ongoing process because, though the organism brings parts of itself into its environment, it does not "bring the life-process itself into the environment."[113] Thus, to bring the 'I' into experience is to get hold of the life process, the living reality of the concrete subject, in some way. To understand such a possibility, implicit in Mead's thought, it will be necessary to return briefly to his account of time as presented in the previous chapter, this time in explicit reference to the self. As was seen in the previous discussion of temporality, Mead holds that we can go back directly a few moments in our experience, but beyond that we are dependent upon memory images.[114] Our specious present is, as Mead notes, very short. However, it is not a knife-edge present. The specious present includes within it the past and the future, thus allowing for the direct experience of change. "We do experience passing events; part of the process of the passage of events is directly there in our experience, including some of the past and some of the future."[115] And, as seen in the previous chapter, the sense of change in the specious present to which the biological individual is always tied is incorporated into the very core of our sense of the functional present.

An example which Mead gives as an analogy for self-awareness is most revealing of his hesitancy to follow through for his analysis of the self the implications of his own analysis of temporality, for in giving an example which would seem made-to-order to highlight the direct sense of change, he ignores this aspect. In the example he points out that, "We sense a ball falling as it passes, and as it does pass part of the ball is covered and part is being uncovered. We remember where the ball was a moment ago and we anticipate where it will be beyond what is given in our experience."[116] Mead concludes that the same holds of ourselves, for to look back and see what we are doing involves getting a memory.[117] However, what the falling ball analogy clearly points out is that in addition to remembering where the ball was a moment ago, there is a direct sense of the falling ball as it passes, a direct sense of part of the ball in the process of being covered and part in the process of being uncovered, a direct sense of change that is incorporated into the sense of the functional present. And, as was also indicated in the previous chapter, the specious present, as defined in terms of the act, represents the stage of reconstruction. Thus, the sense of change which is incorporated into the functional present includes the sense of reconstructive activity. This direct sense is 'there,' and in relation to the self would seem to be a sense of the passing from the 'I' to the 'me', a process rooted in the biological individual or concrete subject tied to the specious present and the direct sense of change, a sense of change which is incorporated within a wider present but "which is never lost."[118] This direct sense of change illustrated by the analogy, rather than the memory upon which Mead focuses, would seem best to explain why Mead can hold that the falling ball analogy explains how, on the basis of "experience we distinguish that individual who is doing something from the 'me' who puts the problem up to him."[119] That sense of movement is 'there' in the present, an I-me dynamic in an ongoing, continuous development, an I-me dialogue which is rooted in, and evinces the temporal vitality of, the "biologic individual" or concrete subject, and which is a continual uncovering and covering of its ongoing development. Thus, it is true that the " 'I' does not appear *in the same sense* in experience as does the 'me'."[120] The 'I', as Mead states, "does not get into the limelight,"[121] but neither is it hiding behind stage. To look back and see what we are doing does, as Mead states, involve memory, yet the sense of the ongoing I-me dynamics, though not seen, though not an object of knowledge, is yet precisely that, sensed.

To clarify this point further, the ensuing discussion will leave Mead's falling ball analogy and turn again to his general concept of sociality as the stage of transition or phase of adjustment between the arising of the novel within the old order and the reorganization which gives rise to the new. The term "sociality," as was seen in the previous chapter, refers not to the new order or to the old order, but to the process of adjustment in which the novel occurrence belongs both to the old order which provides the conditions for its emergence and the new order which accommodates it and renders it continuous with what came before. Sociality is the very character of the present, and its temporal character is essential to the nature of the self.

Applying this concept of sociality as constitutive of the present to the issue at hand, the 'I', as representing the present, represents as well the emerging novelty of the present. "It is because of the I that we are never fully aware of what we are, that we surprise ourselves by our own actions."[122] The novel response of the 'I' is the emergent event, the conditions for which are provided by the past 'me' system, and whose coming to be requires a new 'me' system which comes to terms with the emergent event by incorporating it. In this period of adjustment, the novel, which emerges as novel out of the old system, is accommodated by the new system which, in its adjustment, reinstates it as continuous with what came before. The novel response of the 'I' in the present emerges from the old 'me', and as an emergent could not be predicted from the old 'me'. To this emerging novelty a new 'me' must adjust. The change from the old 'me system' to the new 'me system' is brought about by a process of adjustment in the present, and the transition from the old 'me' to the new 'me' via the emergence of the novelty of the 'I', a process of adjustment involving the ontologically grounded temporal vitality of the concrete subject, is immediately experienced, in its covering and uncovering, through the experience of change in the passing present. For Mead as for Merleau-Ponty, reflection is rooted in the ontologically grounded temporality of the lived body. An adequate account of the reflection constitutive of selfhood therefore must incorporate the features of temporality.

It has been seen that any 'me' contains attitudes partially shaped by the past creativity of an 'I'. Beth Singer, in giving a much needed recognition to the role of the 'I' as partially constitutive of the 'me', distinguishes between a social and an individual 'me', the internalized attitudes of the community or generalized other and the cumulative fund of individuated attitudes taken by the 'I'.[123] These two dimensions of the 'me' are important to distinguish, but, as Singer would agree, are in principle impossible to disentangle, for the previous attitudes or actions of the 'I' have changed the generalized other even as the generalized other has influenced the actions or attitudes of the 'I'. The 'me' is an inseparable fusion and funding of the historically changing, developing circumstances or social contexts in which one finds oneself and one's own ongoing unique responses which both alter the social dimension and make its incorporation into the 'me' uniquely one's own. As Mead stresses,

> The individual, as we have seen, is continually reacting back against this society. Every adjustment involves some sort of change in the community to which the individual adjusts himself. . . . Great figures in history bring out very fundamental changes. These profound changes which take place through the action of individual minds are only the extreme expression of the sort of changes that take place steadily through reactions which are not simply those of a "me" but of an "I". These are changes that take place gradually and more or less imperceptibly.[124]

What Singer seems to be attempting to capture is the sense of the object self as a whole as representing not just conformity or stability but past creativity. But the sense of creativity that once was is not possible without the sense of creativity, and creativity is located in a passing present. H. S. Thayer points out that for Mead the 'I' as the creative pole in internal dialogue has its very genesis in memory,[125] but, again, it is perhaps difficult to remember what one has never experienced. In the sense of the emerging novelty of the 'I' and the accompanying adjustment of the 'me', the sense of one's creativity passes into the sense of having once been.

What the above indicates is that not only is the 'I' not hiding behind the stage of the present, but neither can the 'me' be pushed from it. Mead illicitly conflates the temporal dimensions of the 'me' by confounding the 'me' as a pole in the dialogical stretch of the temporal present with the 'me' as an earlier self thematized in memory through a "second level" self-reflection. This happens, at least in part, because he illicitly separates or "compartmentalizes" his insights concerning the dialogical nature of the self and his perceptive analyses of temporality. Such a separation cannot be made, for the dialogical nature of the self is ontologically grounded, via the lived body, in the dimensions of sociality that constitute the nature of time.[126]

The fundamental concern of reflection is not to attempt the impossible task of catching the 'I' as an object of thematized reflective awareness, not to engage in retrospection, remembering what one said or did or thought, but to carry on an inner dialogue, and to anticipate and critically evaluate its intended probable results. The inner I-me dialogue as it operates in a passing present funded with possibilities emerging from a past and oriented toward a future is nonthematic in that the reflexivity is not thematically aware of itself. The 'I' addresses and responds to the 'me' as object, but without being thematically aware of its own reflexivity, though it can have a *sense* of reflexivity *in the process of* bending back upon itself. In the active engagement in internal dialogue taking place in the passing present, there is a sense of the covering and uncovering, a sense of the "dialogical stretch," of the temporal present. This sense of the cognitive dialogical stretch is ontologically grounded in the temporal dynamics of the biologic individual, the concrete, decentered subject, with which the self is in a sense most identified,[127] and which subtends any cognitive or dialogical I-me relation. Thus, Mead can state that "the life-process itself *is* brought to consciousness in the conduct of the individual form, in his so-called 'self-consciousness.' "[128]

Mead's analysis of time, when related to the self, points to the need for a focus on the temporal import of the distinction between retention and memory in a way similar to that presented by Merleau-Ponty. Mead stresses that the self, as an object found in memory, can be an object found through "immediate memory." Immediate memory, however, is very different from the direct grasp of the immediate past as it is *present within* the passing present. Retention in a passing present is not memory, not even immediate memory. The dialogical stretch of the self in the passing present involves retention. In this passing present there is at once a direct sense of the past and the future and of the move from one toward the other which underlies both memory and expectation. And, in avoiding any vestiges of discrete moments, it must be remembered that time is not a "thin" linear direction, but rather the sedimentations of the past are ingredient in the funded present, thus entering into the retentions of the present involved in the dialogical stretch, a stretch ontologically grounded in the ongoing temporal dynamics of the lived body with its dimensions of sociality.

Here it must be stressed that the nonthematic sense of self functioning is not caught in the problematics of psychical awareness to which Mead so strongly objects. His understanding of the sense of the cognitive self as a sense ultimately rooted in the ongoing temporal dynamics of the concrete or decentered subject renders such a problem spurious. The ongoing nonthematic sense of self does not parallel experience in any way but infuses experience with the living dynamics through which experience is "my experience." What is sensed in experience is thus not an awareness running parallel to ongoing activity, but the life process of the ongoing function of the creativity of the present passing into the sedimented character of the past, and the temporal vitality of this process permeates the I-me dialogue of cognitive activity, of corporeal intentionality in the process of bending back upon itself, providing the running current of awareness which Mead attempts to explain in terms of a series of rapidly changing 'me's' of moments immediately past.

Though Mead recognizes the self as inherently temporal, as incorporating a past oriented towards a future, his discussion of the I-me distinction is not infrequently couched in peculiarly atomistic terms, a tendency implicit in his discussion of the rapidly changing series of 'me's' in terms of which he attempts to exhaust the running current of awareness,[129] to explain the awareness of self as always an awarenss of "the moment passed,"[130] but never of the passing. This problem is highlighted in Mead's discussion of the child's assumption of diverse roles. Though Mead stresses that even "the simplest form of being another to one's self . . . involves a temporal situation,"[131] this temporal situation takes a strange twist, for he claims that "it is in this field that the continuous flow breaks up in ordered series. . . . Time with its distinguishable moments enters, so to speak, with the intervals necessary to shift the scene and change the costumes. *One cannot be another and yet himself except from the standpoint of a time which is composed of entirely independent elements.*"[132] What this statement would seem to indicate, taken in conjunction with Mead's perceptive analyses of temporality, is that the very constitution of the self is distortive of the true nature of temporality. Mead, in his discussion of the self in terms of the 'I' and the 'me' seems inadvertently to have shifted the scene and changed the costumes of time, thus dealing with the 'I' as the locus of a momentary present detached from the direct sense of change and from the dynamics of sociality which constitute all temporal presents. This relapse allows for an invisible 'I' which catches a past 'me' in reflective activity characterized by discrete moments, but does not allow for an 'I' which, as representing the emerging creativity of the concrete subject in a temporally extended present characterized by the features of sociality, is experienced in its "covering and uncovering" in the span of adjustment in which it is in the process of passing from a 'me' which provided the conditions for its novel activity to a 'me' which comes to terms with the novelty and renders it continuous with what came before. Mead's tendency to ignore the features of temporality which his own analysis has revealed is perhaps motivated by his concern to avoid all remnants of psychical contents or of an intuited 'I'. Yet, as has been previously stressed, it is precisely his understanding of temporality and of the temporal nature of the lived body as decentered subject which has undercut the very possibility of the types of positions to which he objects.[133] The nonthematic awareness of the functioning constitutive of selfhood does not deny the outward directedness of direct awareness, does not allow for an intuited 'I' or for psychical contents over against an objectively perceived world or self, but for a sense of the decentered corporeal subject and the cognitive dynamics it grounds.

Mead's ambivalence concerning the relation of self and temporality can be found in the following claims, which at first glance are similar but which have radically different implications. He holds that "we are aware of ourselves, and of what the situation is, but exactly how we will act never gets into experience until *after* the action takes place."[134] Yet, in dealing with the self as a structure in terms of process, he also states that "we are finding out what we are going to say, what we are going to do, by saying and doing, and *in the process* we are continually controlling the process itself."[135] In contrast to the former claim, this latter statement, as well as his entire discussion of temporality, would seem to indicate that the action gets into our experience not *after*, but *as*, it is taking place. This view allows Mead to say that as the response taking place appears in experience it is *not* totally as memory experience.[136] Thinking, for Mead, itself lies "betwixt and between the old system and the new,"[137] and in the "betwixt and between," which constitutes the present, one does not experience just a series of remembered 'me's', but the passage from an old 'me' to a new 'me' via the novel activity of the 'I'.

The roots of this ambivalence in Mead's thinking concerning the nature of the self in relation to temporality can perhaps be traced to his dual uses of *sociality* and his characterization of each in terms of temporality. As was noted earlier,[138] Mead uses *social* or *sociality* in the intrasystematic sense of being with other objects or organisms in the same system and in the intersystematic sense of being in two systems at once. The self must of course be understood as "social" in both senses. As Mead characterizes the distinction in terms of temporality, however, the second sense of *sociality* involves passage, while the first represents a system as it can conceivably be taken at an instant: As he states:

> The difference between these two dimensions of sociality is temporal. A system can conceivably be taken at an instant, and the social character of the individual member would in that instant be what it is because of the mutual relationships of all members. On the other hand, an object can be a member of two divergent systems only in passage, in which its nature in one system leads to the transformation which its passing into another system carries with it. In the passage itself it can be in both.[139]

Mead, in his discussion of the self, seems more often than not to deal with the self in terms of the abstraction of instants, forgetting that any discussion of the self which draws from this view of time is ultimately an abstraction from the sense of lived temporal passage.

It has been seen that the living dynamics of the decentered subject, the biological or existential dimension of the self which can function both as an 'I' and a 'me', is at once both and neither. It is neither in that it substends the I-me congitive distinction and is that which gives rise to it. It is both in that this lived body functions both as an 'I' and as a 'me'. Mitchell Aboulafia finds an ambiguity in Mead's use of the 'I', claiming that Mead views it on the one hand as merely a functional distinction, while on the other hand he views it as the source of real novelty and as rescuing us from determinism.[140] There is, however, no ambiguity if it is remembered that the 'I' as functional is the function of the creativity of the lived body. The 'I' and the 'me' emerge as two dimensions of the concrete subject which, in its vital functioning as creativity passing into sedimentation, provides the ontological grounding for the sense of the dialogical stretch. Mead thus notes that the distinction between the 'I' and the 'me' is functional in that it is made "from the point of view of conduct itself."[141] The 'I' and the 'me' represent "two distinguishable phases"[142] of the activity of the lived body that I am.

Tugendhat has pointed out that the exercise of roles cannot handle the question, Who do I want to be?, not in the sense of "a good teacher," or "a good parent," but in the sense of "What kind of a person do I want to be?[143] Habermas attempts to capture this sense of concreteness which goes beyond particular roles through the distinction between role identity and ego-identity, holding that this lies in the distinction between past and future: what kind of a person I have become as opposed to what kind of person I want to be.[144] These accounts of Mead may at first seem to merely involve a somewhat more restricted sense of role taking than is intended by him, for it may be held that the kind of person I want to be is handled by the kind of integration of roles I want to achieve. The very sense of the question as to "the kind of person I want to be," or "the kind of integration of roles I want to achieve," however, seems to require not only more than the exercise of a series of specific roles but also more than any integration of roles. The sense of what Habermas calls "ego identity" as opposed to role identity would seem to lie not in a distinction between the past and the future, but in the sense of the decentered self as the source of the role taking—the ontological "thickness" or living reality which takes, integrates, and changes roles but which can never be exhausted through this expression. Mead's brief focus on the biological dimension of the self that is never lost is the implicit focus on what Merleau-Ponty calls the "existential self," the decentered subject or vital concrete system of unique intentionality which operates in a present funded with the past and oriented toward the future.

Until now the discussion of the lived body, the decentered subject, has focused mainly on the dimension of creativity. The ensuing discussion will turn from this to the funded or sedimented dimension of the lived body or decentered subject which gives rise to the I-me dialogue of reflective awareness.

Mead holds that because the 'me' is an object of reflection, in unreflective moments, the 'me' disappears.

> At times the individuals are so immersed in what they are doing, so caught up in the world, that they do not reflect on themselves and their actions; the 'me' disappears. 'Where we are intensely preoccupied with the objective world, this accompanying awareness disappears. We have to recall the experience to become aware that we have been involved as selves, to produce the self-consciousness which is a constituent part of a large part of our experience.'[145]

Critics of Mead have interpreted this as indicating not just the lack of reflective consciousness of self but the very absence of self.[146] However, it should be noted that though the 'me' has disappeared from such experience, Mead holds that we have indeed been involved as selves. This self-involvement can best be understood by focusing on another facet of this type of immersion in what one is doing. Mead holds that in such intense situations, experience of memories frequently occur. As he illustrates:

> Tolstoi as an officer in the war gives an account of having pictures of his past experience in the midst of his most intense action. There are also the pictures that flash into a person's mind when he is drowning. In such instances there is a contrast between an experience that is absolutely wound up in outside activity in which the self as an object does not enter, and an activity of memory and imagination in which the self is the principle object.[147]

In the above example it should again be noted that Mead does not state that the self is "relocated" but rather the self *as an object* is "relocated." And here again, Mead's understanding of temporality becomes relevant. As was seen in the previous chapter, a past is a past only in relation to a present. If we could recapture the past as it was, it would be a present that once was, not a past. Similarly, memory of the past is always from the perspective of the present, it is not a reliving of the past. The memories of a past self are memories as essentially related to, and emanating from, a present self. As Mead illustrates, "When one recalls his boyhood days he cannot get into them as he then was, without their relationship to what he has become."[148] These are images of my past because they are viewed from the perspective of a present self. These situations indeed do not involve a present self that is a thematic object of reflection, nor do they involve a self actively but nonthematically engaged in dialogue in a present dialogical stretch. They involve, however, a present nonreflective sense of self, of the decentered subject as that to which my past is inherently related as my past, and which, at any moment, can give rise to the cognitive I-me dynamics relative to the present situation through the disruption of ongoing activity. Indeed, it is significant to note that Mead's examples of highly intense situations are not of those requiring thoughtfulness or deliberation but of those requiring precisely the opposite, the kinds of situations which one might say, in common parlance, require that one "act rather than think."

Mead also gives examples of situations involving either no awareness of self as an object,[149] or a "relocation" of self, because the activity is highly habitualized, as in the case of driving a car along an often-traveled route. Although highly habitualized behavior, as not requiring deliberation, has much in common with Mead's examples of highly intense behavior, there is a special problem involving extremely habitual activity. In this type of situation it may seem that the ongoing adjustment to novelty inherent in sociality does not take place, even nonreflectively. Thus, the sensed flow of the temporal dynamics involved in reconstructive activity, which at any moment can give rise to the emergence of the I-me cognitive dialogical relation, would seem to have disappeared, for there would seem to be no such activity. Yet, there can be no present without novelty and adjustment, the constituents of that sociality which characterizes any present in its passage. Thus, there can be no situation which does not involve some novelty emerging from a sedimented past and passing into new sedimentations, or, in other terms, some novel response of the 'I' emerging from an old 'me' and giving rise to a new 'me', even though the adjustment be minimal. Mead recognizes this in his claim that:

> The resulting action is *always* a little different from anything which he could anticipate. This is true even when he is sim-

ply carrying out the process of walking. The very taking of his expected steps puts him in a certain situation which has a slightly different aspect from what is expected, which is in a certain sense novel. That movement into the future is the step, so to speak, of the ego, of the 'I'. It is something that is not given in the 'me'.[150]

As noted earlier in this section, Mead holds that the extreme opposite of the limit of subjectivity in the radical breakdown of a situation is a state which *"approaches* objectivity." Perfect objectivity, however, as that kind of situation in need of no ongoing adjustment whatsoever, could not be truly temporal. Every experience, even the habitual, is tinged with novelty and a sense of accompanying adjustment, due to the very nature of time. In highly habitual behavior, the novel response of the lived body brings about an unreflective adjustment in terms of the sedimentations which enter into the funded activity of the concrete subject. There is a nonreflective sense of the lived dimensions which underlie a possible I-me cognitive relation and which can bring about reflection at any time, reflection most likely to occur if a problem emerges which cannot be handled by highly habitualized behavior.

Mead holds that the self is made up of a "structure of attitudes" as opposed to "a group of habits."[151] Here the emphasis is on structure as opposed to group, not on attitudes as opposed to habits. As Mead emphasizes, attitudes are habits when we look toward the past, and early adjustments when we look toward the future.[152] Attitudes become habitualized in the sedimentations of the self, and such habitualized, organized attitudes or habits or response provide the funded or sedimented structure which limits, but does not determine, the novel response that can emerge. It has been seen that at times the emerging novelty and the resulting adjustment in the dynamics of the self are so rooted in the sedimentations of past organizations of attitudes, even if originally structured through different types of activities, that reflection need not occur. The nonreflective awareness could be called either prereflective or postreflective. It involves a prereflective organization of activities in that it is that which is not, but can be, brought to reflective awarenss. Yet, this awareness is postreflective in that the very biological organization which is presently operating either in an extremely habitual or extremely intense nonreflective mode is what it is because of the structural organization growing out of activities of previous reflections, a structural organization which allows the bipolar dynamics of adjustment in the above cases to be carried out without reflective awareness.[153]

It can be seen, then, why Mead states that "there is no self unless there is *the possibility* of regarding it as an object to itself," a possibility for which "the body is an integral part."[154] Or, as he elsewhere states, "self-conciousness refers to the *ability* to call out in ourselves a set of definite responses which belong to the others of the group."[155] Once selfhood has developed, this ability or possibility is always there, and in the situations illustrated by Mead is experienced in the present as the nonreflective awareness of the temporally constituted dynamics of adjustment of the lived body, a nonreflective awareness which can give rise at any moment to the cognitive I-me dialogical relation when required, and which grounds the sense of the temporal dialogical stretch.

Here two interrelated points must be stressed. First, the nonreflective experience prior to the development of selfhood is very different from the nonreflective experience which occurs after selfhood has arisen, for the latter involves an organization of ongoing adjustments structured by past I-me dynamics, a concrete decentered subject embodying the sedimentations of past dialogical activities. Without the dialogical reflective level the social organization which enters into the sense of the concrete decentered subject capable of self-reflection could not come to be. Second, because of this, the nondialogical awareness of the self in its ongoing temporal dynamics is quite different than the experience which Mead attributes to James and Cooley and to which he so strongly objects. For his objection lies in the fact that "the individual need not take the attitudes of others toward himself in these experiences, since these experiences merely in themselves do not necessitate his doing so, and unless he does so, he cannot develop a self."[156]

Rather, the sense of self which fringes experience is possible only through the taking of roles and the incorporation of the generalized other within the behavioral structure of the lived body. For Mead, the development of selfhood is essentially cognitive or dialogical, and any nonreflective awareness of self presupposes the cognitive structure involved in taking the role of the other. But the very structure of the self as cognitive is rooted in the temporal features of the lived body. The I-me, subject-predicate, cognitive, reflective, or dialogical relation is rooted in the dimensions of creativity and sedimentation of the lived body. The unity of the decentered corporeal subject in its dimensions of creativity and sedimentation is the unity of temporal experience rooted ultimately in the sense of the directionality of temporal passage. Yet such a unity can become the unity of *my* experience only through the cognitive activity involved in taking the role of the other. Time consciousness, role taking, and self-awareness are inseparably linked. The sense of the unity and directionality of the concrete self is founded ultimately in the sense of the unity and directionality of time.

It has been seen that a nondialogical sense of self as the lived body or decentered subject comes to the fore in the polar extremes of experience, when it is functioning in situations which require its most creative dimensions and in situations which call for its most habitual or "instinctive " dimensions. The sense of self in the former situation is the sense of decentered corporeal subjectivity creatively functioning in the span between the radical breakdown of a situation and the beginning reconstruction of its own mode of behavior as well as of a part of its world. The sense of self in the latter circumstance is the sense of unified organization of ongoing adjustment in which the sedimented dimension of the self plays the dominant role, living out the interplay of the other and my response through the organized activity of the concrete decentered subject. A sense of the fittingness is 'there' without the need for reflection, though the rupture of such a sense, the disruption of the fit, brings about a return to dialogical consciousness. In this way, Mead is not open to the claims either that in the former case he inconsistently allows for a self that is directly accessible to cognition or reflection, or that in the latter case there is no self-awareness whatsoever, and indeed, even no self. In neither case is there dialogical relation involving the I-me polarization of subject and object, but a sense of the lived body which, as indicated above, is in diverse ways both and neither. It is neither in that it subtends the I-me dialogical relation, and is that which gives rise to it. It is both in that this lived body functions both as an 'I' and as a 'me'. Even in dialogical consciousness, the sense of the nonthematic I-me reflective or cognitive activity taking place in the dialogical stretch of the temporal present, the sense of the passing of the 'I' from the old 'me' out of which its novelty arose into the new 'me' which renders it continuous with what came before, is pervaded by the sense of the temporally organized vitality of the lived body.

And, in none of these cases is there a psychical awareness of contents paralleling ongoing activity in an objectively 'there' world. In 'psychical immediacy', the objectivity has broken down. There is no ongoing activity or objects for the sense of the creativity leading to the reconstruction of contents to parallel. In the nonreflective activity of ongoing adequate or habitualized adjustment, the nonreflective sense of self as temporally structured decentered bodily subject does not parallel experience of objects but fringes it, pervades its very tone and texture, making my experience precisely *my* experience, my memories precisely *my* memories. In the nonthematic dialogical consciousness of the temporal present, the temporally founded sense of deliberative activity is again not some awareness paralleling what is taking place in the world, though neither is it a reflection on what one was or thought or did in a moment past, but rather it is a sense of the way one experiences a world in the temporal present. None of these cases deny the outward-directedness of consciousness. And, in none of these cases is the awareness of the temporal vitality of the lived body something opposed to the perceived world but rather something situated within the perceived world, partially constitutive of its character, and oriented toward it. The sense of one's existence in the world is the sense of the temporal dialogical stretch, whether the dialogue is fully operative at the cognitive level or incipient in the dynamic interplay of the creative and sedimented dimensions of the lived body. This sense of one's existence in the world is a sense of the temporally constituted decentered subject, which is at once a way of knowing and a way of being.

In this chapter it has been seen that though Merleau-Ponty's existential self and Mead's cognitive self may at first seem to lie at opposite ends of the spectrum, Merleau-Ponty's focus on the existential self contains the structure for and beginning development of a cognitive view of the self, while Mead's cognitive self is rooted in the lived body with its existential dimensions. Through the mutually clarifying insights offered by these two philsophers in their respective approaches, Merleau-Ponty's latent doctrine of the self can be brought into explicit focus, while Mead's doctrine of the self can be placed within a broader context which helps clarify or resolve certain ambiguities and inconsistencies in his writings. What results both emerges from, and gives added significance to, a fundamentally shared vision of selfhood. For Mead and Merleau-Ponty alike, the self is inherently intersubjective or social, incorporating the role of the other in its very structure. And, for both philsophers, the temporality of the lived body, through which the self emerges as essentially temporal, requires an account of self, not only in its existential but also in its cognitive dimensions, which is consistent with their respective accounts of time. They share a vision of the self that provides a new understanding of subjectivity, a contemporary understanding of a decentered subject which undercuts the problematics of the various versions of an intuited 'I', of a transcendental ego, or of psychical contents paralleling or replacing an objective reality, and which inextricably interweaves the sense of one's self with the sense of one's existence in an intersubjective world. This vision of the self, however, remains basically incomplete without a focus on its interrelation with issues of language and freedom. The ensuing chapters will successively turn to these topics.

5. THE LIFE
OF LANGUAGE

SINCE FOR MEAD AND MERLEAU-PONTY alike language is interwoven with the emergence of selfhood within a shared world, it can be expected that their respective understandings of langauge will have key affinities. For each, language is a type of gesture which is intimately incorporated into the lived body and the lived world, is inseparably intertwined with thought, and, as lived, incorporates both settled tradition and present creativity. Because of this, they both oppose all vestiges of reductionism in the approach to language, as well as all attempts to uproot it from lived experience as a derived, abstract, scientific objectification. It is to Merleau-Ponty's development of these features of language that the ensuing discussion will first turn.

Merleau-Ponty, in his phenomenology of language, emphasizes the speaking subject and meaning involved in speech and rooted in the body. For it is through meaning that speech, like gesture, opens upon a community and upon the lived world which gives speech and language a pivot. In the broader dimensions of language and speech, there is a language-meaning (*langagière*) "which effects the mediation between my as yet unspeaking intention and words, and in such a way that my spoken words surprise me myself and teach me my thoughts. Organized signs have their immanent meaning, which does not arise from the 'I think' but from the 'I am able to.' "[1] In his early considerations of language, Merleau-Ponty emphasizes speech as a type of gesture, a treatment of which reveals the implications of speech in relation to body and to world.

While Merleau-Ponty does not explicitly treat the relation between gesture and animal behavior as Mead does, he emphasizes the continuity between the human and animal organisms, the emergence of the human from the animal in a nonreductionistic way, and the uniqueness of human or symbolic behavior as a distinctive human structure.[2] As such, this human level of structure of behavior as symbolic and as the immersion "in the world by means of the body itself is connected with the order of the significant."[3] Thus, although Merleau-Ponty distinguishes human behavior as distinctively symbolic from animal behavior, this latter is virtual and operative in human behavior. Just as the animal's presence transforms the physical world, introducing meanings such as "food" and "hiding place," so too does the presence of the human in the animal world bring in new meanings. Within human behavior, meanings arise that are transcendent in relation to anatomical apparatus and to the "body as a mere biological entity,"[4] in the sense that they go beyond the natural configuration to the human as symbolic. And yet the animal and strictly biological dimensions exist in the human, but in the human structural unity which transforms them in their entirety, as seen in chapter 4. Merleau-Ponty thus shows that in the human makeup the so-called animal and the human are interwoven, so that there is no animal (in the human) without it being human, and no human which is not animal.

> Everything is both manufactured and natural in man, as it were, in the sense that there is not a word, not a form of behaviour which does not owe something to purely biological being—and which at the same time does not elude the simplicity of animal life, and cause forms of vital behaviour to deviate from their pre-ordained direction, through a sort of *leakage* and through a genius for ambiguity which might serve to define man. Already the mere presence of a living being transforms the physical world, bringing to view here 'food', there a 'hiding place', and giving to 'stimuli' a sense which they have not hitherto possessed. *A fortiori* does this apply to the presence of man in the animal world. Behaviour creates meanings which are transcendent in relation to the

anatomical apparatus, and yet immanent to the behaviour as such, since it communicates itself and is understood.[5]

Within this context of meaningful human behavior, including the relation between speech and gesture, the nature of the connection between gesture and its meaning is revealed. The gesture, as a bodily and behavioral expression, manifests its meanings immediately so that, for example, a gesture of anger does not make one think of anger, but rather, is anger itself. This understanding is made possible by the commonly shared and intersubjective world. Thus, individuals experiencing an angry face or gesture do not need recourse to feelings of their own or to their own gestures to understand its meaning. Nor is anger or any other such attitude "a psychic fact hidden behind the gesture," for the meaning is immediately expressed in the gesture; nor is it experienced as the quality of a thing, such "as the color of the carpet," for it is experienced as human within the human structure of behavior.[6] Yet humans fail to comprehend well the gestures of animals or even of primitive people because there must be some coincidence "with the inner possiblities" and some meaningful communal background or world for a gesture to be experienced as meaningful. It is against this commonness of background that an originary gesture fits and can be understood and interpreted.

> The meaning of a gesture thus 'understood' is not behind it, but rather is intermingled with the structure of the world outlined by the gesture, and which I take up on my own account. It is arrayed all over the gesture itself—as, in perceptual experience, the significance of the fireplace does not lie beyond the perceptible spectacle, namely the fireplace itself as my eyes and movements discover it in the world.[7]

And, as seen in the last chapter, the overlapping of my body with that of the other is possible because the lived body of the other, its gestures, conduct, corporeal intentions and significances are grasped by direct access through the perception of the lived body as one with the intentions of my own body, as prolongations of my own intentions and as entailing an affinity central to the lived body and human exsistence precisely as primordial generality, as pre-personal, and as "two sides of one and the same phenomenon."[8] At this intentional and intersubjective level, the intentions are corporeal without specifying a particular body as subject. The other, in this context, appears "as the completion of the system."[9] As Merleau-Ponty states:

> The communication or comprehension of gestures comes about through the reciprocity of my intentions and the gestures of others, of my gestures and intentions discernible in the conduct of other people. It is as if the other person's intention inhabited my body and mine his. The gesture which I witness outlines an intentional object. This object is genuinely present and fully comprehended when the powers of my body adjust themselves to it and overlap it.[10]

It is in this context that Merleau-Ponty relates gestures to cinema, in that movies present directly the conduct, behavior, or way of being in the world which we can see in gesture and gaze.[11]

Thus for Merleau-Ponty the link between gesture and speech expressed through the body in a common world does not simply mean that meaning and speech or words are *like* gestures and their meanings, but rather, that they *constitute* indeed a type of gesture, as he says in the following text:

> The spoken word is a genuine gesture, and it contains its meaning in the same way as the gesture contains its. This is what makes communication possible. . . . What I communicate with primarily is not 'representations' or thought, but a speaking subject with a certain style of being and with the 'world' at which he directs his aim. Just as the sense-giving intention which has set in motion the other person's speech is not an explicit thought, . . . so my taking up this intention is not a process of thinking on my part, but a synchronizing change of my own existence, a transformation of my being.[12]

Speech and gesture can be further correlated in that speech is related to what it expresses in the same way as a gesture is related to its goal or to what it expresses. Merleau-Ponty goes on to observe that "signification arouses speech as the world arouses my body,— by a mute presence which awaken my intentions without deploying itself before them."[13] Before turning the discussion to body and world entailed in speech, the relation of speech as gesture to thought will be discussed, dispelling a certain misconception about speech.

For Merleau-Ponty speech does not simply express an already completed thought, but rather accomplishes or completes thought. Instead of two independent realms external to one another and coming together, thought can exist only if it is actualized by speech. "There is thus, either in the man who listens or reads, or in the one who speaks or writes, a *thought in speech* the existence of which is unsuspected by intellectualism."[14] Thus, speech, rather than merely the denomination of already recognized objects, is precisely the recognition of objects; "the word bears the meaning, and, by imposing it on the object, I am conscious of reaching that object."[15] The gestural meaning immanent in speech leads to and is incorporated within the conceptual meaning. It is clear according to this interpretation that speech and thought enjoy an internal rather than external relation, as the intellectualist would have it, so that the sense and the word are together or "intervolved" in such a way that the word is the external existence of the thought. Thus, the word is the presence and body of thought in the phenomenal world. Thought is not an internal thing existing independently of the world and of words,[16] but rather, thought and expression are seen to be simultaneously constituted. This power of expressing draws from the entire cultural store, and the body lends itself to speech as to a gesture becoming a habit within the context of a common world.

Since putting things in words accomplishes or completes thought, speech as gesture has a meaning and a world. It is the world which gives constancy and anchor to the language, just as the qualities of a thing are rooted in the constancy of the thing, which in turn is rooted in the constancy of the world. This underlying meaning network or world in language defies translation and gives significance to the language. This is what makes Merleau-Ponty reject the notion of language as simply a system of signs in the abstract. The reason a language finally

> intends to say and does say (*veut dire et dit*) something is that all the signs together allude to a signification which is always in abeyance when they are considered singly, and which I go beyond. ... Each of them expresses only by reference to a certain mental equipment, to a certain arrangement of our cultural implements, and as a whole they are like a blank form we have not yet filled out, or like the gestures of others, which intend and circumscribe an object of the world that I do not see.[17]

The child who learns language has acquired a manner and style of behaving in the significant world, and not "the sum of morphological, syntactical, and lexical meanings."[18]

Language involves the individual's "taking up a position in the world of his meanings," the cultural life borrowing its structures from the natural life. The "phonetic gesture," just as the pattern of my bodily behavior or any gesture, gives the object a significance for me and for others. The human body can be defined by the specific property of "appropriating . . . significant cores which transcend and transfigure its natural powers,"[19] toward a new form of behavior which is the symbolic power or behavior of expression, making communication possible, as seen above.

Communication transpires among speaking subjects within a world. Further, "we live in a world where speech is an institution. For all these many commonplace utterances, we possess within ourselves ready-made meanings."[20] Such sedimented and available meanings arising from former acts of expression set up a common world among speaking subjects within which context the words refer, just as in the case of gestures in relation to the perceived world. The linguistic gesture, like gestures in general, gives its meaning, which reveals its world. "The spoken word is a gesture, and its meaning, a world."[21] In a specific culture, speech as gesture is sedimented, constituting the common world which engulfs the communicators who contact each other in a common world. It is to the central role of the lived body in the world as the context of such behavior and as the anchor of speech that the discussion will now turn.

This central role of the body in the world is seen to be paralleled in the world of language, where the body is also central for speaking. Thus, Merleau-Ponty refers to the body as "expression,"[22] in the sense that

> my body is the seat or rather the very actuality of the phenomenon of expression (*Ausdruck*) and there the visual and auditory experiences, for example, are pregnant one with the other, and their expressive value is the ground of the antepredicative unity of the perceived world, and, through it, of verbal expression (*Darstellung*), and intellectual significance (*Bedeutung*). My body is the fabric into which all objects are woven, and it is, at least in relation to the perceived world, the general instrument of my 'comprehension'.[23]

Just as the world arouses the body, so too speech is an instance of corporeal intentionality involving significations arousing speech. "It is my body which gives significance not only to the natural object, but also to cultural objects, like words."[24]

As the field of action is open for the body, so too the linguistic world is open for the body, so that the role of the body in speech is similar to that in action.[25] As the hand moves to the cup of coffee offered to me, so too my "whole body system"[26] is involved in concentrating to find and to say the word. Thus, the body is the vehicle or the expression of symbolic systems which transcend its strictly biological activity as well as the significance in natural gestures, all of which would "collapse if ever the body ceases to prompt their operation and install them in the world and our life."[27] The originary and creative dimension of speech is prior to this sedimentation and becomes sedimented as past acts of speech. Yet, indeed, this sedimented world and sedimented language provide the context for creativity in speaking and expressing: "What nature does not provide, cultural background does."[28]

For Merleau-Ponty, living language includes sedimented language and sedimented speech as well as creative or originary language and creative speech. The sedimented as past is still as such part of the lived whole. Just as the present was seen in the analyses of time to contain past presents by way of sedimentation, so too here, Merleau-Ponty, in a parallel fashion, understands sedimented language as one essential dimension of lived language or as speech now sedimented, as part of the whole of language which is appropriated in speaking. In a real sense, the speaker has his language, just as the language, which precedes the speaker, engulfs the speaker. This reciprocity pervades lived language. One must then say that language is already there as a repository before the speaker, but likewise, it is projected by the speaker both as repository and as living, creative, and continuously speaking. This lived whole includes language as repository or residue of acts of speech and language as productive or creative. Thus lived language does not preclude the originary and creative dimension which itself is prior to and becomes part of the deposit of sedimentation. Sedimented language and sedimented world provide the context for creativity in speaking and expressing, for "breaking the silence."[29] Language is revelatory and expresses nascent significance or birth of meaning. "In its live and creative state, language is the gesture of renewal and recovery which unites me with myself and others.

We must learn to reflect on consciousness *in* the hazards of language."[30] This reflects the much quoted distinction which Merleau-Ponty makes: "Or again one might draw a distinction between a *speaking word* and a *spoken word*. The former is the one in which the significant intention is at the stage of coming into being."[31] while the latter relates to already developed expression.

In discussing how such acquired meanings come to be constituted, Merleau-Ponty raises the further question about the accidental character of the link between the verbal sign and its meaning, as shown by the existence of numerous languages. Although there is arbitrariness in language between a word and its meaning, it is not total since there is some connection between the unique character of each individual language and its specific world. Further, he attacks the position which takes the nonlinguistic gesture to be natural and the linguistic to be conventional by showing that neither the so-called natural gestures expressing emotions nor the emotions themselves are natural. The fact that humans share the same organs and nervous systems to express emotions does not mean that the same signs are employed in different cultures. "What is important is how they use their bodies, the simultaneous patterning of body and world in emotion. . . . It is no more natural, and no less conventional, to shout in anger or to kiss in love than to call a table a 'table'. Feelings and passional conduct are invented like words."[32] These so-called conventions presuppose "an earlier means of communication and language must be put back into this current of intercourse"[33] in which its gestural sense expresses this world, as so many ways of the body living the world. Hence, what must be seen is that language as gesture reveals a meaning in relation to world, and it is this latter which is not entirely arbitrary, so that the "full meaning of a language is never translatable into another,"[34] nor can one completely absorb another language to the same extent as the one in which one lives as one's own. Even for people who are fluent in several langauges, the variations of unique worlds are not completely assimilated, and one does not ever belong to two worlds at the same time.

It can be seen, then, that Merleau-Ponty opposes two mutually exclusive interpretations of language, empiricist or mechanistic psychology and intellectualism, both of which have similar philosophical assumptions. According to the reductionist accounts of speech and language, there is no speaking subject, but rather, "a flow of words set in motion independently of any intention to speak"[35] so that human speaking is like the electric lamp becoming incandescent. While it is the case that Merleau-Ponty roots speech in the prereflective and pre-personal perceptual realm and in existence as meaning giving, this activity does not prescind from the individual person. He explicitly disavows the empiricists' interpretation of the meaning of words as given with the stimuli or with the states of consciousness which they simply name, or the view that "the shape of the word, as heard or phonetically formed, is given with the cerebral or mental track."[36] Similarly, he rejects outright the intellectualist position according to which the words are self-contained and the thoughts, already independently constituted, come to words. There is a kinship between empiricist or mechanistic psychologies and the intellectualist position since, as Merleau-Ponty contends, both make it impossible for the word or speech to have meaning or significance in a nonreductionistic sense of the fullness of meaning. Consequently, according to Merleau-Ponty, "we refute both intellectualism and empiricism by simply saying that the word has a meaning."[37]

In the context of such rejections, Merleau-Ponty's phenomenology of language similarly brings into focus the experience of language in contast to the sciences which focus upon language as derived, objectified, and abstract. This contrast is much the same as that between the objective body and the lived body, objectified world and lived world, and objective time and lived time. Just as the centrality of the lived body was revealed in being in the world, so too the centrality of lived language is brought to the fore as the foundation for all other considerations of language, and is involved in that very centrality of the lived body.

Merleau-Ponty, as seen above, in developing a phenomenology of speech and lived language, which includes sedimented and originary language, opposes the interpretation of language by the sciences of language as first and foremost an object of thought. For him, language is not merely a closed system or the sum of morphological, syntactical, and lexical meanings, but, rather, is first lived, and as such gives rise to a phenomenology of language including both its sedimented and creative moments. He explicitly affirms the impossibility of simply juxtaposing the two perspectives, "language as an object of thought and language as mine"[38] or as lived. He goes on: "As soon as we distinguish, alongside of the objective science of language, a phenomenology of speech, we set in motion a dialectic through which the two disciplines open communications."[39] This attempt to keep a dialogue with those sciences, although consistent with his dialogue with the sciences of psychology, physiology, sociology, and the human sciences in general, is rendered difficult by a failure on his part, as Ricoeur points out, to take into account that for structuralism language is an autonomous system. Ricoeur emphasizes that it is precisely this structuralist presupposition which excludes the possibility of any phenomenology of language and speech, for, if language is focused on as an empirical object, and signs are simply unities in relation to other signs in the whole system, then the constitution of the sign (word) is such that a phenomenology of speech is completely excluded. Signification and a subject have little place in such a theory of language. Thus, Ricoeur considers structuralism to levy a challenge to phenomenology: "The challenge consists in this, that the notion of signification is placed in a field other than the intentional aim of a subject."[40] If, as Ricoeur contends, these are antinomical views dealing with the same phenomenon, the confrontation between them cannot result in the mere juxtaposition or opposition of one to the other that Merleau-Ponty attempts.[41]

The question remains what such a phenomenology can do in relation to the semiological sciences.[42] Merleau-Ponty's interest was not so much to find the positive value to these sciences or to develop an opening in their presuppositions of closure as it was to develop a phenomenology of language and speech in a positive direction. He fails, however, as Ricoeur indicates,[43] to take them seriously on their own ground and deal with their assumptions. But the text of the lecture, "On the Phenomenology of Language," indicates his clear acceptance of semantic priority and creativity in language against the absolute presuppositions of structuralism. Further, the link of language to gesture as meaningful and as involving world sketches the radical difference between this view of language and that of structuralism,[44] and at once points toward affinities with Mead's understanding of language in relation to gesture, to thought, and to action.

Mead explains the origins and function of language by examining its role in the social process. As he states, language "has to be studied from the point of view of the gestural type of conduct within which it existed without being as such a definite language. And we have to see how the communicative function could have arisen out of that prior sort of conduct."[45] For Mead, language, thought, and action are inseparably intertwined in the ongoing social act constituted by the "conversation of gestures." Because

Darwin studied animal gestures—facial, bodily, and vocal—Mead finds his work of particular importance. But he takes issue with it in its key respects, for Darwin concluded that these gestures were expressions of emotions. Mead objects that Darwin and psychologists of the day who were interested in the way individuals communicate through acts assumed that such acts "had a reason for existence because they expressed something in the mind of the individual. It is an approach like that of the philologist. They assume that language existed for the purpose of conveying certain ideas, certain feelings."[46] Mead did not deny that there is an emotional dimension in the instinctive acts found in animal communication, but denied that they were mainly the expression of emotions or, more generally, that the gesture was an expression of any internal feelings or psychological states. Language, for Mead as for Merleau-Ponty, is not a vehicle for communicating private meanings or ideas or states of consciousness. Rather, language is a social process and grows out of gestures which, as the vehicle for eliciting responses from other animals, are parts of social acts. Mead agrees with Wundt here that the gestures of animals are not expressions of emotions but rather means of eliciting response, but argues that Wundt's psychophysical parallelism could not account for the emergence of the language gesture.[47] Wundt presupposed selves to explain the social process of communication, while according to Mead, the emergence of selves must be explained in terms of communication within an ongoing social process.

Indeed, Mead identifies even expressions of the emotions with the beginnings of social acts and accounts for their value from this perspective.[48] He speaks approvingly of James's view of the emotions, which "comes back to the reaction to the motor attitudes of the organism itself,"[49] yet it is with Dewey that he is most in agreement, for Dewey holds that some inhibition of action is always involved.[50] Mead claims that while there is no independent self-contained emotion which the overt gesture expresses, the overt gesture does not cause the emotion. Rather, the emotion is intertwined with the beginning phase of the gesture and emerges with the inhibition of action. Thus he holds, for example, that clenching the fist does not represent a psychical fact of anger, nor does it cause the anger, but rather the anger arises with the inhibition of the act of striking, and is immediately expressed in the clenching of the fist.[51] And, just as the relation between a linguistic gesture and its meaning will be seen to have a certain arbitrariness, limited by a world of social interaction, so too are the gestures immediately expressive of emotions to be understood. As Mead states concerning the expression of emotions, "Our position implies that these expressions have arisen out of social contact and are in a sense created by social conduct."[52] Thus, though Mead emphasizes the common physiological basis for the emotions in all human beings, he is in agreement with Merleau-Ponty that where social conduct of certain types varies, the gestures which embody the emotions and are their expression will vary as well. Nonlinguistic gestures are not merely natural, anymore than linguistic gestures are merely arbitrary, for both emerge in the context of social interaction.

As noted in earlier chapters, Mead holds that back of all gestures lie tendencies to act. Gestures are the beginnings of acts,[53] and as such are informative about the probable future phases of the act. Gestures are anticipatory of what is to follow, and thus serve as means of eliciting response even before there is awareness of meaning. Language itself is a gesture, a gesture which is conscious and significant. As Mead states, "Language as a set of significant symbols is simply the set of gestures which the organism employs in calling out the response of others."[54] As noted earlier, the logical structure of meaning is found in the triadic or "threefold relationship of gesture to adjustive response and to the resultant of the social act which the gesture initiates."[55] Thus, the meaning which language expresses is objectively present in social interaction and is not a content of mind or consciousness.[56]

While the conversation of gesture does not necessarily involve consciousness of meaning, language emerges out of gesture when consciousness of meaning attaches to the gesture. Language, as a social process that grows out of gesture and includes awareness of meaning, is broader than speech, for it includes sign language, or the gestures made by little children before they can utilize articulate speech. These are significant gestures. "When the child points at food he is doing the same thing that he would be doing if he asked for it, and this is a different thing from the whining of the dog."[57] Mead holds that though language could grow out of any set of gestures,[58] the vocal gesture is of special importance. As he observes, "We cannot see ourselves when our face assumes a certain expression. If we hear ourselves speak we are more apt to pay attention. One hears himself when he is irritated using a tone that is of an irritable quality, and so catches himself."[59] The peculiar importance of the significant vocal gesture or significant symbol over other significant gestures is that "it affects the individual who makes it just as much as it affects the individual to whom it is directed. . . . The individual who speaks in some sense takes the attitude of the other whom he addresses. . . . It is through this sort of participation, this taking the attitudes of other individuals, that the peculiar character of human intelligence is constituted."[60] What we say has the same meaning for us as it does for the group to whom it is addressed. Mead notes, though, that while the vocal gesture has a peculiar importance in that it reacts upon the individual making it in the same way that it reacts upon another, "this is also true in a less[er] degree of those of one's own gestures that he can see or feel."[61]

Neither sign language nor written language are primary modes of communication, but they have the same character of the vocal gesture, that is, the user responds or tends to respond as others tend to respond to it.[62] Both hand-movements and speech appeal to our eye or ear as well as to those of others and provide situations in which we become definitely self-conscious.[63] As Mead observes, "One sees one's self using the gestures which those who are deaf make use of. Of course the same is true of any form of script. But such symbols have all been developed out of the specific vocal gesture, for that is the basic gesture which does influence the individual as it influences others."[64] As Mead observes, "We are continually following up our own address to other persons by an understanding of what we are saying, and using that understanding in the direction of our continued speech."[65]

Mead points out that though nonhuman animals have vocal gestures used in the social context, these are not significant symbols, for the user of the vocal gesture does not respond to its own stimulus in the same way as the other hearers of the gesture respond. There are, however, social situations in which the conduct of one animal does affect others in carrying out acts in which all are engaged. "In some degree the animal takes the role of the other and thus emphasizes the expression of its own role."[66] Further, "many of the acts of these lower forms are as highly complex as many human acts which are reflectively controlled."[67] Mead finds the difference to lie in the distinction between instinct and impulse. The instinct can be quite complex, yet different elements of the whole process are so rigidly organized together that a blockage at any point frustrates the entire undertaking. "It does not leave the parts of the whole free for recombination in other forms. Human impulses, however, are generally susceptible to such analysis and recombination in the presence of obstacles and inhibitions."[68]

This points to one of the key functions of language, giving us control in the organization of the act.[69] And control over the organization of the act includes reconstruction when the act is blocked, an activity which lies between the impulse and consummatory stages of the act, and which involves both speech and the hand. Though language involving the hand is secondary to speech, the hand plays a crucial role in the development of language. "Speech and the hand go together in the development of the social human being."[70] The growth of language and the manipulation of objects,[71] though different, are inseparably intertwined. Both language and the hand involve the means to the attainment of ends which lie between the impulse and consummatory stages of the act. "The multitude of possible responses which constitute mediate things that lie between our impulses and their consummations opens up the field of indication and reference out of which language can arise, though the two processes undoubtedly work together."[72] For Mead, the conversation of gestures and the appearance of objects within experience "are two basic and complementary logical aspects of the social process."[73]

This role of language in controlling and reconstructing ongoing activity is possible because in the human, as opposed to lower-animal forms, there has been an "internalization" of the communicative process which constitutes thinking and selfhood. As seen in the previous chapter, the I-me dynamic of selfhood is essentially dialogical in nature. The presence in the conduct of the individual of the tendencies to act in the same way as others act,[74] which is basically brought about by the vocal gesture, is "responsible for the appearance in the experience of the individual of a social object, i.e., an object answering to complex reactions of a number of individuals, and also for the appearance of the self. Indeed, these two appearances are correlative."[75] Mead's theories of language and of roles as discussed in previous chapters are inseparably interrelated and provide the interwoven fabric for the emergence of selfhood.[76] As Mead stresses the import of the linguistic gesture:

> I know of no other form of behavior than the linguistic in which the individual is an object to himself, and, so far as I can see, the individual is not a self in the reflexive sense unless he is an object to himself. It is this fact that gives a critical importance to communication, since this is the type of behavior in which the individual does so respond to himself.[77]

This interrelationship among the internalization of the conversation of gestures, role taking, selfhood, reconstructive ability, and language is expressed in Mead's claim that:

> the internalization in our experience of the external conversations of gestures which we carry on with other individuals in the social process is the essence of thinking; and the gestures thus internalized are significant symbols because they have the same meanings for all individual members of the given society or social group, i.e., they respectively arouse the same attitudes in the individuals making them that they arouse in the individuals responding to them: otherwise the individual could not internalize them or be conscious of them and their meanings. As we shall see, the same procedure which is responsible for the genesis and existence of mind or consciousness—namely, the taking of the attitude of the other toward one's self, or toward one's own behavior— also necessarily involves the genesis and existence at the same time of significant symbols or significant gestures.[78]

Though speech plays a crucial role in Mead's position, he disagrees with Watson's view that all our thinking is vocalization. According to this view, thinking is "merely starting to use certain words." Though Mead holds that this is in a sense true, "Watson does not take into account all that is involved here, namely that these stimuli are the essential elements in elaborate social processes and carry with them the value of those social processes."[79] As Mead is careful to point out, mental processes do not lie in words, but are part of a process that is going on between organism and environment: "Out of language emerges the field of mind,"[80] but language itself is possible because of "the triadic relation on which the existence of meaning is based."[81] The partial truth of Watson's claim lies in the fact that thinking involves starting to use certain words. There is an internal relation between thinking and speaking. Speech is thinking out loud, while silent thought is "silent speech," and gains its structure through language. But contrary to Watson's "merely," both thinking and speaking are rooted in and express the character of the social process, whether one is speaking to oneself or to others. Language involves, "even when language makes thought possible, a co-operative social process."[82]

Language, as part of the social act, is not merely descriptive but creative. Through its reconstructive role, indicated above, it actively enters into the constitution of new facts, new situations.

"It is an implement for that purpose."[83] Language as creative of new situations, emerges from the reconstructive activity of individuals. "By using significant symbols, we get the attitude, the meaning, within the field of our own control, and that control consists in combining all these various possible responses to furnish the newly constructed act demanded by the problem."[84] Yet this does not imply that there can be a private language, for two reasons. First, language is temporal and thus partakes of the features of temporality. As such its creativity occurs within a funded context arising out of the sedimentations of past creativities. With words, as with all human behavior, "we build out at both limits," thus incorporating the past and creatively structuring the future, and in the process bringing about a new past with its new sedimentations. Any creativity of language emerges in a present rich with the past. We are born into a common language which we creatively appropriate.

Second, language conveys thinking, and both language and thought are social or intersubjective. Language creates new situations by creating new meanings that are embodied in new ways of acting, giving rise to new sharable experiences, which, as sharable and workable, are at once objective and "universal." Because language is inherently temporal and is internally related to thought, Mead's entire theory of expression echoes his view of the self. As he notes,

> A person asserting his rights on a certain occasion has rehearsed the situation in his own mind. He has reacted toward the community and when the situation arises he arouses himself and says something already in his mind. But when he said it to himself in the first place he did not know what he was going to say. He then said something that was novel to himself, just as the scientist's hypothesis is a novelty when it flashes upon him.[85]

Like Merleau-Ponty, Mead holds that though there is a certain arbitrariness in any language between a word and its meaning, because langauge is tied to the specific character of a world of social interaction, this arbitrariness is limited. As Mead observes, "If you conceive of the mind as just a sort of conscious substance in which there are certain impressions and states, . . . then a word becomes purely arbitrary. . . . There seems to be absolute freedom of arrangement and language seems to be an entirely mechanical thing that lies outside of the process of intelligence."[86] Contrary to this view, the system of symbols called a language connotes much more than the "minute phonetic elements."[87] Rather, though there is a great range in our use of language, "whatever phase of this range is used is a part of a social process, and it is always that part by means of which we affect ourselves as we affect others and mediate the social situation through this understanding of what we are saying."[88]

Thus, Mead characterizes language, as the "field of a fifth dimension" of experience.[89] He forcefully brings this home in the following:

> A person learns a new language, and as we say, gets a new soul. He puts himself into the attitude of those that make use of that language. He cannot read its literature, cannot converse with those that belong to that community, without taking on its peculiar attitudes. He becomes in that sense a different individual. You cannot convey a language as a pure abstraction; you inevitably in some degree convey also the life that lies behind it. And this result builds itself into relationship with the organized attitudes of the individual who gets this language and inevitably brings about a readjustment of views.[90]

Language is expressive of a manner or style of behaving in a significant world. To truly appropriate a language is to understand the language, and that involves, ultimately, to live the life of the language, to live the social process it expresses.

For Mead as for Merleau-Ponty, humans have a fundamental common world because they all participate in the human process of significant communication. As Mead states, in discussing the various levels and types of generalized others, "the one which is the most inclusive and extensive is, of course, the one defined by the logical universe of discourse (or system of universally significant symbols) determined by the participation and communicative interaction of individuals. . . . it enables the largest conceivable number of human individuals to enter into some sort of social relation, however indirect or abstract it may be, with one another—a relation arising from the universal functioning of gestures as significant symbols in the general human social process of communication."[91] As he explains, this transcends the bounds of different languages and different racial and national customs, lead-

ing to the further and larger context of social relations and interactions of civilization as a whole.[92] Any particular unique
language expresses a particular unique way in which this logical
universe of discourse is embedded in the social appropriation of a
concrete world.

The above discussion has revealed that for Merleau-Ponty and
Mead alike, language cannot be divorced from the intentions of
the speaker. In this way they similarly deny the popular claims
both that words simply name states of consciousness or bring already self-contained thoughts to expression, and also that language
is either an autonomous system or a closed system of morphological, syntactical, and lexical meanings. Rather, language grows out
of gesture and is itself a form of gesture which embodies meanings
expressive of social praxis within a common world and which is
incorporated into the very nature of selfhood. Language is temporally constituted, and as such incorporates the temporal dimensions of sedimentation and creativity by which it changes and
grows. They both view language as intimately interwoven with
the experience of a world and as partaking of the features of commonness and uniqueness evinced in the very concept of world, for
they each reveal a common world for language and for all those
who communicate with langauge, as well as a certain uniqueness
of the world of a particular language. Thus, language, for Merleau-
Ponty and Mead alike, is not only central in relation to concrete
human existence, but also partakes of, and is partially constitutive
of, its key features. It remains now to see the way in which human
freedom shares a similar centrality.

6. THE PATTERN OF FREEDOM: THE DIVERSITY OF INTERWOVEN THREADS

BECAUSE THE RESPECTIVE understandings of freedom by Mead and Merleau-Ponty are closely linked with the issues of selfhood and temporality, it can again be anticipated, as with the previous chapter on language, that there will be close affinities between the two positions. And indeed, for both, freedom is always situated freedom because of the nature of the self and the nature of temporality, and it involves the functioning of the entire corporeal decentered subject in its various dimensions. Additionally in this chapter, however, and analogously with those on self and temporality, it will be seen that while Merleau-Ponty's focus on freedom is more narrowly situated than is that of Mead, the former's intense existential focus helps highlight an important dimension implicitly operative in Mead's discussion of freedom. And Mead's broader pragmatic focus will be seen to complement rather than contradict the existential focus of Merleau-Ponty. This broader focus includes the strong and inextricable pragmatic linkage of freedom with values, traces of which can be found unexplicated in Merleau-Ponty's position, as well as the key pragmatic theme of scientific method. These broader issues will in turn afford the opportunity for a final brief glance at the complementary nature of the respective frameworks of Mead and Merleau-Ponty.

Merleau-Ponty understands human freedom to be incorporated within the temporal sense of human existence which itself essentially entails the lived body and the lived world. Such a context opposes any interpretation of a transcendental consciousness with absolute decisions or of human existence as reduced to a thing caught up in causal relationships and determined by external factors. "There is never determinism and never absolute choice, I am never a thing and never bare consciousness."[1] That nothing determines individuals from outside is not due to the fact that nothing acts upon them *ab extra*, but, rather, to the fact that they are from the start outside themselves and open to the world. As he says: "Freedom exists in contact with the world, not outside it."[2] Thus, there is an interplay between the individual's decisions and the situation and roles that the individual appropriates. Freedom, rather than simply an act or a specific choice, emerges within the context of a field as an existential project or commitment which precedes deliberation.

This existential project is the lived dimension of existence prior to and more originary than the derived active dynamism of personal decision. Further, the possibilities which personal decision chooses are already directed, on a more originary, intersubjective level,[3] by the course of events in which each concrete individual participates. Thus, freedom emerges first as the situated unfolding of possibilities. Personal activity is receptive to and creative from this level of existential project which both feeds such activity of freedom and itself is directed and nourished by it. Thus, such personal activity arises from the existing individual's interaction in the fullness of a concrete situation to which freedom, as receptive, reveals a dimension which is diametrically opposed to Sartre's absoluteness of freedom.

Merleau-Ponty adamantly refuses to go along with Sartrean negative and absolute freedom.[4] Although any role or any project can be redirected or destroyed, freedom, precisely as situated, receptive, and positive, implicitly subsists in the fundamental commitment in which existence takes place. Yet in this existential commitment on the level of the common world, the commitment of the individual entails freedom prior to that of an explicit decision.[5] Thus, it is from such a concrete situation that the individual sometimes slowly becomes aware of latent decisions already made, as in the cases of someone pondering a marriage possibility or belaboring a vocational or professional decision. In such cases, the individual at some point realizes that the commitment has already been made on that concrete, existential level and simply remains to be appropriated within an explicit decision. Freedom in this context is always a meeting of the pre-personal with the individual's decisions. "We are involved in the world and with others in an inextricable tangle. The idea of situation rules out absolute freedom at the source of our commitments, and equally, indeed, at their terminus."[6] Freedom, then, in a sense is found at that level before the individual's personal and individual decisions, since any individual is situated in an ongoing stream of history within which coexisting individuals make a lived commitment. Thus, in a sense, "we choose our world and the world chooses us."[7] The individual is born into an already constituted world, but one which is never completely constituted. Within that context, the individual has to make a choice of a concrete manner of being in the world, the latent intentions of which will now be further clarified.

Merleau-Ponty explicitly employs a distinction between express intentions and general intentions throughout his treatment of freedom in contrasting individual intentions and the existential project from which they arise. Entailed here is the now famous distinction between intentional acts and operative intentionality, both of which are rooted in being in the world or crossing over to world as one sense of transcendence as seen above. The examples of fatigue in climbing, inferiority complex, class consciousness, and revolution all shed light on specific and concrete being in the world and the various ways in which one's freedom allows a personal stance in being in the world and, as well, express intentions rooted in it, as will become clear.

The choice to climb a mountain or a mound of rocks and the intentional dimensions latent within that choice can be seen to exemplify, within being in the world, the relation between intentional acts and operative intentionality and the express intention and the general intention incorporated within that relation. The fatigue resulting from climbing, with the different stances toward fatique taken by different participants in such activity, shows something essential about personal being in the world. For, although equally and intensely exhausted, some persons might reach a point where fatique is simply accepted and transformed so that they are willing to go on, even though they are dirty, tired, and sweaty, allowing, perhaps even enjoying, the fatique with its sweat, grime, and grind, while others must stop because they dislike the fatique (which may not be any worse or even as bad), and because they have chosen differently their manner of being in the world. Likewise, such a choice is manifest in the case of someone with an inferiority complex which has become over the years a privileged response or has taken on a "specific weight."[8] Yet this sedimented response also can be overturned by freedom, which gears itself to our situation instead of destroying it, and which can redirect our existence by actualizing other possibilities than those privileged as sedimented or habituated, as mentioned above.

> I am free in relation to fatique to precisely the extent that I am free in relation to my being in the world, free to make my way by transforming it. But here once more we must recognize a sort of sedimentation of our life; an attitude towards the world, when it has received frequent confirmation, acquires a favored status for us. Yet since freedom does not tolerate any motive in its path, my habitual being in the world is at each moment equally precarious, and the complexes which I have allowed to develop over the years always remain equally soothing, and the free act can with no difficulty blow them sky-high.[9]

Within such a stance in being in the world, other facets of freedom emerge, such as the limits of and obstacles to freedom projected within such intentional acts, as well as already contained in operative or lived intentionality. Freedom "comes into being in the act of accepting limits and to which the least perception, the slightest movement of the body, the smallest action, bear incontestable witness."[10] On the other hand, it is precisely this situation which affirms freeedom in its restrictions. Concerning this limit and affirmation, Merleau-Ponty says: "All involvement is ambiguous because it both affirms and restricts a freedom: my undertaking to do a certain thing means both that it would be possible for me not to do it and that I exclude this possibility."[11] And here his discussion of the obstacles of freedom set by freedom itself must be dealt with in further clarifying the distinction between express intentions and general intentions.

Obstacles emerge from the project of freedom itself, which, in its projections, sets bounds to itself. The project to climb the rocks is what forces some rocks to emerge as obstacles to the project and others as providing a path to go between. The express intention is the intention to climb these rocks, while the general intention evaluates "the potentialities of my environment."[12] This latter is tied to the "natural self," i.e., the self in nature, which is situated on earth in the environment, and for whom some things are large and others small—all of the time, whether I have decided to climb them or not. This is related to the lived body in its concrete situatedness. Thus, general intentions are general in a double sense, first as including simultaneously all possible objects in a system, so that "if the mountain appears high and upright, the tree appears small and sloping";[13] and, secondly, in the sense that they are not mine in that "they originate from other than myself."[14] Further, they hold as such for all subjects like myself. Thus, as psychology has shown, there are within us favored shapes or forms and spontaneous evaluations. According to Merleau-Ponty, "without the latter, we would not have a world, that is a collection of things which emerge from a background of formlessness by presenting themselves to our body as 'to be touched', 'to be taken', 'to be climbed over'."[15] Hence, while there are no obstacles in themselves, the self which qualifies them as obstacles is not acosmic, but an incarnate existence which constitutes a basic significance of world, and which provides the ground for every deliberate meaning-giving activity. And such general intentions pre-exist express intentions, as the following discussion further reveals.

The existential project is the place of these intentions, so that, for example, the revolutionary project does not initially result from an explicit judgment or from deliberately posing an end or goal. According to Merleau-Ponty, the existential project is primary in relation both to the revolutionary intention and the class-consciousness intention. For these are first lived as concrete being in the world before coming to a head in the explicit formulation or express intention, and even without being explicitly conscious of them. The actual taking a position in relation to class and to revolution comes about and matures in coexistence before it enters formally into a movement with objective ends and explicit expression. The intellectual project and positing of ends is simply a culmination of the existential project.[16] This lived context involves evaluation of the situation and its entailments and takes an implicit stance in relation to advantages and disadvantages. There is a realization of a life synchronized with the life of the town laborers in which all share a common lot. This phenomenon manifests the conflation of the individual's decisions and the sustaining existential project, as will be further elaborated in relation to the anonymity mentioned above.

On a fundamental level within general existence, a class can be lived prior to awareness of it. An anonymity of this generality and of this individuality intermesh, with the presence to self being mediated through the generality which surrounds us in our coexistence.[17] Merleau-Ponty contends that reflection reveals me to myself "as identical with my presence in the world and to others, as I am now realizing it: I am all that I see, I am an intersubjective field, not despite my body and historical situation, but, on the contrary, by being this body and this situation, and through them, all the rest."[18] Such an attempt to describe myself throws into focus an "anonymous flux, a comprehensive project"[19] and as yet unqualified as, for instance, a "working man" or "middle class." Further, it can be seen that around individuality, there is a generality or sociality which shares in the anonymity of the individuality. Thus, being in the world bears a double anonymity: "Each one of us must be both anonymous in the sense of absolutely individual, and anonymous in the sense of absolutely general."[20] And it is within the common world and as a generalized concrete subject that coexistence must be understood.

Although it is "I" who give significance, direction, and future to my life,[21] my being in the world bears an anonymous life with a significance which I have not constituted, but which is rooted in an anonymous intersubjective level. The significance of events is the concrete project of a future emerging within social coexistence from the general or impersonal (the *On* or *Das Man*) before any personal decision comes on the scene, indicating a certain dialectic or reciprocity of levels in the conferral of significance on events or on history. This means that humans confer on history its significance, but first on the existential level below that of personal decision, so that, in a sense, history itself first puts forward that significance, as can be seen in the example of Napoleon. Ten years after the revolution in France, it was time historically for someone to assume leadership, and, by personal decision appropriating the significance of recent events, to redirect the course of events. The meaning-giving, according to Merleau-Ponty, is not merely centrifugal, which is why the subject of history is not merely the individual. "There is an exchange between generalized and individual existence, each receiving and giving something. There is a moment at which the significance which was foreshadowed in the One, and which was merely a precarious possibility threatened by the contingency of history, is taken up by an individual."[22] According to Merleau-Ponty this holds true for all evaluations, so that the express and the general intentions must be brought to the fore in clarifying fundamental attitudes in the world in relation to freedom. As he states in another place: "It is a matter of understanding that the bond which attaches man to the world is at the same time his way to freedom."[23] And this "way to freedom" entails values and morality which, though fundamental to Merleau-Ponty's philosophy of existence, are not explicitly developed. Values in relation to freedom can be thematically explicated.

Merleau-Ponty's fundamental thesis of the primacy of perception is the point of first focus for dealing with his view of values, for it is within perception and from the perceived world that values emerge and originate, so that "the experience of perception is our presence at the moment when things, truths, values are constituted for us."[24] Thus, it is from the perceived world that values first are constituted in coexisting, as he says: "The perceived world is the always presupposed foundation of all rationality, all value and all existence."[25] Merleau-Ponty has insisted in his thesis of the "primacy of perception" that he is only trying to bring rationality to earth, and not to destroy reason. What has been destroyed is only the belief that reason has an absolute hold on truth and value in the abstract, that scientific objectivity is the privileged domain of rationality and its own ground, and that its truth is for all time. Reason, brought down to earth, is thus confined to temporal and worldly conditions. Yet this does not destroy truth or value, and gives room for freedom precisely in that context of temporal existence. For freedom is at the heart of temporal human existence as such in its sweeping unfolding in the world, directing and being directed by the concrete situation.

Thus, on this primordial level freedom entails values and morality. For from this concrete and temporal ongoing existence as the situated flux of heritage, values are first appropriated prereflectively and pre-personally and are taken up and lived. Evaluation transpires on this level. As seen above, there is acquisition and possibility. World, meaning, and values, already appropriated as an ongoing whole within the deep-seated perceptual realm, can involve a process of reevaluation and reconstitution or can incorporate new meanings and new values in certain situations.

Values which are derived from a world are first lived on the prereflective and existential level. This existential level, however, rather than simply passive to already made values, is itself creative as well as receptive in the constitution of values. While values are expressed first on the existential level of possibilities, the personal decision of the individual comes to appropriate and redirect them in an authentic way. Thus the reciprocity between personal decison and existential project highlights the creativity and receptivity of the individual on both levels.

Thus, it should be clear that morality and values consist neither "in the private adherence to a system of values,"[26] nor to values or moral principles already established and given, but rather emerge on the receptive, creative, existential level.[27] Further, Merleau-Ponty denies absolute values. He accepts, in some subtle way, a scale of values, but only from a particular point of view.[28] As for the scale of values differing according to different points of views, questions arise as to whether this constitutes relativism and whether there are on the level of the concrete some privileged positions. For Merleau-Ponty this fullness and ambiguity of the moral context of values does not result in an unadulterated relativism, but rather, brings to the fore the total situation of the acting persons, who must take up the values of the situation and direct life in terms of them, or creatively adapt them in finding their own way. For him, true morality consists not in "following exterior rules or in respecting objective values," but rather in attunement to and actually living the real value dimension found in our existence, including good faith, loyalty to promises, respect for others.[29] Within this context individuals can move forward only by being what they are at present and by living time, incorporating decisions within the generality of existence and the temporal situation. It is to the correlation between the pre-objective present and presence, essentially involving time and entailing the existential project, that the discussion will now turn.

Existential freedom is situated in the flux of time and thus is rooted in the field of the present in passage, which itself contains all pasts and the stirring of the unfolding of the future. This "thickness of the pre-objective present"[30] in relation to presence and to time as the existential sense of human life—the field of the present where "we find our bodily being, our social being, and the pre-existence of the world" and at the same time the basis for our freedom—is the context for the solution of all problems of transcendence.[31] Freedom rests at the core of transcendence understood in both senses,[32] as the presence or weddedness or crossing over to the world, and as the passing of the present into the past from the future. The concrete and living present is rooted in presence which is rooted in time as the sense of existence.[33] Time, rather than an external attribute, is an essential characteristic of human existence, as also is freedom. And the essence of this temporal subject, constituted with freedom essential to it at its core, is bound up with "that of the body and that of the world"[34] because human existence is bodily and is in the world. Further, freedom has its roots in time which is the origin of spontaneity and acquisition or sedimentation, for time, as the sense of human existence, entails the passage from future to past in such a way as to actualize the possiblities of existence in being in the world projected on that level by human existence. The world which provides the field for freedom, and the body which keeps the world alive, are involved in the dynamism of interaction between the individual's decisions and the generality which underlies them.

From the backdrop of Merleau-Ponty's focus on the situated freedom of a social, temporal self, the discussion will turn to Mead's own pragmatic approach to the issue of freedom, and to its inextricable link with considerations of value and scientific method. The role of freedom in Mead's philosophy has been questioned from two diverse directions. Interpretations of the self which view the 'I' as somehow outside of experience find Mead's account of freedom inadequate.[35] Secondly, and perhaps more widely accepted, are the claims that Mead is, in spite of his talk about freedom, a social determinist because of his emphasis on the generalized other, the 'me' component of the self.[36] Thus it can be seen that one's understanding of Mead's concept of freedom flows directly from one's interpretation of the self in its I-me dimensions. The following discussion presupposes the previous interpretations of Mead's concept of the self and of his understanding of the temporality in which it is rooted.

The 'I', it has been seen, represents the novel, the emergent, the unexpected. Freedom, however, does not lie in unbridled novelty or wild or impulsive behavior. Impulsive conduct is uncontrolled conduct.[37] Mead holds that to act freely is to be governed by one's self rather than by external causes, but here it must be remembered that without the social dimension, the internalized generalized other, the 'me', there is no self. For Mead, freedom requires control over one's actions, self-determination. This is possible only through the use of reflective intelligence, which involves the dialogical relation between the novel actions and choices of the 'I' and the social dimension, the generalized other, the past, the 'me'. Thus, freedom does not lie in being unaffected by others[38] and by one's past, but in the way the 'I' uses the 'me' in its novel decisions and actions. The 'me' calls for a certain sort of an 'I'. The 'me' is in a sense a censor, "but the 'I' is always something different from what the situation itself calls for. . . . The 'I' both calls out the 'me' and responds to it."[39] The 'me' evaluates the acts of the 'I', and the self-evaluations of the 'me' embody social values which are incorporated into the self through its ability to take the role of the other or the attitude of the other. The significance of this interrelationship is that if the self "did not have these two phases there could not be conscious responsibility."[40] This interrelationship incorporates the ability to "talk to himself in terms of the community to which he belongs and lay upon himself the responsibilities that belong to the community," the ability to "admonish himself as others would," the ability to "recognize what are his duties as well as what are his rights."[41] The 'me' represents the social controls internally operative within the self. For Mead, self-criticism is fundamentally social criticism.

Here it must be remembered that these controls have themselves resulted not just from the internalization of the attitudes of the other but from the effect on these attitudes of the past responses of the 'I'. Not only is the 'I' not enslaved by or determined by the 'me', but the 'me' has itself been formed in part from the past creative acts or perspectives of the 'I'.[42] The 'I' as agent enters into the organization of attitudes which constitute the generalized other. Further, it determines what roles it takes, and how they are appropriated and organized, and hence altered. It also selects that upon which it directs its interests and concerns, and chooses its mode of response. The 'me' represents present possibilities for future activities which limit but do not determine the choice to be made. Thus, for Mead as for Merleau-Ponty, what yields the possibilities for present choice is a product of the conditions into which individuals are thrown, their past, their traditions, the generalized other with which they interact, and also their own creative responses to these conditions, responses which in turn have reshaped them. My freedom is limited by the constraints of my past and by the generalized other into which I am thrown, for these limit the range of possibilities open for my choosing. Yet this range has been partially shaped by previous free acts. The response of the 'I' changes the organization of attitudes of the 'me', which in turn resituates or alters the possibilities for future choices.

Mead's concept of freedom is intimately interrelated with the concepts of reflective intelligence and moral agency. Freedom originates from the self and involves self-determination based on reflective intelligence. It is tied to the sense of the moral as responsibility to rational action. The temporal foundations of freedom can best be approached via Mead's concept of moral necessity. He holds that though the " 'me' represents a definite organization of the community incorporated in our own attitudes, and calling for a response," the response that occurs "is something that just happens. There is no certainty in regard to it. There is a moral necessity but no mechanical necessity for the act."[43] Mead's understanding of moral necessity can be seen in his characterization of, and agreement with, a particular aspect of the way Bergson "rescues freedom." As he characterizes this rescue, "The coming of the future into our conduct is the very nature of our freedom. We may be able to get the reason for everything we do after the act, according to the mechanical statement; but to see conduct as selective, as free, we must take account of that which is not yet in position to be expressed in terms of a mechanical statement."[44] Or, as he states in discussing his own position, "At the future edge of experience we project the causal mechanism into the future, but always as the condition of the future that has been selected, not as the condition of the selection."[45] And thus, "the causal structure of the set or environment that is selected in no way determines the selection that is made."[46] Moral necessity involves precisely that which is not necessitated. We can look back, give reasons, say why we acted as we did, view the act in its continuity with the past, though in its occurrence it was a novel event, the 'I's' "movement into the future" which "we cannot tell in advance."[47] Moral necessity occurs in a passing present oriented toward the future, while mechanical necessity involves the statement of the past.[48] Moral necessity is the self-controlled step into the future in a world full of present possibilities emerging from a past. As Mead states,

> The moral necessity lies not in the end acting from without, nor in the push of inclination from within, but in the relation of the conditions of action to the impulses to action. The motive is neither a purely rational, external end, nor a private inclination, but the impulse presented in terms of its consequences over against the consequences of these other impulses. The impulse so conditioned, so interpreted becomes a motive to conduct.[49]

Moral necessity thus involves the free play of rational choice rooted in the vital drives of the lived body.[50] Such rational choice, in weighing consequences, must take into account the environment, the social dimension, the 'me'. Freedom, then, lies in the contextually set selection of an oncoming future. Freedom is always situated freedom. Freedom is not capricious; nor is moral necessity conformity to the past. Freedom and moral necessity are two sides of the same coin. They each involve the creativity of choice within a concrete or existential context set by present possibilities emerging from a past.

Freedom at its fullest involves rational choice in the actualization of possiblities, but this is precisely moral conduct at its fullest. Mead holds that moral awareness is the most concrete awareness in that there is no phase of life that may not become a condition or phase of conduct, and thus moral conduct reaches its highest expression "in the estimation of every possible content of the individual and his situation."[51] Moral awareness permeates experience, and all experience is value laden to some degree, for the consummatory phase of the act is partially constitutive of the very nature of human activity. Human experience as anticipatory, is also ultimately consummatory, and, as rationally organized is, for Mead, the foundation of happiness.[52] The moral dictum implies that individuals fully recognize the conflict between the consequences of an impulse and the consequences of all the other social processes that go to make them up,[53] and thus, to live according to the moral dictum "is simply to live as fully and consciously and as determinedly as possible."[54] The 'I' can make a rational choice, a choice not stemming from blind compulsion or outmoded ideals, because it is aware of the possible consequenes of the choice. This involves, ultimately, "the full interrelationship of the self and the situation."[55] Thus, moral action is rational action in terms of an estimation of consequences within a situation constituted by organism-environment interaction, a situation which provides the matrix of possibilities for intelligent choice.

The estimation of conflicting consequences leads to the reconstruction of a situation which resolves the conflicting demands. Mead holds that out of the reconstruction of the conflict and the recognition of the consequences it involves, "the immediate statement of the end appears."[56] The motive itself arises within this context of reconstruction, for, as was seen above from the perspective of the discussion of moral necessity, "the motive does not arise from the relations of antecedently given ends of activities, but rather . . . the motive is the recognition of the end as it arises in consciousness."[57] The motive and end arise together in the reconstructive act. For this reason, if abstract valuations are used instead of concrete valuations, they are usually inadequate, "as the abstract external valuations are always the precipitations of earlier conduct."[58] As Mead states this in more general terms, "We cannot interpret the meaning of our present through the history of the past because we must reconstruct that history through the study of the present."[59]

External, fixed ends do not provide incentives to moral action, but rather the reservoir of moral power lies in the vitality of the impulses behind the various interests. Because the power of moral action comes from the vitality of the purposive organism, not from the activities which serve as the occasion of their expression, and even more so not from static ideals, Mead can claim that "the good reasons for which we act and by which we account for our actions are not the real reasons."[60] At times these different aspects are not necessary to distinguish, for they work in harmony. However, at times our underlying attitudes change enough that they cannot connect with former occasions for conduct or with accepted ideals, and "uneasiness and friction" arise within the individual. At these times, Mead states, "our minds[61] . . . fall behind the profound development that is taking place underneath."[62] Indeed, Mead holds that profound social reconstruction can take place "back of our minds" before our minds can analyze the situation in terms of the new attitudes. There is a "mental lag."[63] For Mead, as for Merleau-Ponty, existential intentions are lived, at times without our being explicitly conscious of them, before being brought to explicit formulation as an object of choice.

Too much of a mental lag between underlying changing attitudes and awareness of needed changes in ideals and occasions for expression of attitudes can lead to complexes and compulsions.[64] These disintegrate the individual into fragmented elements, thereby diminishing free activity. "We cannot gather ourselves together when we do not feel free."[65] Thus, according to Mead, there are degrees of freedom in proportion to the extent to which the individual becomes organized as a whole.[66] The "felt" fragmentation or unification operative in nonreflective awareness, "underneath" reflection, underlies the degrees of freedom expressible through consciously directed choice, and in authentic freedom, explicit choices must be in harmony with the changes, often profound, "taking place underneath."

Mead's stress on the 'I' in the exercise of freedom may seem to indicate that habitual behavior, behavior which manifests the 'me' as a "conventional, habitual individual"[67] cannot be free. This, however, is not the case. The 'me', it has been seen, is a structure of habits that are at once a sedimentation of one's past[68] and an orientation toward the future. It is "the self we refer to as character."[69] These habits define how one would probably act in specific types of situations with the consequences they imply. In the area of value, this can be understood as general tendencies to act in specific types of situations when motivated by particular types of ends, as well as general tendencies to be motivated by particular types of ends. If the network of habits which constitute the sedimented dimension of the lived body provide an integrative unification, then nonreflective habitual behavior is free. Thus, while "in freedom the personality as a whole passes into the act. . . . [t]his does not necessarily spell creation, spontaneity."[70] It does, however, involve previous reflective reconstructive activity.[71] Further, as seen in chapter 4, even the most ingrained habits of response involve minimal novelty and reconstructive activity, for they not only reflect sedimentations of previous creative activity but also involve, in their step toward the future, the dimensions of sociality constitutive of the temporal present. Thus Mead can claim that the need for moral action "is simply the necessity of action at all."[72] Networks of habits are partially sedimentations of one's own past reconstructive acts and, to the extent and for the time that they work in providing an integrative function, they are expressions of an individual's achievement of freedom. The self, it has been seen, is both an 'I' and a 'me'. The self has the dimensions of creativity and conformity. And freedom lies neither in the 'I' nor in the 'me', in the creativity or in the conformity, but in the proper relation between the two, and while both aspects are essential to the self in its full expression, "the relative values of the 'me' and the 'I' depend very much on the situation." Sometimes it is important to act in a habitual or a socially conforming way, sometimes it is important to be highly creative.[73]

The 'I', as the creative dimension of the lived body, gives the sense of freedom, of agency.[74] This experiential sense of freedom and agency in its relation to the experience of temporality is indicated in Mead's claim that at the future edge of experience there is readiness to accept control of what is taking place, and *this itself is "a datum of experience."*[75] It is the sense of the "living act which never gets direclty into reflective experience" as an object.[76] With the development of selfhood, the sense of the temporal present becomes the sense of one's own agency. The sense of freedom in the passing present is the sense of agency, not a grasp of any particular content. Here it must be remembered that the sense of the novelty of the 'I' is the sense of its passing from an old 'me' out of which its novelty has arisen into a new 'me' which accommodates it and renders it continuous with what came before, the sense of novelty arising out of a context of past conditions and passing into a context of new conditions. Thus, though the 'I', as representing the creative dimension of the lived body, represents the sense of freedom, of agency, yet such a sense ultimately involves the sense of the entire existential subject, for freedom is always situated freedom, just as it was seen in previous chapters that the temporal sense of novelty in general is the sense not of sheer novelty in a discrete or isolated present[77] but of sociality, which involves the "betweenness" of past and future. The very sense of freedom in the passing present, then, is the sense of situated freedom, founded in the temporality of the lived body, the body that I am. The temporal dynamics which permeate the dynamics of the lived body provide the conditions for freedom. We are, ontologically, free. But, authentic freedom must be won through the integrative function of rational self-control.

In the breakdown of the workable value situation, in the reconstruction and reintegration of values, the sense of subjectivity functioning comes to the fore.[78] Thus, there is the opportunity for a new integration that more adequately fulfills the demand for self-fulfillment through rational reconstruction permeated with the vitality of a new sense of the subjectivity which must fit into the reconstructed situation. As was seen in chapter 4, the creative functioning of decentered, concrete subjectivity is the source of the reflective I-me distinction through which this vital, corporeal subjectivity attempts to grasp itself as an object. It is this sense of decentered subjectivity which we are continually trying to realize through conduct and which we can never get fully before ourselves in reflection.[79] It is that which is never exhausted in the exercise of roles and which cannot be totally confined within role identity.[80] In the functioning of subjectivity[81] "novelty arises and it is there that our most important values are located. It is the realization in some sense of this self that we are continually seeking," and we do not know just what its energy and possibilities are.[82] We surprise ourselves by our actions and choices because of the novelty of the 'I', but the 'I' as the dimension of creativity operates within a present rich with the possibilities presented by the past, by the 'me' as the social and sedimented dimension of the decentered subject. Not only can we not know in advance the novel choices to be made by the 'I', but neither can we exhaustively grasp in its concrete entirety the range of possibilities open to it in even the most limited of circumstances, because we can never exhaustively grasp the richness of the intentional possibilities of the lived body, of corporeal subjectivity functioning in its temporal dynamics, through any number of objectifications of it as an object 'me' to an observing 'I'. The 'me' as representing the object pole of the cognitive relation is by definition always the object, never the subject, but an object which can never be exhaustively grasped, just as no object can be exhaustively grasped. As Mead stresses, "Many of the aspects or features of this entire pattern do not enter into consciousness."[83]

Tugendhat sees Mead's understanding of freedom in the sense of self-determination as one-sided. He claims that it recognizes the explicit or implicit process of deliberation aiming for an objectively justified preference, but does not recognize that "the process of adducing grounds must come to an end when decisions about one's life are at issue; thus the decision retains an irreducibly volitional or subjective aspect."[84] He concludes that an adequate concept of responsibility and autonomy "consists in a specific way of choosing that is not exhausted in the reflective self-relation, but is essentially determined by it."[85] Yet Mead recognizes this aspect not just for decisions about one's life but in a more general sense, since no amount of deliberation can determine the exact form which any decision will take. Nor can deliberation necessarily determine the general nature of the decision, since for Mead, as for Merleau-Ponty, the explicit decision may stem from possibilities latent in the present which have never been brought to conscious awareness, possibilities which may lead to a nonreflective commitment toward a particular line of action which explicit choice appropriates but which reflection cannot exhaust. This is precisely what lies implicit in Mead's understanding of moral necessity discussed above. The "essential determination" of action by self-reflection does not exhaust the process of choosing, though after the choice one can look back and provide the "deliberative reasons" for the choice. The response of the 'I' is rooted in the vital intentionality of corporeal subjectivity, and this concrete functioning can never be exhausted by deliberative awareness. The sense of the temporal flow of corporeal intentionality functioning provides a nonreflective sense of workable adjustment in the decision process which underlies and overflows deliberative reasoning, thus bringing rationality down to its foundation in existence, the "development taking place underneath," the reconstructive activity "back of our minds," the wellspring of concrete creativity and adjustment which eludes explicit breakdown and is inexhaustible by any amount of self-reflective or deliberative activity. Freedom, like selfhood, involves self-conscious deliberation, but freedom, selfhood, and rationality itself are ultimately rooted in the non-reflective[86] sense of temporal, corporeal, subjectivity functioning.

While Mead rejects the notion of fixed, absolute values and moral norms, he opposes relativism as well.[87] The energies of the self cannot successfully be confined within the constraints of a generalized other which stifles its development. As Mead states: "The individual in a certain sense is not willing to live under certain conditions which would involve a sort of suicide of the self in its process of realization." At these times the 'I' reconstructs the society, and hence the 'me' which belongs to that society.[88] Yet one never stands as a pure 'I' in opposition to the generalized other,[89] for

> The only way in which we can react against the disapproval of the entire community is by setting up a higher sort of community which in a certain sense out-votes the one we find. A person may reach a point of going against the whole world about him; he may stand out by himself over against it. But to do that he has to speak with the voice of reason to himself. He has to comprehend the voices of the past and of the future.[90]

In brief, he has remained in the most inclusive generalized other, the universe of discourse,[91] and must use this to comprehend what possibly can be in the light of what has been. For Mead, there is always novelty and change, but novelty and change within the context of tradition and continuity.

Mead views the demand for freedom always as the demand to move "from a narrow and restricted community to a larger one, that is larger in the logical sense of having rights which are not so restricted."[92] And growth of community involves growth of self. When we allow value conflicts and their possible resolution to be stated in terms of old selves, the moral problem takes on the character of a necessary sacrifice either of one's self or of the other. A proper consideration of the problem, however, should involve a reconstruction of the situation in such a way that there is no conflict among selves, but rather the emergence of enlarged and more adequate selves. "Solution is reached by the construction of a new world harmonizing the conflicting interests into which enters the new self."[93]

Mead sees this process as "logically identical" with the replacement of an inadequate scientific hypothesis by a new one that overcomes previous problems and conflicts. There is a "complete parallel" holding between the social situation and the situation of the scientist. "The scientist has his own hypothesis, and the question is, Is it the one on which the community as a whole can act or work? The individual is trying to restate his community in such a way that what he does can be a natural function in the community."[94] The difference lies in the fact that moral situations deal with concrete human interests "in which the whole self is reconstructed in its relation to the other selves whose relations are essential to its personality."[95] The expansion of the self involves the larger incorporation of other selves, an expanded generalized other which becomes a part of one's own self, for as has been seen, the self is distinguishable but not separable from other selves. Thus Mead claims that freedom is the expression of the whole self which has become entire through the reconstruction which has taken place.[96] In this way, "Freedom lies definitely in a reconstruction which is not in the nature of a rebellion but in the nature of presenting an order which is more adequate than the order which has been there."[97]

The importance of scientific method in the moral situation can be indicated through two of Mead's claims. The first involves the universalizing dimension of ideals:

> To the degree that any achievement of organization of a community is successful it is universal, and makes possible a bigger community. In one sense there cannot be a community which is larger than that represented by rationality. . . . That which is fine and admirable is universal—although it may be true that the actual society in which the universality can get its expression has not arisen.[98]

As Mead relates this to science,

> Now there is nothing so social as science, nothing so universal. Nothing so rigorously oversteps the points that separate man from man and groups from groups as does science. There

cannot be any narrow provincialism or patriotism in science. Scientific method makes that impossible. Science is inevitably a universal discipline which takes in all who think. It speaks with the voice of all rational beings. It must be true everywhere; otherwise it is not scientific. But science is evolutionary . . . there is a continuous process which is taking on successively different forms.[99]

The ongoing reconstruction of the social situation in terms of a more encompassing perspective which works in integrating previously conflicting segments, providing an enlargement of self corresponding to the new ideal, is precisely the operation, within the sphere of values, of scientific method. This represents the fullest expression of freedom[100] through the universalizing dimension of rationality. Freedom is tied to the sense of the moral as responsibility to rational action, and this is precisely responsibility to the method of science, for the operation of scientific method is the operation of impartial intelligence.[101] Scientific method can be dismissed only by dismissing intelligence itself,[102] though "unfortunately, men have committed this sin against their intelligence again and again."[103]

Scientific endeavor best reflects creative reconstruction, impartial intelligence[104] and the ideal of universality—not universality as a "philosophical abstraction," a final completion, a metaphysical assumption, or a fixed form of the understanding,[105] but as the "working character" of its claims, claims which are always subject to reconstructive change.[106] These features of free activity manifest in scientific method provide, for Mead, the basis for a doctrine of rights which can be natural rights,[107] without the traditional entanglement with notions of atomic individuals or natural law.[108] And these features of free activity are also the ingredients of Mead's understanding of democracy as the political expression of the functioning of experimental method. Any social structure or institution[109] can be brought into question through the use of social intelligence guided by universalizing ideals, leading to reconstructive activity which enlarges the situation and the selves involved, providing at once a greater degree of authentic self-expression and a greater degree of social participation. Democracy, for Mead, involves not a particular form of government but a particular type of self.[110] In this way, democracy provides for a society which controls its own evolution. Any organization of roles involves a shared value or goal, and the overreaching goal of a human society, according to Mead, is precisely "this control of its own evolution."[111]

Thus, the ultimate "goal" involving the working character of universality is growth or development, not final completion. This in turn indicates that neither democracy nor the working ideal of universality can imply that differences should be eliminated or melted down,[112] for these differences provide the necessary materials by which a society can continue to grow. Though the generalized other indeed represents social meanings and social norms, social development is possible only through the dynamic interrelation of the unique, creative individual and the generalized other. Thus Mead holds that "the value is the contribution of the individual to the situation, even though it is only in the social situation that the value obtains."[113] Moral intelligence is social intelligence, though social intelligence is not possible without individual creativity. As can be seen from Mead's entire analysis of the self, the freedom of the individual and the constraints of the generalized other are not two isolatable entities, but rather two poles in a dynamic temporal process which becomes manifest as two poles within the self and two poles within the society. The proper functioning of these two inseparable, dynamically interrelated poles results in authentic freedom. Thus Mead can hold that freedom can thrive only in a society characterized by the reign of law and the sense of responsibility.[114] Freedom is the ability to regulate and reconstruct conduct through the creative development of universalizing norms and ideals. Mead's strong emphasis on the activity of the scientist in relation to the exercise of freedom and moral responsibility lies in the fact that in both areas "the individual functions in his full particularity, and yet in organic relationship with the society that is responsible for him."[115]

Mead's strong emphasis on scientific method here points toward some concluding remarks concerning the relation between the positions of Mead and Merleau-Ponty. Nowhere in Mead's writings is the method of the scientist as the model for understanding human activity more prominent than in his study of freedom and values, yet nowhere can the contents of the respective fields be found to be more disparate. Thus, this chapter points out perhaps more clearly than any before the way in which for Mead scientific method, as the method of experimental inquiry, is a method which takes experience on its own terms, so to speak, refusing to reduce away any area of lived experience to the second-level objectifications of any particular science. It has been seen that the method of science is, for Mead, the pragmatist, operative in all arenas of life because it is expressive of the dynamics of life itself. It involves a noetic creativity which is constitutive of a world of objects, and which is embodied in or directs one's anticipatory activity, the fulfillment of which in the ongoing course of experience constitutes truth as workability. Further, an examination of scientific method as the process of experimental inquiry has been seen to indicate for Mead precisely the need to return to lived experience as the grounding level for scientific contents, for any world of scientific objects is constituted through second-level reflections rooted in lived experience, and the truth of the claims manifest within it are verified through a return to lived experience. Thus, as has been seen, the phenomenological and experimental or instrumental threads of Mead's pragmatism are inextricably intertwined.

If Mead is correct in his understanding of the pervasive features of human activity as incorporating the dynamics of scientific method, then the descriptive interpretations of Merleau-Ponty's phenomenological focus on human existence should include those features Mead finds to be characteristic of the lived activity of the scientist. This has been seen to in fact be the case. Or, perhaps conversely stated, if, as Merleau-Ponty holds, there is really a pervasive structure to all human activity, and any one instance can become the intitial focal point for the phenomenological examination which yields its pervasive features, then Mead's understanding of the dynamics of scientific inquiry as indicative of the dynamics of human existence can well be expected to converge with Merleau-Ponty's own analyses of concrete human existence. Thus, Mead and Merleau-Ponty are each led, through their respective types of approach, to similar understandings of the central features of human existence and of the relationships among the various levels of human experience.

Yet their different approaches, which have been seen throughout this work to lead to convergences of the above type, point also toward a major divergence which has been seen to characterize their respective positions. This divergence came to the forefront most markedly in chapter 3, where it was seen that Mead's analyses of temporality led him to a metaphysics of nature as a speculative explanation of the features of lived experience, a path which Merleau-Ponty's phenomenological approach refused to follow. Even here, however, the divergence was not indicative of an irreconcilable conflict between their respective positions but pointed toward the possibility of an extension of their rapport. The remaining comments will highlight this possibility and its significance, which have been briefly intimated in various places in this work, most notably in chapter 3, but which are elusively present throughout.

Merleau-Ponty's direct and explicit antagonism against speculative philosophy is tied to his reaction to philosophical interpretations of empirical science which illicitly reified its contents and led to reductionist understandings of humans and nature. This antagonism is a specific instance of his more general attack on any attempt to provide speculative philosophical explanations in terms of any sort of absolutes or of realities detached from us.[116] Yet Merleau-Ponty's position can allow for the possibility of a different type of speculative metaphysics rooted in the lived level of our bond with the real. This is evidenced in his assertion that "the starting point of 'explanations', in so far as they are legitimate," must be sought in the thickness of lived experience.[117] Just as Merleau-Ponty stresses description in empirical science and scientific method, yet allows for second-level explanations rooted in description, so it would seem that he also could allow for the possibility of speculative explanation in philosophy, but only if such explanation is rooted in description of lived experience and verified in the return to lived experience. Indeed, as was stressed earlier, it is precisely a concern to avoid the pitfall of reifying the events of science that leads to Mead's own ambivalence concerning the speculative extension of the temporal features of human existence.

Mead's metaphysics of sociality is a speculative metaphysics of nature, but not the nature of the natural scientist, which is a construct built up as a second-level elaboration of the measurable. It has been seen that Mead, like Merleau-Ponty, has truly gotten away from the problem of the Galilean fallacy of projecting the mathematical model onto the world and then allowing as facts only what that model will allow to emerge. Mead's metaphysics of sociality is clearly a philosophy of nature in the sense of nature before natural science, that level of nature to which I in my experience am fundamentally bound, which is one with my body in that it is accessible only through the commerce and union my body has with it. And, Mead, like Merleau-Ponty, has learned from the reductionist fallacy the more general lesson that any speculative philosophy is inadequate if not grounded in and constantly nourished by the level of the full richness of lived experience, a richness which belies the philosophical tradition of illicit reifications and false dichotomies.

Focusing on Mead from the perspective of Merleau-Ponty's phenomenological approach helps highlight the way in which Mead's speculative metaphysics of sociality, both in its method of development and in its content, is intimately intertwined with the dynamics of concrete human existence. Thus, Mead's metaphysics of sociality can be seen as central to and as strengthening the systematic character of his thought rather than as a later, somewhat irrelevant appendage.[118] And focusing on Merleau-Ponty's rootedness in lived experience from the direction of Mead's pragmatic approach helps highlight the manner in which a contemporary interpretation of speculative metaphysics is viable within the context of Merleau-Ponty's phenomenology, thus offering his perspective an added dimension in its approach to fundamental philosophical issues. The possibility for this broadly based reciprocal enrichment, which grows out of the shared and complementary dimensions of their specific concerns, may well turn out to be the most fruitful of all.

NOTES

INTRODUCTION

1. John J. McDermott, *The Culture of Experience: Philosophical Essays in the American Grain* (New York: New York University Press, 1976), p. 160 (recently reissued by Waveland Press).

2. John J. McDermott, *Streams of Experience: Reflections on the History and Philosophy of Americn Culture* (Amherst: The University of Massachusetts Press, 1986), p. 142.

3. Joseph Margolis, *The Persistence of Reality*, vol. 2, *Science Without Unity: Reconciling the Human and Natural Sciences* (Oxford and New York: Basil Blackwell Ltd., 1987), pp. 74, 77.

4. Maurice Natanson, *The Social Dynamics of George H. Mead* (The Hague: Martinus Nijhoff, 1973). This book reflects the strong influence of Natanson's teacher, Alfred Schutz.

5. Hans Joas, *G. H. Mead: A Contemporary Re-examination of His Thought* (Cambridge, Massachusetts: The MIT Press, 1985).

6. G. H. Mead, *The Philosophy of the Present*, ed. Arthur Murphy (La Salle, Illinois: Open Court, 1959), p. 98. Italics Added.

7. Sandra B. Rosenthal and Patrick L. Bourgeois, *Pragmatism and Phenomenology: A Philosophic Encounter* (Amsterdam: B. R. Grüner, 1980)

8. Patrick L. Bourgeois and Sandra B. Rosenthal, *Thematic Studies in Phenomenology and Pragmatism* (Amsterdam: B. R. Grüner, 1983)

CHAPTER 1

1. This does not imply a reductionistic naturalism resulting from the illicit reification of scientific contents, but rather the naturalism of the lived experience of nature before science.

2. G. H. Mead, *Mind, Self, and Society*, ed. Charles Morris (Chicago: The University of Chicago Press, 1934), p. 10.

3. This is not to deny that Mead's brand of behaviorism has metaphysical underpinnings, a point which will be developed explicitly in later chapters but which is implicit throughout the entire work.

4. *Ibid.*, p. 2.

5. Mead, *Philosophy of the Present*, p. 69. Mead's concept of emergence involves his concept of sociality and its temporal features. The development of this, however, will be postponed till chapter 3.

6. Mead, *Mind, Self, and Society*, pp. 227–28. Even rudimentary organic activity is inherently social. This point is implicit within the above discussion, but it will not be developed until chapter 3.

7. Mead, *Philosophy of the Present*, p. 36.

8. See John Dewey, "The Reflex Arc Concept," *The Early Works*, vol. 5, ed. Jo Ann Boydston (Carbondale: Southern Illinois University Press, 1972), pp. 96–109. (Quoted by Mead in "The Definition of the Psychical," *Mead: Selected Writings*, ed. Andrew Reck, New York: Bobbs-Merrill Co., 1964, pp. 36–37.)

9. G. H. Mead, *The Philosophy of the Act*, ed. Charles Morris (Chicago: The University of Chicago Press, 1938), p. 404.

10. Ibid.

11. G. H. Mead, *Movements of Thought in the Nineteenth Century*, ed. Merritt Moore (Chicago: The University of Chicago Press, 1936), p. 346.

12. Maurice Natanson, *The Social Dynamics of George H. Mead* (The Hague: Martinus Nijhoff, 1973).

13. Mead, *Mind, Self, and Society*, pp. 7–8.

14. Ibid., pp. 4–6.

15. Ibid., p. 5.

16. Ibid., pp. 4–6.

17. Mead, *Movements of Thought*, p. 404.

18. Mead, *Philosophy of the Present*, p. 161.

19. Mead, *Mind, Self, and Society*, p. 332.

20. Mead, *Philosophy of the Present*, p. 35.

21. Maurice Merleau-Ponty, *The Structure of Behavior*, trans. Alden Fisher (Boston: Boston Press, 1963).

22. It must be remembered that Merleau-Ponty, in spite of his critique of the sciences from the phenomenological perspective, employs the objective sciences in a more positive way than is often appreciated. Spiegelberg notes this in saying: "What is perhaps most characteristic of the early Merleau-Ponty is the concrete and painstaking manner in which he uses science as his point of departure and works his way methodically to the place where only a new philosophical solution can do justice to the problem posed by it. This is particularly true of his first work, in which he leads the reader from an objectivist behaviorism via gestalt psychology to a new phenomenology of gestalt. C.f. Herbert Spiegelberg, *The Phenomenological Movement*, vol. 2 (The Hague: Martinus Nijhoff, 1965), p. 540. Also, see the essays in *The Primacy of Perception*, translated and edited by James Edie (Evanston: Northwestern University Press, 1964); and *Themes From the Lectures at the College of France 1952–1960*, translated by John O'Neill (Evanston, Illinois: Northwestern University Press, 1970); and many other works.

23. As seen in the above section of this chapter, this cannot be confused with introspection. The intentional character of experience would militate against that.

24. Maurice Merleau-Ponty, *The Primacy of Perception*, p. 24. Herbert Spiegelberg states regarding Merleau-Ponty's interpretation of Watsonian behaviorism: "Merleau-Ponty believes that John Watson himself wavers between a materialistic interpretation of behavior in terms of physiology and an 'environmental' one which sees in it a relation between man and his world, the vision of man as a debate and a constant coming to terms (*explication*) with a physical and social world." (*La Structure du Comportement* (Presses Universitaire de France, 1942) 3, note) Spiegelberg, *The Phenomenological Movement*, pp. 540–41.

25. Merleau-Ponty, *Primacy of Perception*, p. 24. Merleau-Ponty recognizes that Gestalt psychology confuses scientific method with the limited quantitative aspect of the mechanistic universe at once reductivistic of and thus inadequate to animal and human phenomena. His chief concern is to criticize the overclaim for the objective quantification of science in these instances and their failure to yield to a descriptive account demanded by the fullness of the phenomenon. In spite of this limit and its failure to disassociate psychological science from quantitative and objectivistic results or content, this gestalt psychology has achieved a philo-

sophical significance worthy of note, as he says: "It has again put into question the classical alternative between 'existence as thing' and 'existence as consciousness', has established a communication between and a mixture of objective and subjective, and has conceived of psychological knowledge in a new way, no longer as an attempt to break down these typical ensembles but rather an effort to embrace them and to understand them by reliving them." "The Metaphysical in Man", in *Sense and Non-Sense*, trans. Hubert L. Dreyfus and Patricia Allen Dreyfus (Evanston, Illinois: Northwestern University Press, 1964), p. 86.

26. Merleau-Ponty, *Structure of Behavior*, p. 201.

27. The "natural attitude," as used by phenomenologists, is the attitude presupposed by reductionistic and naturalistic science according to which the foundations of knowledge and of reality are not questioned, but assumed. The shift or change of focus, effected by the reductions employed by phenomenological method, is an attempt to get away from this natural attitude in an attempt adequately to account for meaning. This aspect of the phenomenological reduction, however, is not necessarily opposed to all naturalisms, keeping in mind the ambiguities in the use of this label. Also, this technique of changing focus is not intended to "cut off" intentions from their referents, but rather, simply to change focus.

28. Ibid., p. 4.

29. Maurice Merleau-Ponty, *Phenomenology of Perception*, trans. Colin Smith (New York: The Humanities Press, 1962), p. 7.

30. Ibid.

31. Ibid., pp. 7–8.

32. Merleau-Ponty, *Structure of Behavior*, p. 224.

33. Merleau-Ponty first introduces the notion of form in a lower level in ibid., p. 47. "It is not a question of risking one hypothesis among others, but of introducing a new category, the category of 'form', which, having its application in the inorganic as well as the organic domain, would permit bringing to light the 'transverse functions' in the nervous systems of which Wertheimer speaks and whose existence is confirmed by experience without a vitalist hypothesis. For the 'forms', and in particular the physical systems, are defined as total processes whose properties are not the sum of those which the isolated parts would possess. More precisely they are defined as total processes which may be indiscernable from each other while their 'parts' compared to each other, differ in absolute size; in other words the systems are defined as transposable wholes."

34. Ibid., p. 13, and ch. 1 n. 10.

35. Ibid.

36. Ibid., p. 31.

37. Ibid., p. 103.

38. Ibid., pp. 102–3. "Precisely the preceding observations show that we cannot treat reactions to the structure of the situation as derived or give a privilege of objectivity to those which depend on elementary excitations. For instance, the excitations received on the sensory terminations and the movements executed by the effector muscles are integrated into structures which play a regulating role in their regard. These structural processes account for the laws of learning which we formulated above: since they establish a relation of meaning between situation and response, they explain the fixation of adapted responses and the generality of the acquired aptitude. In the stimulus-response schema, they bring into play not the material properties of the stimuli, but the formal properties of the situation: the spatial, temporal, numerical and functional relations which are its armature. It is to the extent that relations of this kind emerge and become efficacious by themselves that the progress of behavior is explicable."

39. "*Behavior*, inasmuch as it has a structure, is not situated in either of these two orders. It does not unfold in objective time and space like a series of physical events; each moment does not occupy one and only one point of time: rather, at the decisive moment of learning, a 'now' stands out from the series of 'nows,' acquires a particular value and summarizes the groupings which have preceded it as it engages and anticipates the future of the behavior; this 'now' transforms the singular situation of the experience into a typical situation and the effective reaction into an aptitude. From this moment on behavior is detached from the order of the in-itself (*en soi*) and becomes the projection outside the organism of a *possibility* which is internal to it. The world, inasmuch as it harbors living beings, ceases to be a material plenum consisting of juxtaposed parts; it opens up at the place where behavior appears." Merleau-Ponty, *Structure of Behavior*, p. 125.

40. Ibid., p. 184.

41. Ibid., p. 181.

42. Ibid.

43. Ibid., p. 180.

44. Ibid., p. 176.

45. Merleau-Ponty's use of *phenomena* or *phenomenal* must not be interpreted in the context of phenomenalism, for that is a position totally alien to his phenomenology. For Merleau-Ponty clearly denies the distinction between the phenomenon and noumenon in Kant, and interprets the phenomenon to already yield the real.

46. Ibid., p. 201.

47. Mead, *Philosophy of the Act*, p. 3.

48. Ibid., p. 24.

49. Ibid., p. 23.

50. Mead, "The Mechanism of Social Consciousness," *Selected Writings*, p. 134.

51. Mead, *Philosophy of the Act*, p. 12.

52. Ibid., pp. 147–48.

53. Ibid., p. 149.

54. The above discussion is mainly concerned with the separation of space and time in the estabishment of the object of perception, rather than with the nature of time per se. This latter issue will be postponed till chapter 3.

55. This point will be developed in chapter 4.

56. Mead, *Philosophy of the Act*, p. 109.

57. Ibid., p. 151.

58. Ibid., p. 110.

59. Ibid., p. 16

60. Ibid., p. 186.

61. Ibid., p. 147.

62. Ibid., p. 110.

63. Ibid., p. 186.

64. Mead, *Mind, Self and Society*, p. 154n.

65. Mead, *Philosophy of the Act*, p. 24.

66. Ibid., pp. 361–62. It should perhaps be stressed at this point that by *physical object* or *physical being* in this context is not meant the derived objects of scientific knowing but rather the things encountered in everyday perceptual experience.

67. Ibid., p. 115.

68. Jürgen Habermas, *The Theory of Communicative Action, II*, trans. Thomas McCarthy (Boston: Beacon Press, 1987), p. 28.

69. Mead, *Philosophy of the Act*, pp. 115–16.

70. Ibid.

71. Mead, *Philosophy of the Present*, pp. 116–17.

72. Ibid.

73. Ibid., p. 152

74. This correlation is best made with Merleau-Ponty's extended use of intentionality, which he states as follows: "Beneath the 'intentionality of the act', which is the thetic consciousness of an object . . . , we must recognize an 'operative' intentionality which makes the former possible, and which is what Heidegger terms transcendence." Merleau-Ponty, *Phenomenology of Perception*, p. 418.

75. Ibid., p. 25.

76. Merleau-Ponty, *Structure of Behavior*, p. 175.

77. The orientation of Merleau-Ponty's phenomenology of perception with this thesis is to oppose views of perception according to which it is a simple result of the action of external things on our body as well as against those insisting on the autonomy of consciousness. (Merleau-Ponty, *The Primacy of Perception*, p. 3.)

78. Ibid., p. 25.

79. Ibid., p. 15.

80. Ibid., p. 13.

81. Ibid., p. 14.

82. Ibid., p. 25.

83. Merleau-Ponty sets the stage for the development of insight into the structure of meaning in relation to perception in *The Structure of Behavior*, p. 224. For a good orientation and summary of his analyses of perception, see: Merleau-Ponty, *The Primacy of Perception*, pp. 12–42.

84. Those elements entailed in his account of perceptual activity must be distinguished and extricated from his entirely different context of accounting for spacial distance and contact as lived, where the first concern is to reveal the full dimensions of perception without distortion from the presupposed stance of objective science. Thus, his first focus is to contrast the here-now in perception in relation to lived depth and distance with the accounts of derived and objective depth and distance by empiricists and rationalists. This lived and primordial depth is prior to depth as relation among objects or contents, revealing a rootedness of sizes and dis-

tances in a pre-objective realm in which depth is grasped as a possibility of a subject involved in the world. This lived dimension of distance is the presupposed context for interpreting distance experience as operative in Merleau-Ponty's analysis of perceptual behavior.

85. Ibid., p. 12.

86. Merleau-Ponty, *Phenomenology of Perception*, pp. 138–39.

87. Ibid., 265.

88. Ibid.

89. Merleau-Ponty, *Primacy of Perception*, p. 14.

90. Although Merleau-Ponty emphasizes vision throughout his writings, this emphasis exemplifies rather than denies the truth of contact experience, for vision in his account grasps the resistence of things perceived.

91. This facet of sensibility will be discussed further in the next chapter.

92. Merleau-Ponty, "Eye and Mind," *Primacy of Perception*, p. 167.

93. This point involves more explicit developments of Merleau-Ponty's later philosophy where he attempts to deal with subjectivity and reflective self-consciousness in a more basic and originary reflection as flesh, the place and occasion for the emergence of being.

CHAPTER 2

1. There it was seen that this relation of the object to its environment established all objects, even the objects of contact experience, as involving the features of distance perception.

2. G. H. Mead, *The Individual and the Social Self: Unpublished Work of George Herbert Mead*, ed. David Miller (Chicago: The University of Chicago Press, 1982), p. 29.

3. Mead, *Movements of Thought*, p. 388.

4. "Concerning Animal Perception," *Psychological Review* 14 (1907), *Selected Writings*, p. 78.

5. Mead notes, however, that "we use the nicer discriminations of the eye to define these congruences." *The Philosophy of the Act*, p. 175.

6. Ibid., p. 197.

7. Ibid., p. 363.

8. Mead, "The Definition of the Psychical," *Selected Writings*, p. 37.

9. Mead, *Philosophy of the Act*, p. 127ff.

10. Ibid., p. 337.

11. Ibid., pp. 132–33.

12. Ibid., p. 131.

13. Mead, *Philosophy of the Present*, p. 172.

14. Mead, "The Genesis of the Self and Social Control," *Selected Writings*, p. 272.

15. As will be seen in chapter 4, the concept of subjectivity plays an important role in Mead's understanding of the self, but not in any sense which places subjective contents in consciousness set over against an objective order.

16. Mead, *Philosophy of the Act*, pp. 131–32.

17. Ibid., p. 362

18. Ibid., p. 365.

19. Ibid., p. 128.

20. Mead, *Philosophy of the Present*, pp. 116–17.

21. Ibid., p. 117.

22. Merleau-Ponty, *Phenomenology of Perception*, p. 209.

23. Merleau-Ponty, "The Primacy of Perception and its Philosophical Consequences." The central thesis and development of this lecture, although not explicitly dwelling on the role of the body, focuses on the primacy of perception involving sensation and world.

24. See: Merleau-Ponty, *The Structure of Behavior.* The whole of *The Structure of Behavior* leads to vital intentionality in terms of human behavior.

25. Merleau-Ponty, *Phenomenology of Perception*, p. 212.

26. Ibid., p. 213.

27. "Sensation is intentional because I find that in the sensible a certain rhythm of existence is put forward . . . and that, following up this hint, and stealing into the form of existence which is thus suggested to

me, I am brought into relation with an external being, whether it be in order to open myself to it or to shut myself off from it." Ibid., pp. 214–15.

28. Ibid., p. 214.

29. In this regard, Merleau-Ponty says, "We must rediscover, as anterior to the ideas of subject and object, the fact of my subjectivity and the nascent object, that primordial layer at which both things and ideas come into being." Ibid., p. 219.

30. Merleau-Ponty, *Structure of Behavior* p. 224.

31. Ibid., See pp. 220–24, especially p. 224.

32. Merleau-Ponty, *Phenomenology of Perception*, p. 321.

33. Ibid., p. 58.

34. Ibid., p. 4.

35. Ibid., p. 233.

36. Ibid., p. 233–234.

37. Ibid., p. 236. This point is developed in explicit detail in Merleau-Ponty's later works in the direction of his phenomenological ontology.

38. This view corrects one possible way of interpreting his earlier view of the *tacit cogito* in a subjectivistic direction. In chapter 4 on the self, Merleau-Ponty will be seen to reject his earlier view of the *tacit cogito* as some kind of latent self-presence.

39. Merleau-Ponty, "Eye and Mind," *Primacy of Perception*, p. 164.

40. *The Visible and the Invisible*, pp. 267–69; p. 147.

41. Ibid., p. 139.

42. Ibid., pp. 259–69.

43. The other direction of analysis is that of the world, which will be undertaken in the last section of this chapter.

44. Mead, "A Pragmatic Theory of Truth," *Selected Writings*, p. 340.

45. The focus on the significance of social behavior and language for the development of the awareness of meaning will be postponed until the discussion of the genesis of the self in chapter 4 and language in chapter 6. The present discussion focuses on the role of meanings in informing the sensing dimension of experience.

46. Mead, *Philosophy of the Act*, p. 635.

47. Ibid., p. 85.

48. Ibid., p. 633.

49. Mead, "Image or Sensation," *The Journal of Philosophy* I, pt. 2 (1904), p. 606.

50. Ibid.

51. Mead, "Concerning Animal Perception," *Selected Writings*, p. 390.

52. Mead, "Image or Sensation," *Selected Writings*, p. 606; *Philosophy of the Act*, p. 223.

53. Mead, *Mind, Self, and Society*, p. 338.

54. Mead, *Philosophy of the Act*, p. 335.

55. This triadic relationship can be seen to be analogous to the interplay of gesture in the social emergence of meanings, a threefold relationship of gestures of first organism, gesture of second organism, and gesture to subsequent phases of the given social act. Mead, *Mind, Self, and Society*, p. 80. This will be discussed in chapter 4 as it pertains to the emergence of selfhood.

56. Mead, "The Mechanism of Social Consciousness," *Selected Writings*, p. 134.

57. Mead, *Philosophy of the Act*, p. 392.

58. Ibid., p. 118.

59. Mead, *Mind, Self, and Society*, p. 332.

60. Merleau-Ponty, *Structure of Behavior*, p. 58.

61. For a summary of his analysis of perception, see: Merleau-Ponty, *The Primacy of Perception*, pp. 12–42. See also our discussion of the internal structure of meaning in: "Mead and Merleau-Ponty: Meaning, Perception and Behavior," *Analecta Husserliana*, 1990 Vol. XXXI, pp. 401–409.

62. Merleau-Ponty, *Phenomenology of Perception*, pp. 326–27.

63. Ibid. This specifically human environment will be further considered in the next section of this chapter in the context of 'world'.

64. Ibid., p. 327.

65. Ibid., p. 185.

66. Ibid., p. 142.

67. Ibid.

68. Ibid., p. 145.

69. Ibid. The field as 'world' will be the focus of the next section of this chapter.

70. Ibid., p. 144.

71. Ibid., p. 146.

72. Ibid., p. 53.

73. Ibid.

74. Mead, *Philosophy of the Act*, p. 35.

75. Ibid., p. 107.

76. Ibid., p. 331. As will be shown in the next chapter, this universe of events cannot be equated with the contents of science.

77. Ibid., p. 348.

78. Ibid., p. 275.

79. Ibid., p. 174.

80. Mead, *Individual and the Social Self*, p. 31.

81. Mead, *Philosophy of the Act*, p. 114.

82. Ibid., p. 348.

83. Ibid., p. 215.

84. Ibid.

85. Natanson, *Social Dynamics*, pp. 82–83.

86. Mead, *Philosophy of the Act*, pp. 64–65.

87. Mead, "A Pragmatic Theory of Truth," *Selected Writings*, pp. 341–42.

88. Mead, "Scientific Method and the Individual Thinker," *Selected Writings*, pp. 205–9.

89. Mead, *Philosophy of the Act*, p. 32.

90. Mead, *Pragmatic Theory of Truth,*" *Selected Writings*, p. 340.

91. Ibid., p. 328.

92. Ibid.

93. Mead, *Movements of Thought*, p. 350.

94. Mead, "Pragmatic Theory of Truth," *Selected Writings*, p. 331.

95. Ibid., 334.

96. Ibid., p. 330.

97. Mead, *Movements of Thought*, p. 344–45.

98. Mead, "Pragmatic Theory of Truth," *Selected Writings*, p. 344.

99. Ibid., pp. 341–42.

100. Mead, "Scientific Method and the Individual Thinker," *Selected Writings*, pp. 211–12.

101. Mead, "Pragmatic Theory of Truth," *Selected Writings*, p. 338.

102. This point was developed from a different direction in chapter 1.

103. Mead, "Scientific Method," *Selected Writings*, p. 209–10.

104. Mead, "Pragmatic Theory of Truth," *Selected Writings*, p. 328.

105. Ibid., p. 338.

106. Ibid.

107. Mead, "Scientific Method," *Selected Writings*, p. 210.

108. See chapter 1.

109. Merleau-Ponty investigates sensation in the *Phenomenology of Perception* for the sole purpose of elaborating the vital relation of the perceiver to his body and to his world. Merleau-Ponty, *Phenomenology of Perception*, p. 208.

110. Maurice Merleau-Ponty, *Primacy of Perception*, p. 15.

111. Ibid., p.12.

112. In referring to these different worlds, Merleau-Ponty should be understood to focus on different aspects or dimensions of the lived world, rather than to splinter world into multiple worlds. Since he deals with these various aspects of the lived world as "worlds," they will be dealt with similarly in the text, but with the prior understanding that there is a lived world with various dimensions; the natural world and things, the human world and other people, the cultural world and cultural objects, etc.

113. Merleau-Ponty, *Phenomenology of Perception*, p. 57. Merleau-Ponty states: "Our task will be, moreover, to rediscover phenomena, the layer of living experience through which other people and things are first given to us, the system 'Self-others-things' as it comes into being, to reawaken perception and foil its trick of allowing us to forget it as a fact and as perception in the interest of the object which it presents to us and of the rational tradition to which it gives rise."

114. It is precisely this "independent" aspect of the world as already there which Merleau-Ponty comes to develop explicitly in his later, more ontological considerations.

115. Hans Joas claims that phenomenology's life-world, unlike Mead's world that is there, aspires to an absolute beginning. (G. H. Mead: A Contemporary Re-examination of His Thought, p. 208). This is exemplative of the way in which Joas's attempts to indicate radical differences between Mead's view and that of phenomenology in general usually turn out to involve the transcendental phenomenology of Husserl, and are inapplicable to existential phenomenology.

116. Merleau-Ponty, *Phenomenology of Perception*, p. 313 (italics added). It is not because constant colors are perceived beneath the variety of lightings that the existence of things are believed in, nor is the thing a collection of constant characteristics. Merleau-Ponty indicates that impressions or qualities are not the constants of perception: "Far from its being the case that the thing is reducible to constant relationships, it is in the self-evidence of the thing that this constancy of relationships has its basis" (ibid., p. 302). Thus, there are no independent and discrete properties or elements or impressions in need of synthesis, since all the properties or qualities of a thing form a system united in the thing, but not as a unifying substratum posited by thought. A quality is never merely a quality, but the quality of a certain object (ibid., p. 313), so that "perception goes straight to the thing" (ibid., p. 305) and bypasses the quality.

117. Ibid., p. 144.

118. Ibid., p. 145.

119. Ibid., p. 326–27.

120. Ibid., p. 326.

121. Ibid.

122. Ibid., p. 350.

123. The title of part 1 is "The Body," and that of part 2 is "The World as Perceived," the last two chapters of which focus on the lived body.

124. Ibid., p. 203.

125. Ibid., 303. This sense of transcendence will be further dealt with in chapter 3, on time. Transcendence basically means that consciousness is constituted in such a way as to be rooted in and cross over to that world which is not itself, even though consciousness can only be in the world in a sense. It also means that the object of perception is inexhaustible and cannot be totally grasped from any particular perspective.

126. Ibid., p. 298. As Merleau-Ponty says in another place: "Thus, the thing is correlative to my body and, in more general terms, to my existence, of which my body is merely the stabilized structure" or style of anticipation rooted in the body (ibid., p. 320). Although the body is borne toward certain experience, i.e., tactile, by all of its surfaces and all of its organs, simultaneously, and carries with it a typical structure of tactile 'world', the thing is presented as an inter-sensory entity. The object which presents itself to the gaze or touch arouses a motor intention which aims at the thing itself and not at the body. The significance of the thing "inhabits that thing" (ibid., p. 319).

127. But this overcoming of the problem of the other requires distinguishing it "from the objective body as set forth in works on physiology." Such a conception of body does not allow significance and intentionality "to dwell in molecular edifices or masses of cells" as a thing (ibid., p. 351).

128. But this is precisely because, along with the perceiving subject, I find in myself a pre-personal subject. The character of the pre-personal aspect of the subject and the internal relation between consciousness and the lived body and between the lived body and that of the other will be fully explored in chapter 4.

129. Ibid., p. 354.

130. Ibid., p. 353. This point will be further developed in chapter 4.

131. Ibid., p. 347.

132. Ibid., p. 327.

133. Ibid., p. 321.

134. "It has already been seen above in this chapter that what distinguishes the human world from the animal environment is that for the human, life understands an infinite number of possible environments. . . . so that the human and the natural are seen to be interwoven . . . since the natural world is the structure or schema or horizon of things, and as such, is interwoven with the human cultural world." Ibid., p. 327.

135. It will be seen in chapter 4 that Merleau-Ponty contends that the constitution of the other person is not sufficient to elucidate that of

society, which is not merely an existence involving two or more people, but rather a coexistence involving an indefinite number of consciousnesses (*Phenomenology of Perception*, p. 349).

136. Ibid., p. 362.

137. Ibid., p. 364. *Ursprung* here means origin.

138. Merleau-Ponty says: "We are inextricably and confusedly bound up with the world and with others" ("Metaphysics and the Novel," in *Sense and Non-Sense*, trans. John O'Neill (Evanston, Illinois: Northwestern University Press, 1970) p. 36). In another place, he says: "neither error nor doubt ever cut us off from the truth, because they are surrounded by a world horizon which the teleology of consciousness invites us to resolve" (*Phenomenology of Perception*, p. 398).

139. For Merleau-Ponty, truth is tied to sedimentation, which will be explored in chapter 4, and to the present, as seen in the following text: "Truth is another name for sedimentation, which is itself the presence of all presents in our own. That is to say that even and especially for the ultimate philosophical subject, there is no objectivity which accounts for our super-objective relationship to all times, no light that shines more brightly than the living present's light" "On the Phenomenology of Language," in *Signs*, trans. Richard C. McCleary (Evanston, Illinois: Northwestern University Press, 1964), p. 96.

140. Merleau-Ponty, "The Philosopher and Sociology," *Signs*, p. 109.

141. "Field of presence," as a technical term, will be clarified in the next chapter.

142. Merleau-Ponty, *The Prose of the World*, ed. Claude Lefort, trans. John O'Neill (Evanston, Illinois: Northwestern University Press, 1973), p. 107.

143. Merleau-Ponty, *Primacy of Perception*, p. 25.

144. Merleau-Ponty, *Prose of the World*, p. 106.

145. Merleau-Ponty can be seen to remain faithful to this situatedness and field of presence and truth even in his latest thinking: "It is a matter of understanding that truth itself has no meaning outside of the relation of transcendence, outside of the *Ueberstieg* toward the horizon—that the 'subjectivity' and the 'object' are one sole whole, that the subjective 'lived experiences' count in the world, are part of the *Weltlichkeit* of the 'mind' are entered in the 'register' which is Being, that the object is nothing else than the *tuft* of these *Abschattungen*" (The Visible and the Invisible, ed. Claude Lefort, trans. Alphonso Lingis (Evanston, Illinois: Northwestern University Press, 1968), p. 185.

146. As Sallis put it, he provides "an ontological rehabilitation of the sensible" (John Sallis, *Phenomenology and the Return to Beginnings*, (Pittsburgh: Duquesne University Press, 1973), p. 55; Merleau-Ponty, *Signs*, pp. 166–67. Merleau-Ponty now forfeits any *tacit cogito* prior to transcendence in favor of a more fundamentally conceived transcendence understood as "'I belong to myself' while belonging to the world" (Quoted in Sallis, p. 66; Merleau-Ponty, *Phenomenology of Perception*, p. 407). Such a view of transcendence relates world and being, a concern of the later writings of Merleau-Ponty.

147. See Sallis, *Phenomenology and the Return of Beginnings*, pp. 54, 61; and Merleau-Ponty, *The Visible and the Invisible*, p. 27.

CHAPTER 3

1. Hans Joas holds both that Heidegger, as opposed to Mead, has an individualistic understanding of the constitution of time consciousness, and that Mead offers an objection to the phenomenological enterprise in general. See: *G. H. Mead: A Contemporary Re-examination of His Thought.* Irrespective of the question of the accuracy of the first point, this individualistic approach cannot be attributed to Merleau-Ponty's phenomenology. The features of specific phenomenological approaches which Mead rejects are rejected by Merleau-Ponty as well. Joas himself at times offers a more limited objection directed mainly against Husserl. See especially pp. 69, 189, 197.

2. Merleau-Ponty, "The Concept of Nature, I," *Themes From the Lectures at the College of France 1952–1960*, trans. John O'Neill (Evanston, Illinois: Northwestern University Press, 1970), p. 86.

3. Merleau-Ponty, "Einstein and the Crisis of Reason," *Signs*, p. 193.

4. Ibid., p. 197.

5. Ibid., pp. 196–97.

6. Ibid.

7. Ibid., p. 197.

8. Ibid., p. 196.

9. Ibid.

10. See: Ibid., p. 196. In another place, Merleau-Ponty affirms this very clearly: "Bergson made perception the fundamental mode of our relation to being" ("Everywhere and Nowhere," *Signs*, p. 155). Bergson, in Merleau-Ponty's interpretation, would be distorted if his description of

perceived being in *Matter and Memory* were minimized. Rather than relate things to images in a restrictive sense of the "physical" or of souls,
"he says that their fullness beneath my gaze is such that it is as if my
vision developed in them rather than in me" Further, Merleau-Ponty sees
that Bergson establishes a reciprocity between the being and the perceiver
so that being exists "for me" and at once, the perceiver exists "for being."
"Never had the brute being of the perceived world been so described"
("Bergson in the Making," *Signs*, p. 185). In *Duree et Simultaneite* he
pierces into the perceived world.

11. Merleau-Ponty, "Bergson in the Making," *Signs*, p. 185.

12. Ibid.

13. Merleau-Ponty, "Einstein and the Crisis of Reason," *Signs*,
p. 196.

14. Ibid., p. 195.

15. Merleau-Ponty, "The Concept of Nature, I," *Themes From the
Lectures*, p. 86.

16. Merleau-Ponty, "Bergson in the Making," *Signs*, p. 186.

17. Ibid., p. 185–86. In *Themes from the Lectures* Merleau-Ponty
can be seen to correlate the singularity of the individual observer's point
of view with philosophical simultaneity. "Perceived time is, of course, sol-
idary with the observer's point of view, but *by this fact* it constitutes the
common dimension for all possible observers of one and the same nature.
And this is so, not because we are constituted so as only to *attribute* to
other observers an expanded or foreshortened time relative to our own—
but rather the very contrary, in the sense that in its singularity our perceived time announces to us other singularities and other perceived times,
with the same rights as ours, and in principle grounds the philosophical
simultaneity of a community of observers. In place of Laplace's dogmatic
objectivity, pledged upon the inheritance of all thinking subjects in the
same core of being which remains amorphous but with whose presence
they experiment from within the situation to which they belong.
   With all the more reason, a consideration of the sciences which Au-
guste Comte and Cournot called cosmological—that do not fix themselves upon constant relations but regard them as a means to
reconstructing the development of the world, and, for example, of the so-
lar system—would lead one to establish a regression of eternal ideologies
in which nature is an object identical with itself and finally the emergence of a history—or, as Whitehead said, of a 'process'—of nature."
Merleau-Ponty, "The Concept of Nature, I," *Themes From the Lectures*,
pp. 86–87.

18. Merleau-Ponty, *Phenomenology of Perception*, p. 276n.

19. As will be seen in the next section of this chapter, this is the transcendence constitutive of time.

20. Merleau-Ponty refers to Bergson's depiction of the body as "an instantaneous section made in the the becoming of consciousness." Ibid., p. 79n.

21. Ibid., p. 79n. The following text, which further elaborates on Bergson's view of lived time and upon its corporeal unity as Merleau-Ponty sees it, reveals the relationship between lived time, the pre-personal level, and freedom, the latter two fitting within the focuses of the next two chapters. "If consciousness snowballs upon itself, it is, like the snowball and everything else, wholly in the present. If the phases of movement gradually merge into one another, nothing is anything in motion. The unity of time, space and movement cannot come about through any coalescence, and cannot be understood either by any real operation. If consciousness is multiplicity, who is to gather together this multiplicity in order to experience it as such, and if consciousness is fusion, how shall it come to know the multiplicity of the moments which it fuses together? ... What is for us primary and immediate, is a flux which does spread outwards like a liquid, but which, in an active sense, bears *itself* along, which it cannot do without knowing that it does so, and without drawing itself together in the same act whereby it bears itself along—it is that 'time which does not pass' of which Kant somewhere speaks. For us, then, the unity of movement is not a real unity. But neither is multiplicity real, and what we object to in the idea of synthesis in Kant, as in certain Kantian texts of Husserl, precisely that it presupposes, at least theoretically, a real multiplicity which consciousness has to surmount. What for us is primary consciousness is not a transcendental Ego freely positing before itself a multiplicity in itself, and constituting it throughout from start to finish, it is an I which dominates diversity only with the help of time, and for whom freedom itself is a destiny, so that I am never consciousness of being the absolute creator of time, of composing the movement through which I live, I have the impression that it is the mobile entity itself which changes its position to another. This relative and prepersonal I who provides the basis for the phenomenon of movement, and in general the phenomenon of the real, clearly demands some elucidation. Let us say for the moment that we prefer, to the notion of synthesis, that of synopsis, which does not yet point to an explicit positing of diversity." *Phenomenology of Perception*, p. 276n.

22. Ibid., p. 265.

23. Ibid.

24. Quoting Husserl, *Prasenzfeld*.

25. Ibid., p. 265.

26. Ibid., p. 138.

27. Merleau-Ponty, "The Concept of Nature, I," *Themes From the Lectures*, p. 86.

28. Mead, *Philosophy of the Present*, p. 32.

29. Mead refers always to Whitehead's early works, not to *Process and Reality.*

30. Mead, *Philosophy of the Present*, p. 43.

31. Ibid., pp. 43, 49.

32. Ibid., p. 49.

33. Ibid., pp. 20–21.

34. Mead, *Philosophy of the Act*, pp. 636–37.

35. Mead, *Movements of Thought*, p. 325.

36. Such a constitution was discussed in the previous chapters.

37. Mead, *Movements of Thought*, p. 60.

38. Ibid., p. 316.

39. Mead, *Philosophy of the Present*, pp. 60–61.

40. Ibid., p. 57.

41. Ibid., p. 112.

42. This will be developed in some detail in the following chapter, on self. Its function in the constitution of the perceptual object was indicated in chapter 1.

43. Mead, *Philosophy of the Present*, p. 62.

44. Supra, p. 56.

45. Merleau-Ponty, *Phenomenology of Perception*, p. 424.

46. Ibid., p. 410.

47. Ibid., p. 411.

48. Ibid., p. 412.

49. The time of such an independent realm, however, should be considered, in a sense at least, too full or too rich for there to be time, rather than too empty, as is often alleged. According to such an account, that emptiness results from the interpretation of future as "not yet," of the

past as "no longer," and of the consequent collapse of the present as the infinitesimally small result. Merleau-Ponty contends that in a certain sense, "time is, therefore, not a real process, not an actual succession" out there which humans are content to measure and record (ibid., p. 412). Merleau-Ponty contends that, in introducing the "not yet" and the "no longer," the non-being of time is removed, so that only the present is considered in terms of being, thus rendering such a limited account to deal with time as related to being and not to non-being.

50. Ibid., p. 433.

51. Merleau-Ponty here invokes the distinction between the Gestalt of the circle and the signification 'circle', with the "latter . . . recognized by an understanding which engenders it as the place of points equidistant from a center, the former by a subject familiar with his world and able to seize it as a modulation of that world, as a circular physiognomy. We have no way of knowing what a picture or a thing is other than by looking at them, and their *significance* is revealed only if we look at them from a certain point of view, from a certain distance and in a certain *direction*, in short only if we place, at the service of the spectacle, our collusion with the world." Ibid., p. 429.

52. Ibid., p. 429.

53. Ibid., p. 419.

54. Ibid., p. 424.

55. Ibid., p. 417.

56. Ibid., p. 418.

57. Ibid., p. 424.

58. Ibid., p. 415.

59. Ibid., p. 419.

60. Merleau-Ponty gives his own twist of interpretation to phenomenological terms, making them existential structures of experience, while he adamantly rejects any transcendental element throughout his *Phenomenology of Perception*, just as he has done at the end of *The Structure of Behavior,* cf. p. 224. It is precisely this existential turn of phenomenology, with its inclusion of the practical and affective dimensions of intentional corporeal existence, which makes a link possible between his brand of phenomenology and the pragmatism of Mead. Such a link is not possible between Mead and Husserlian transcendental phenomenology.

61. Merleau-Ponty, *Phenomonology of Perception,* p. 419.

62. Ibid. "Temporality temporalizes itself as future—which lapses into-the-past-by-coming-into-the-present." (Ibid., p. 420. Merleau-Ponty quoting Heidegger, *Sein und Zeit.*)

63. Ibid., pp. 420–21.

64. Ibid., p. 421.

65. Ibid.

66. Ibid., p. 427. Merleau-Ponty affirms this in the context of clarifying the sense of passive synthesis, a term which he retains even though he has great misgivings about it. He firmly rejects any hints at the passivity or receptivity to multiplicity, rather than being its initiator. He says: "A passive synthesis is a contradiction in terms if the synthesis is a process of composition, and if the passivity consists in being the recipient of multiplicity instead of its composer. What we meant by passive synthesis was that we make our way into multiplicity, but that we do not synthesize it. Now temporalization satisfies by its very nature these two conditions: it is indeed clear that I am not the initiator of the process of temporalization; I did not choose to come into the world, yet once I am born, time flows through me, whatever I do. Nevertheless this ceaseless welling up of time is not a simple fact to which I am passively subjected, for I can find a remedy against it in itself, as happens in a decision which binds me or in the act of establishing a concept. It withholds me from what I was about to become, and at the same time provides me with the means of grasping myself at a distance and establishing my own reality as myself. What is called passivity is not the acceptance by us of an alien reality, or a causal action exerted upon us from outside: it is being encompassed, being in a situation—prior to which we do not exist—which we are perpetually resuming and which is constitutive of us. A spontaneity 'acquired' once and for all, and one which 'perpetuates itself in being in virtue of its being acquired' is precisely time and subjectivity." Ibid., p. 427.

67. Ibid., p. 430.

68. Ibid., p. 416.

69. Ibid., pp. 416–17.

70. Ibid., p. 417.

71. Ibid., p. 420.

72. Ibid., p. 430.

73. And, since, as Heidegger says, "temporality temporalizes itself as future-which-lapses-into-the-past-by-coming-into-the-present," the unity

of time is also on that prior level (Ibid., p. 420). Merleau-Ponty here is quoting Martin Heidegger, *Sein und Zeit*.

74. Merleau-Ponty, *Phenomonology of Perception*, p. 421.

75. Ibid., p. 415n. "Bergson can therefore only compress or expand the series of 'present moments'; he never reaches the unique movement whereby the three dimensions of time are constituted, and one cannot see why duration is squeezed into a present, or why consciousness becomes involved in a body and a world." Ibid., p. 79n. Merleau-Ponty explains further: "If, in virtue of the principle of continuity, the past still belongs to the present and the present already to the past, there is no longer any past or present. If consciousness snowballs upon itself, it is, like the snowball and everything else, wholly in the Present." Ibid., p. 276n.

76. Ibid., p. 415.

77. Ibid., p. 422.

78. Ibid., p. 418.

79. "The ontological world and body which we find at the core of the subject are not the world or body as idea, but on the one hand the world itself contracted into a comprehensive grasp, and on the other the body itself as a knowing-body." Merleau-Ponty, Ibid., p. 418.

80. As will be seen in the treatment of the self in the next chapter, time for Merleau-Ponty is the origin of both the body and the other: "Others and my body are born together from the original ecstasy," lived time.

81. Ibid., p. 410.

82. This sedimentation as primal acquisition provides the foundation of personal acts, requiring, first, that the past which gets established be carried over into the present at a level beneath that of personal acts. It is precisely the structure of retention by which the past is retained nonthematically in the present. "What is true, however, is that our open and personal existence rests on an initial foundation of acquired and stabilized existence. But it could not be otherwise, if we are temporality, since the dialectic of acquisition and future is what constitutes time." Ibid., p. 432. Sedimentation in relation to time and to self will be discussed in the next chapter.

83. Ibid., p. 426.

84. This was seen in the first section of chapter 2.

85. Merleau-Ponty, *The Visible and the Invisible*, pp. 267–68. Thus it can be seen that Merleau-Ponty's later development still has time at its center.

86. Mead, *Philosophy of the Present*, p. 11.

87. Ibid., p. 90.

88. Ibid., p. 23.

89. Ibid.

90. Mead, *Philosophy of the Act*, pp. 333–35.

91. Ibid., p. 21.

92. Ibid., p. 65.

93. Mead, *Philosophy of the Present*, p. 70.

94. Ibid., p. 49.

95. Ibid., p. 47.

96. Ibid., pp. 114–16.

97. Mead, "The Nature of the Past," *Selected Writings*, p. 350.

98. Ibid.

99. The term "specious present" can be quite misleading. Mead does not mean by this a false or pseudo-present, but rather the temporal spread of the present as opposed to a present characterized in terms of the abstractions of knife-edged moments. A specious present contains within itself past, present, and future.

100. Mead, *Philosophy of the Present*, p. 88.

101. Ibid.

102. Ibid.

103. Mead, *Philosophy of the Act*, p. 220.

104. Ibid., p. 221.

105. Mead, *Philosophy of the Present*, pp. 87–88.

106. Ibid.

107. Mead, *Philosophy of the Act*, pp. 65–66. The discussion of self, in the next chapter, will refer to Mead's falling ball example, which similarly exemplifies the specious present, but as directly related to the issue of self-awareness.

108. Ibid., p. 331.

109. Mead, *Mind, Self, and Society*, p. 351.

110. Mead, *Philosophy of the Present*, p. 13.

111. Mead, "The Nature of the Past," *Selected Writings*, p. 349.

112. This point, touched upon in the present context, will be developed at some length in the next chapter.

113. Joas, *G. H. Mead: A Contemporary Re-examination of His Thought*, p. 175.

114. Ibid., p. 188.

115. Mead, *Philosophy of the Present.*, p. 52.

116. Ibid., p. 13.

117. Ibid., p. 105.

118. Ibid., p. 61.

119. Mead, "Scientific Method," *Selected Writings*, p. 210.

120. Ibid., p. 210. Mead also objects to epistemology, but what he is objecting to is the limited view of epistemology as the attempt to bridge the gap between a subject and object. Thus, he states that "the epistemologist starts . . . with the immediate experience of the individual and attempts by way of this cognitive reference to reach a world outside of the individual's experience." (*The Philosophy of the Present*, p. 108). Yet, he proceeds to offer his own pragmatic epistemology, which undercuts this problem.

121. According to Joas, "Mead considers a cosmology, in the sense of a comprehensive scientific view of the world, possible if it is not conceived of as a theory of a nature which is independent of humanity." *G. H. Mead: A Contemporary Re-examination of His Thought*, p. 186.

122. See chapter 1.

123. Mead, *Philosophy of the Act*, pp. 277–78.

124. Thus, the present work does not attribute Mead's diverse statements concerning the extent of application of some of his central concepts to an historical development of his thought but to an inherent ambivalence of his attitude toward speculative metaphysics.

125. Mead, *Philosophy of the Act*, p. 344.

126. Ibid., p. 165.

127. Mead, *Philosophy of the Present*, p. 86. This point will be developed in the chapter on the self.

128. Ibid., p. 65.

129. Ibid., p. 52.

130. Mead, *Movements of Thought in the Nineteenth Century*, p. 317.

131. Mead, *Philosophy of the Act*, p. 340.

132. Mead, *Philosophy of the Present*, p. 175.

133. Ibid., p. 48.

134. Ibid., p. 23.

135. Ibid., pp. 14–16.

136. Ibid., pp. 15–16.

137. Ibid., p. 12. Emphasis added.

138. Ibid., p. 26.

139. Ibid., pp. 173–74.

140. Ibid., pp. 17–18. Emphasis added.

141. Ibid., p. 66.

142. Mead, *Philosophy of the Act*, p. 362.

143. This point will be discussed at some length in the next chapter.

144. Mead, "The Nature of the Past," *Selected Writings*, p. 352.

145. Mead, *Philosophy of the Present*, p. 106.

146. Ibid., p. 175.

147. Ibid., p. 63.

148. Ibid., pp. 23–24. Emphasis added.

CHAPTER 4

1. Miller opposes Mead's understanding of the self to Husserl's location of the self outside of society and to existentialism's view of the self as isolated and as a passion. Regardless of the question of the validity of Miller's claims here, it should be stressed that Merleau-Ponty's position falls into neither of these two categorizations. David Miller, *George Herbert Mead: Self, Language, and the World* (Austin: The University of Texas Press, 1973), pp. 8–9.

2. Mead's use of the term "social" is different from his use of the term "sociality." The social "is a systematic order of individuals in which each has a more or less differentiated activity" (*The Philosophy of the Present*, pp. 86–87), while "the principle of sociality involves the claim that "the nature of something in one system affects its nature in other systems that it occupies" (*The Philosophy of the Act*, p. 610). Thus, the term "social" represents the intrasystematic, while the term "sociality" represents the intersystematic. Mead is not always consistent in his own use of these two terms, but as will later be seen, he attributes to each a significant temporal difference which influences his understanding of the self.

3. Mead, *Mind, Self, and Society*, p. 357.

4. Mead, "Social Psychology as Counterpart to Physiological Psychology," *Selected Writings*, p. 101.

5. Ibid.

6. Mead, *Mind, Self, and Society*, p. 368.

7. Mead, "Social Consciousness and the Consciousness of Meaning," *Selected Writings*, p. 128.

8. Ibid., p. 131. For purposes of the present discussion, the role of resistance in the constitution of the physical object and the awareness of one's own organism, discussed in chapter 1, need not be reintroduced here.

9. Mead, *Movements of Thought*, p. 380.

10. Mead, *Mind, Self, and Society*, p. 168.

11. Ibid., p. 163.

12. Ibid., p. 173.

13. Ibid., p. 136.

14. Ibid., pp. 171–72.

15. Ibid., p. 140.

16. Mead, "Social Consciousness and Consciousness of Meaning," *Selected Writings*, p. 133.

17. Mead, *Philosophy of the Act*, p. 153.

18. Ibid., pp. 361–62.

19. Ibid.

20. Mead, "A Behavioristic Account of the Significant Symbol", *Selected Writings*, p. 244. Mead holds that the basic tendencies constituting the physiological and biological materials of the human are social; human nature is essentially social throughout. *Mind, Self, and Society*, p. 139n.

21. Mead notes that while he has spoken of these "from the point of view of children," he could, "of course, refer also to the attitudes of more primitive people out of which our civilization has arisen." *Mind, Self, and Society*, p. 152.

22. Ibid., p. 150.

23. Ibid., p. 159.

24. Ibid., p. 151.

25. Ibid., p. 158.

26. Ibid.

27. There are various types of communities, or groups and sub-groups, each inclusive of a respective "generalized other," and determined in socially functional terms. Some are "concrete groups or subgroups, such as political parties, clubs, corporations, which are all actually functional social units in terms of which their individual members are di-rectlly related to one another." There are also "abstract social classes or subgroups, such as the class of debtors and the class of creditors, in terms of which their individual members are related to one another only more or less indirectly, and which only more or less indirectly function as social units." The most inclusive abstract social group is the logical universe of discourse. It "enables the largest conceivable number of human individuals to enter into some sort of social relation . . . a relation arising from the universal functioning of gestures as significant symbols in the general human social process of communication. "Ibid., pp. 157–58. Further, Mead holds that it is possible for inanimate objects to form parts of the gener-alized other in so far as one responds to those objects in social fashion. Ibid., p. 154n. See chapter 2 for the discussion of this last point.

28. Ibid., p. 154.

29. Ibid., p. 179.

30. Although the correlation between world and self is such that one cannot be treated without entailing the other, world is treated in the present chapter only to the extent necessary for an adequate treatment of self, as self was treated only to the extent necessary in the chapter above on world. The correlation of world and self is such that the revelation of one has already begun with the exposition of the other, for, on the one hand, the world is the project of the subject, and at once, the self is the project of the world; and, on the other hand, the self is present to itself only and precisely as transcending to the world. " 'The world is insepara-ble from the subject, but from a subject who is nothing but a project of the world; and the subject is inseparable from the world, but from the world which he himself projects.' As Merleau-Ponty points out in *Signs*, the " 'presence to myself which defines me and conditions all alien pres-

ence' is simultaneously presence to a compresent world which always bears me 'somewhere else' and so requires me to assume once more the search to constitute the bases of my thought and existence. . . . 'It is in communicating with the world that we communicate with outselves.' " *Signs*, p. xv, translator quoting Merleau-Ponty. Merleau-Ponty states: "Our task will be, moreover, to rediscover phenomena, the layer of living experience through which other people and things are first given to us, the sytem 'Self-others-things' as it comes into being, to re-awaken prception and foil its trick of allowing us to forget it as a fact and as perception in the interest of the object which it presents to us and of the rational tradition to which it gives rise." *Phenomenology of Perception*, p. 57.

31. Merleau-Ponty, *Structure of Behavior*, p. 124. "The preceding chapters teach us not only not to explain the higher by the lower, as they say, but also not to explain the lower by the higher." See also pp. 180–84. "The advent of higher orders, to the extent that they are accomplished, eliminate the autonomy of the lower orders and give a new signification to the steps which constitute them. This is why we have spoken of a human order rather than of a mental or rational order." (p. 180.)

32. Ibid., p. 120.

33. Ibid.

34. Merleau-Ponty, *Phenomenology of Perception*, pp. 450–51.

35. "If there is a break, it is not between me and the other person; it is between a primordial generality we are intermingled in and the precise system, myself-the others. What 'precedes' intersubjective life cannot be numerically distinguished from it, precisely because at this level there is neither individuation nor numerical distinction. The constitution of others does not come after that of the body; others and my body are born together from" lived time. Merleau-Ponty, "The Philosopher and His Shadow," *Signs*, p. 173.

36. Merleau-Ponty, *The Phenomenology of Perception*, p. 352.

37. Ibid.

38. Ibid., p. 349.

39. Ibid. The French expression *on*, usually translated as "one," or paraphrased in English, in this context depicts the impersonal, as when it is said that "one says" to translate *on dit*. It is perhaps better to translate this as "one" rather than "we" in the present context, preserving the impersonal dimension which Merleau-Ponty emphasized regarding this level of the lived body.

40. The child living in the symbiotic relationship with its mother has not an aware coherent sense of differentiation between the mothering one and itself, and yet sociality or social interactions or "anonymous col-

lectivity" ("The Child's Relations with Others" in *The Primacy of Perception*, p. 119) is already constitutive long before the emergence of a personal dimension of self. Ibid., pp. 147–49. Also, the baby knows its mother through this lived relationship long before it knows what she looks like. Its perception of meaning precedes all else, for perception always aims at human intentions and meaning structures through which the realities of the world are seized in experience. This primordial intersubjective level, as responsiveness to others from a level in which children do not yet differentiate themselves from others, accounts for and becomes explicitly apparent in children's often attributing to others what belongs to themselves. Further, this process of differentiation of my body as mine or of the 'I' depend upon appropriate social interaction, and thus its emergence is social in origin.

41. Merleau-Ponty, *Phenomenology of Perception*, p. 352.

42. Merleau-Ponty, "The Film and the New Psychology," *Sense and Non-Sense*, p. 58.

43. Merleau-Ponty, *Phenomenology of Perception*, p. 352.

44. Ibid. pp. xvi–xvii.

45. Merleau-Ponty, "Eye and Mind," *Primacy of Perception*, p. 170.

46. This treatment is not first and foremost a treatment of language, which will be the focus of chapter 6. However, in focusing on the appropriation of the personal level, the ability to express personal pronouns is already to have the personal and individuated level.

47. Merleau-Ponty, "The Child's Relations with Others," *Primacy of Perception*, p. 99.

48. Ibid., p. 109.

49. Another case of this phenomenon of identification, according to Merleau-Ponty, is the relation of the child to the mother. This identification involves projection from the child of his own experiences and assimilation of the attitudes of the mother. At this point there is a lack of differentiation between the projection and the assimilation. This is also exemplified by children in families into which another child is born. The youngest child must adapt his grasp of the role of the youngest and eldest, sometimes identifiying with the role of the eldest since the child is no longer the youngest because of the infant, and sometimes, if the child was the youngest of two children, learning the role of the middle child once the infant is born. Merleau-Ponty deals with several examples of children in families into which an infant is born. One of these examples involves a younger of two children showing jealousy when his new brother is born. At first he identifies with the newborn, carrying himself as though he

himself were the infant. When he shortly after identifies with the older brother, he overcomes his jealousy, and adopts all the characteristics of the oldest child, including an attitude toward the infant that is identical with what the older brother's attitude had been to him before the birth of the infant. Thus, he adopts first the role of the infant as the youngest on whom is showered attention, and then the role of the eldest who participates in giving attention to the youngest. Ibid., p. 109.

50. "The acquisition of the imperfect tense at the birth of her little brother indicated that the child was becoming capable of understanding that the present changes into the past. The imperfect is a former present which, moreover, is still referred to as present, unlike the past definite. The imperfect is 'still there.' The acquisition of the imperfect thus presupposes a concrete grasp of the movement from present to past which the child, on her part, was just in the process of achieving in her relations with her family. The fact is, all the verbs she used in the imperfect after the birth of her brother had to do with the baby. The baby *is* what the elder sister *used to be* in the world of the family." Ibid., p. 112.

51. Ibid., p. 150–51. This whole discussion on the acquisition of the use of personal pronouns, especially of the 'I, marks more and more the differentiation of the child from his situation and from others. However, this does not eliminate the intersubjective, pre-personal level of the lived body in the adult as a dimension of the concrete subject.

52. Ibid., p. 151.

53. Ibid., p. 153. This ego is encompassed by what Mead calls "the me."

54. Ibid., p. 114.

55. Ibid., p. 115.

56. Ibid., pp. 117, 118.

57. Ibid., p. 117.

58. Ibid., p. 118.

59. Ibid., p. 119.

60. Ibid.

61. While it is the case that Merleau-Ponty rejects the immanent presence or closed interiority of his early philosophy, the tendency to over-interpret this in his early works should be avoided, since the seeds of its rejection are already in the early work. Because of his own rejection, there is a danger to exaggerate its role in the early works, as well as to overem-

phasize the difference between the early and the late works of Merleau-Ponty. See: *The Visible and the Invisible*, p. 171.

62. Merleau-Ponty, *Phenomenology of Perception*, p. 376.

63. This is what Merleau-Ponty means by saying that "consciousness is transcendence through and through" (Ibid., p. 376), meaning transcending itself in the sense of going beyond itself to world and to things in the world. Thus, this use of *transcendence* is not in any way to be confused with any sense of *transcendental*.

64. This point was developed in chapter 3 in the context of the reflective character of time as the sense of human existence.

65. Ibid., p. 426.

66. Ibid.

67. The concept of sedimentation is central to Merleau-Ponty's philosophy although he seldom thematizes it.

68. Merleau-Ponty, *Phenomenology of Perception*, p. 420.

69. Ibid., p. 424.

70. Ibid., p. 432.

71. Martin C. Dillon, *Merleau-Ponty's Ontology* (Bloomington and Indianapolis: Indiana University Press, 1988), p. 137.

72. Merleau-Ponty, *Phenomenology of Perception*, p. 130.

73. Merleau-Ponty, "The Child's Relations with the Other," *Primacy of Perception*, p. 119.

74. See the previous chapter for a discussion of these points.

75. Further, this deepening could be interpreted as a precursory response to certain deconstructionists' jump into the flux as a rational aversion to bringing it to meaningful articulation. Furthermore, Merleau-Ponty's interpretation of self has given a possible way beyond the question of the failure of time as the sense of being.

76. Mead, *Mind, Self, and Society*, pp. 369–70.

77. Ibid., p. 372.

78. Ibid., p. 353.

79. Ibid., p. 371.

80. See, for example, Ibid., p. 173: "The essence of the self is cognitive."

81. Joas, *G. H. Mead: A Contemporary Re-examination of His Thought*, pp. 64–89.

82. Ibid., pp. 86–87.

83. Ibid.

84. Mead, "The Definition of the Psychical," *Selected Writings*, p. 42.

85. Ibid., pp. 52, 49.

86. Ibid., p. 46.

87. Ibid., p. 49.

88. Ibid., pp. 53–54.

89. Ibid., p. 49.

90. Mead, *Mind, Self, and Society*, p. 136.

91. Mead, *The Individual and the Social Self*, p. 148.

92. Mead, "The Definition of the Psychical," *Selected Writings*, p. 43. *Feeling* here is not a psychological category but an experiential level; the level closest to pure immediacy, most devoid of interpretive elements.

93. Ibid., pp. 50–51.

94. Ibid., pp. 58–59.

95. Ibid., p. 51.

96. Ibid., p. 52.

97. Ibid., p. 58.

98. Ibid., p. 55.

99. See chapter 2 for the discussion of this point.

100. Mead, "The Definition of the Psychical," *Selected Writings*, p. 44.

101. Ibid., pp. 44–45.

102. Mead, "The Social Self," *Selected Writings*, pp. 144ff.

103. Ibid., p. 142.

104. Ibid., p. 142.

105. Mead, *Mind, Self, and Society*, p. 174.

106. Mead, "The Social Self," *Selected Writings*, p. 148.

107. Mead, *Mind, Self, and Society*, pp. 174–75.

108. Mead, "The Social Self," *Selected Writings*, p. 142.

109. Mead, "The Mechanism of Social Consciousness," *Selected Writings*, p. 141.

110. Ibid.

111. Ibid.

112. Mead, *Mind, Self, and Society*, p. 175. Mitchell Aboulafia assimilates the self to the 'me' pole, holding that while Mead often refers to the 'I' and 'me' as self, in other contexts the self is basically the 'me'. *The Mediating Self: Mead, Sartre, and Self-Determination* (New Haven, Connecticut: Yale University Press, 1986.) (See p. 18, n. 18 of his book for his specific statement of this intended use.) As here indicated, however, the self is in a certain sense most identified with the lived intentional body or the biologic dimension in its aspect of creativity, a function identified with the subject 'I' rather than the object 'me'.

113. Ibid., p. 174n.

114. Ibid., p. 174.

115. Ibid., p. 176.

116. Ibid.

117. Ibid.

118. This point was developed in the previous chapter.

119. Mead, *Mind, Self, and Society*, p. 177.

120. Ibid., p. 178.

121. Ibid., p. 174.

122. Ibid., p. 174.

123. Beth Singer, "Rights and Norms," forthcoming in the proceedings of the conference, *American Philosophy: Its Roots and Edges* (College Station, Texas: Texas A & M University Press).

124. Mead, *Mind, Self, and Society*, p. 202.

125. H. S. Thayer, *Meaning and Action: A Critical History of Pragmatism* (New York: Bobbs-Merrill Co., 1968), p. 259.

126. Norbert Wiley, in "Peirce, Mead and the Internal Conversation," a paper presented at the American Sociological Association, August, 1989, makes a distinction between the 'me' as past and the 'me' as object, but in so doing divorces the 'me' as object from temporality.

127. Supra, p. 111.

128. Mead, *Movements of Thought in the Nineteenth Century*, p. 372. Italics added. See supra, pp. 000–000, for the setting of the import of this claim.

129. Supra, p. 110.

130. Mead, "The Social Self," *Selected Writings*, p. 142.

131. Mead, *Mind, Self, and Society*, p. 151.

132. Ibid., p. 376. Emphasis added.

133. This is analogous to the claim made in the previous chapter that Mead's determination to avoid all remnants of the reification of scientific contents, a problem which his speculative metaphysics of temporality in fact undercuts, leads to his hesitancy concerning the cosmic extension of certain of his temporal concepts.

134. Mead, *Mind, Self, and Society*, pp. 177–78. Emphasis added.

135. Ibid., p. 140.

136. Ibid., p. 176.

137. See previous chapter for the "betwixt and between" of sociality.

138. Supra, ch. 4, n.2. As was noted there, he at times explicitly distinguishes between social as intrasystematic and "sociality" as intersystematic, but does not rigorously adhere to this distinction in terminology.

139. Mead, *Philosophy of the Present*, p. 77. This distinction would seem to be implicit in Joas's assertion that "with the concept of 'sociality' Mead emphatically does not mean a general systematic character, but rather the stage of the origination of something new in a present." *G. H. Mead: A Contemporary Reexamination of his Thought*, p. 183.

140. Aboulafia, *The Mediating Self*, p. 25. Aboulafia seems to identify functional and fictional. His generally keenly perceptive analysis runs into this kind of problem with Mead because his way of focusing on Mead in relation to Sartre draws him away from any concern with the centrality of the lived body.

141. Mead, *Mind, Self, and Society*, p. 173.

142. Ibid., p. 177.

143. Ernst Tugendhat, *Self-Consciousness and Self-Determination*, Trans. Paul Stern (Cambridge, Massachusetts: The MIT Press, 1986), pp. 234–48.

144. Habermas, *Theory of Communicative Action, II*, p. 106.

145. Mead, "The Social Self," *Selected Writings*, p. 145.

146. See, for example, Aboulafia, *The Mediating Self: Mead, Sartre, and Self-Determination*, p. 24.

147. Mead, *Mind, Self, and Society*, p. 136.

148. Mead, *The Philosophy of the Present*, p. 30.

149. Mead, *Mind, Self, and Society*, p. 135.

150. Mead, *Mind, Self, and Society*, p. 177. Emphasis added.

151. Mead, *Mind, Self, and Society*, p. 163.

152. Mead, *Philosophy of the Present*, p. 24.

153. As has been previously stressed, even reflective awareness as actively engaged in the dialogical stretch of the temporal present is nonthematic. This is very different from the second level thematization of the 'me' in "self-observation".

154. Mead, *Individual and the Social Self*, p. 148.

155. Mead, *Mind, Self, and Society*, p. 163.

156. Ibid., p. 173.

CHAPTER 5

1. Merleau-Ponty, "On the Phenomenology of Language," *Signs*, p. 88.

2. This human structure of behavior in relation to that of the animal and the physical was treated in previous chapters.

3. Paul Ricoeur, "New Developments in Phenomenology in France: The Phenomenology of Language," *Social Research* XXXIV (1967), p. 10.

4. Merleau-Ponty, *Phenomenology of Perception*, p. 189.

5. Ibid.

6. Ibid., p. 184.

7. Ibid., p. 186.

8. Ibid., p. 354.

9. Ibid., p. 352.

10. Ibid., p. 185.

11. Merleau-Ponty, "Film and the New Psychology," *Sense and Non-Sense*, p. 58. Supra, chapter 3, p. 94.

12. Merleau-Ponty, *Phenomenology of Perception*, p. 183.

13. Merleau-Ponty, "On the Phenomenology of Language," *Signs*, p. 89.

14. Merleau-Ponty, *Phenomenology of Perception*, p. 179.

15. Ibid., p. 177.

16. Ibid., p. 182.

17. Merleau-Ponty, "On the Phenomenology of Language," *Signs*, p. 88.

18. Ibid., p. 88.

19. Merleau-Ponty, *Phenomenology of Perception*, p. 193.

20. Ibid., p. 183.

21. Ibid., p. 184.

22. Ibid., title of chapter 6.

23. Ibid., p. 235.

24. Ibid., p. 235.

25. Ibid., pp. 180–81.

26. Merleau-Ponty, *The Prose of the World*, ed. Claude Lefort, trans. John O'Neill (Evanston, Illinios: Northwestern University Press, 1973), p. 19.

27. Merleau-Ponty, *Themes from the Lectures*, p. 9.

28. Merleau-Ponty, *Phenomenology of Perception*, p. 186.

29. Merleau-Ponty, "On the Phenomenology of Language," *Signs*, p. 89.

30. Merleau-Ponty, *Prose of the World*, p. 17.

31. Merleau-Ponty, *Phenomenology of Perception*, p. 197.

32. Ibid., p. 189.

33. Ibid., p. 187.

34. Ibid.

35. Ibid., p. 175.

36. Ibid.

37. Ibid., p. 177.

38. Merleau-Ponty, "On the Phenomenology of Language," *Signs*, p. 86.

39. Ibid.

40. Paul Ricoeur, "The Question of the Subject: The Challenge of Semiology," *The Conflict of Interpretations: Essays in Hermeneutics*, ed. Don Ihde (Evanston, Illinois: Northwestern University Press, 1974), p. 250.

41. In his own attempt to interarticulate semiology and phenomenology of language, Ricoeur says: "This reanimated phenomenology can not be content with repeating the old descriptions of speech which do not recognize the theoretical status of linguistics and its first axioms, the primacy of structure over process" (Ricoeur, "New Developments in Phenomenology in France," p. 19). For Ricoeur, the conditions imposed by semiology on such a phenomenology of language are such that it is "through and by means of a linguistics of language that a phenomenology of speech is today conceivable. It is in a hand-to-hand struggle with the presuppositions of semiology that it must reconquer: 1) the sense of a relation of transcendence in sign or reference, 2) the sense of its relationship to the speaking subject, and lastly, 3) the origin of the symbolic function itself whereby man is a being-for-sense" (Ricoeur, "New Developments in Phenomenology in France,' " p. 19). But, while demanding that phenomenology account for a theory of structure, for the system or semiological model, i.e., for a theory of the constitution and relation of signs, it is equally true that for Ricoeur semiology must account for meaning or the semantic dimension of language which it fails to recognize.

42. This is a restricted application of the term "semiological," relating particularly to structuralism and psychoanlysis, and is not to be confused with the broader and richer use of "semiology" as a nonreductionistic study of signs. See Paul Ricoeur, "The Question of the Subject: The Challenge of Semiology," *Conflict of Interpretations*, p. 237; pp. 247ff.

43. Paul Ricoeur, "New Developments in Phenomenology in France," p. 12; and ibid., p. 247ff.

44. Within the development of the phenomenology of lived language, the sciences of diachrony and synchrony are derived from lived language as a whole. However, that derivation of the sciences of language in general from the lived language leaves open the question of the particular points of the derivation, for instance, in attempting to face the questions—which Ricoeur insists on confronting in meeting the challenge of semiology—of how diachronic and synchronic linguistics are to be related. "Merleau-Ponty thinks he is in agreement with Saussure when he attributes to him the distinction between 'a synchronic linguistics of speech and a diachronic linguistics of language.' This is obviously an error." Paul Ricoeur, "New Developments in Phenomenology in France," p. 12. This article of Ricoeur reveals implicitly an equivocation in Merleau-Ponty's use of "synchrony" and "diachrony." On the one hand, he reveals the roots of both in lived language, synchrony within speech and diachrony within sedimented language. But this does not preclude their expression within the derived and abstracted langue as the object of the sciences, where the question of their relation and interarticulation remains to be dealt with. Ricoeur reflects an awareness of the lack of treatment of this second level consideration by Merleau-Ponty: "But is language, as the linguists consider it, taken seriously here? The fact that the notion of language as an autonomous system is not taken into consideration here is a serious weakness of this phenomenological analysis. Its treatment of the process of 'sedimentation' puts it into the vicinity of psychological treatments, of the notion of habit, of acquired capacity; but the structural element as such is missing." Ricoeur, pp. 12–13.

45. Mead, *Mind, Self, and Society*, p. 17.

46. Ibid., p. 16.

47. Ibid., p. 42, and p. 42, n. 1.

48. Mead, *Individual and the Social Self*, p. 39.

49. Mead, *Movements of Thought*, p. 396.

50. Ibid.

51. Mead, *Individual and the Social Self*, p. 40. It may be argued that while what Mead is illustrating works with the example of anger, it does not seem to fit within the context of some other emotions. Yet, it must be remembered that Mead has an expanded understanding of the inhibition of the act, such that it is involved in the very constitution of the perceived object. See chapter 1.

52. Ibid., p. 39.

53. Ibid., p. 13.

54. Mead, *Mind, Self, and Society*, p. 335.

55. Ibid., p. 80.

56. Ibid.

57. Mead, *Individual and the Social Self*, pp. 36, 43.

58. Ibid., p. 36.

59. Mead, *Mind, Self, and Society*, p. 65.

60. Mead, *Movements of Thought*, p. 379.

61. Mead, "A Behavioristic Account of the Significant Symbol," *Selected Writings*, p. 243.

62. Mead, *Mind, Self, and Society*, p. 67.

63. Mead, *Individual and the Social Self*, p. 46.

64. Mead, *Mind, Self, and Society*, pp. 67–68.

65. Ibid., p. 140.

66. Ibid., p. 362.

67. Ibid.

68. Ibid.

69. Ibid., p. 13.

70. Ibid., p. 237.

71. See Chapter 1 for the role of the hand in the development of objects of awareness.

72. Mead, *Philosophy of the Act*, pp. 135–36.

73. Mead, *Mind, Self, and Society*, p. 79.

74. By the same attitude, or same response, Mead intends not an absolute sameness but rather a similarity of organization of possible responses which function in the same way.

75. "The Genesis of the Self and Social Control," *Selected Writings*, p. 184.

76. This is true also for Merleau-Ponty, though as was seen in the previous chapter, the function of role taking in the development of selfhood is not as explicitly developed in his position as it is in Mead's philosophy..

77. Mead, *Mind, Self, and Society*, p. 142.

78. Ibid., pp. 47–48.

79. Ibid., p. 69.

80. *Ibid.*, p. 133.

81. Ibid., p. 145.

82. Mead, *Philosophy of the Act*, p. 518.

83. Mead, *Mind, Self, and Society*, pp. 11–14.

84. Ibid., p. 97.

85. Ibid., p. 197.

86. Ibid., pp. 74–75.

87. Mead, *Philosophy of the Act*, p. 518.

88. Mead, *Mind, Self, and Society*, pp. 74–75.

89. The first four are of course time and the three dimensions of space.

90. Mead, *Mind, Self, and Society*, p. 283.

91. Ibid., pp. 157–85.

92. Ibid., p. 273.

CHAPTER 6

1. Merleau-Ponty, *Phenomenology of Perception*, p. 453.

2. Merleau-Ponty, "The War Has Taken Place," *Sense and Non-Sense*, p. 148.

3. Merleau-Ponty, *Phenomenology of Perception*, p. 450.

4. Merleau-Ponty explicitly opposes Sartre on freedom throughout this chapter. He can be seen to oppose the essential points of Sartre regarding freedom: first, the absolute status which Sartre gives to freedom in human existence, and especially his failure to incorporate the situated at the heart of freedom; second, his failure to allow passivity at the heart of freedom; and third, the strictly negative context of freedom. Merleau-Ponty further opposes existential freedom to scientism, according to which things happen in the cause-effect relation and human action gets

subsumed within that context, and to idealism, for which freedom operates outside of nature.

5. This is clear from the case, which Merleau-Ponty invokes, of the prisoner who is tortured to betray friends but who does not do so because of his solidarity with them, springing from mutual values, common cause, or common world resulting from their coexisting and their common commitment at a level of individuality prior to the individual's level of personal decision.

6. Ibid., p. 454.

7. Merleau-Ponty, *Phenomenology of Perception*, p. 454.

8. Ibid., p. 442.

9. Ibid., p. 441.

10. Merleau-Ponty, "Hegel's Existentialism," *Sense and Non-Sense*, p. 70.

11. Merleau-Ponty, "The Battle Over Existentialilsm," *Sense and Non-Sense*, p. 72.

12. Merleau-Ponty, *Phenomenology of Perception*, p. 440.

13. Ibid.

14. Ibid., p. 440.

15. Ibid., p. 441.

16. Merleau-Ponty contends in this context that only the intellectual and propagandist take up and use the derived expression of the revolutionary project as focal point.

17. Ibid., p. 448. "I must . . . apprehend around my absolute individuality a kind of halo of generality or a kind of atmosphere of 'sociality'."

18. Ibid., p. 452.

19. Ibid., p. 434.

20. Ibid., p. 448.

21. These spring from present and past and "in particular from my mode of present and past co-existence" (Merleau-Ponty, *Phenomenology of Perception*, p. 447).

22. Ibid., p. 450.

23. Merleau-Ponty, "Marxism and Philosophy," *Sense and Non-Sense*, p. 130.

24. Merleau-Ponty, *The Primacy of Perception*, p. 25.

25. Ibid., p. 13.

26. Ibid., p. 25.

27. Merleau-Ponty rejects a universal and closed morality given in a neat package of norms. He emphasizes the creativity involved in the appropriation of values, the ambiguity of existence as not given clear direction or complete control to the realm of personal decision of the individual. He says regarding a moral norm: There is no given universality; there is only a presumptive universality" ("The Primacy is Perception," *Primacy of Perception*, pp. 31–32). He simply portrays morality as problematic rather than denying it. He says concerning the ambiguity of the concrete situation of values and morality: "We have unlearned 'pure formality' and learned a kind of vulgar immoralism, which is healthy. The moral man does not want to dirty his hands. It is because he usually has enough time, talent, or money to stand back from enterprises of which he disapproves and to prepare a good conscience for himself" ("the War Has Taken Place," *Sense and Non-Sense*, p. 147).

28. Regarding the absolute value, he admits, in a qualified way, to the absolute value of the person, but adds that when, in military decisions, he had to call an artillery barrage against the enemy, although he might feel positive toward the enemy, he did not accept the absolute value of the person. He is responding here to the question, Do you posit the other as an absolute value? by saying "Yes, in so far as a man can do so." ("The Primacy of Perception," *Primacy of Perception*, p. 35).

29. Merleau-Ponty expresses this in the following text: "True morality does not consist in following exterior rules or in respecting objective values: there are no ways to *be* just or to *be* saved. One would do better to pay less attention to the unusual situation of the three characters in *L'Invitée* and more to the good faith, the loyalty to promises, the respect for others, the generosity and the seriousness of the two principals. For the value is there. It consists of actively being what we are by chance, of establishing that communication with others and with ourselves for which our temporal structure gives us the opportunity and of which our liberty is only the rough outline." "Metaphysics and the Novel," *Sense and Non-Sense*, p. 40.

30. Merleau-Ponty, *Phenomenology of Perception*, p. 433.

31. Ibid. "The solution of all problems of transcendence is to be sought in the thickness of the pre-objective present, in which we find our bodily being, our social being, and the pre-existence of the world, that is, the starting point of 'explanations', in so far as they are legitimate—and at the same time the basis of our freedom."

32. These two senses of *transcendence* were treated at some length in the chapter on time above.

33. As seen in the chapter on time, human existence is present to the world as familiar with it, as at or in the world in action, as already comprehending it in its very forestructure. Thus, in a primary way, originary and lived time are the root of human existence's presence to the world. There is a "relationship of active transcendence between the subject and the world" (Merleau-Ponty, *Phenomenology of Perception*, p. 430). This is the context in which situated freedom fits.

34. Ibid., p. 418.

35. See, for example, Mitchell Aboulafia's *The Mediating Self: Mead, Sartre, and Self Determination*, pp. 15–26; Paul Pfuetze, *The Social Self* (New York: Bookman Associates, 1954), pp. 94–96.

36. This type of criticism comes often from interpreters of Mead in the areas of psychology and sociology, but it is also to be found in the interpretations of philosophers. Andrew Reck indicates the potential problem in *Persons and Community in American Philosophy*, ed. Konstantin Kolenda (Rice University Studies, vol. 66, 1980).

37. Mead, *Mind, Self, and Society*, 211–12.

38. In the area of value, this may seem to take on the overtones of "sympathy" or "empathy," but Mead stresses that what is involved is not "feeling the other's joys and sorrows." And, Mead in fact defines sympathy in terms of the dialogical relation involved in taking the role of the other. See *Mind, Self, and Society*, pp. 298–99.

39. Mead, *Mind, Self, and Society*, p. 178.

40. Ibid., p. 178.

41. Mead, *Movements of Thought*, pp. 375–77.

42. As James Campbell aptly captures this point, "At least in part we choose our 'me'." "George Herbert Mead: Philosophy and the Pragmatic Self," *American Philosophy*, ed. Marcus G. Singer (Cambridge, Massachusetts: Cambridge University Press, 1985), p. 102.

43. Mead, *Mind, Self, and Society*, p. 178.

44. Mead, *Movements of Thought*, p. 317.

45. Mead, *Philosophy of the Act*, p. 348.

46. Ibid.

47. Mead, *Mind, Self, and Society*, p. 176.

48. Mead, "Scientific Method and the Individual Thinker," *Selected Writings*, p. 256.

49. Mead, "The Philosophical Basis of Ethics," *Selected Writings*, p. 87.

50. David Miller analyzes Mead's position in terms of what he calls three levels of morality: the level of impulsive behavior, springing from such instincts as involved in food, shelter, companionship, etc.; the level of conformity to the restraining force of the 'me'; and the reconstructive creativity of the 'I', noting that freedom enters at this third level. *George Herbert Mead: Self, Language and the World*, p. 238. Joas, on the other hand, seems not only to detach what Miller calls the first level from the sphere of morality, but also to claim that for Mead, morality has no biological roots. *George Herbert Mead: A Contemporary Re-Examination of His Thought*, p. 133. Although Mead's range of instincts may well be unacceptable, the biological roots of morality would seem to be rightfully essential to his position.

51. Mead, "The Philosophical Basis of Ethics," *Selected Writings*, p. 84.

52. Mead, *Philosophy of the Act*, p. 136.

53. Mead, "The Philosophical Basis of Ethics," *Selected Writings*, p. 87.

54. Ibid.

55. Ibid.

56. Ibid.

57. Ibid., pp. 85–86.

58. Ibid., p. 93. This discussion interrelates with his understanding of moral necessity, discussed above.

59. Mead, *The Philosophy of the Act*, p. 486.

60. Ibid., p. 480.

61. As he states, "I am not now using the term 'mind' in a technical sense. I refer to the meanings and values which things have for us and the responses they call out." Ibid., p. 479.

62. Ibid., p. 480.

63. Ibid., pp. 480ff.

64. Ibid., p. 480.

65. Ibid., p. 663.

66. Ibid.

67. Ibid., p. 197.

68. Here it must be remembered that this sedimentation of one's past includes both past creativity and past social conformity, past "I's" and past "me's".

69. Mead, "The Social Self," *Selected Writings*, p. 147.

70. Mead, *Philosophy of the Act*, p. 663.

71. Ibid.

72. Mead, "The Philosophical Basis of Ethics," *Selected Writings*, p. 85.

73. Ibid., p. 199.

74. Mead, *Mind, Self, and Society*, p. 177.

75. Mead, *Philosophy of the Act*, pp. 343–44. Italics added.

76. Mead, *Mind, Self, and Society*, p. 203.

77. In such a present, novelty could not be experienced as such.

78. See chapter 4 for the development of this point without a specific focus on the value situation.

79. Mead, *Mind, Self, and Society*, pp. 203–204.

80. This point was discussed in chapter 4 in relation to the claims of Ernst Tugendhat and Jürgen Habermas.

81. Mead's refers here to the 'I', but it is the 'I' as representative of the creative dimension of the body that I am, rather than as representative of a subject over against an object.

82. Mead, *Mind, Self, and Society*, p. 204.

83. Ibid., p. 144n.

84. Ernst Tugendhat, *Self-Consciousness and Self-Determination*, p. 265.

85. Ibid., p. 313.

86. Here it must be remembered that the nonreflective is at once prereflective as regards what is to come, but postreflective in that it incorporates the sedimentations of past reflective activity.

87. The denial of both of these alternatives was seen to be implicit in Merleau-Ponty's incipient value orientation.

88. Mead, *Mind, Self, and Society*, p. 214.

89. As David L. Miller so well states, "No individual, short of insanity, can, as an 'I', stand over against the entire generalized other. That would mean the loss of one's mind and resorting to sheer unsocialized impulses. "The Meaning of Freedom From the Perspective of G. H. Mead's Theory of the Self," *The Southern Journal of Philosophy* 20 (1982).

90. Mead, *Mind, Self, and Society*, pp. 167–68.

91. Ibid., p. 157–58.

92. Ibid., p. 199.

93. Mead, "The Social Self," *Selected Writings*, pp. 148–49.

94. Mead, *The Philosophy of the Act*, p. 663.

95. Mead, "The Social Self," *Selected Writings*, p. 149.

96. Mead, *Mind, Self, and Society*, pp. 162–63.

97. Mead, *Philosophy of the Act*, p. 663.

98. Mead, *Mind, Self, and Society*, pp. 266–67.

99. Mead, *Movements of Thought*, p. 168.

100. Mead, *Philosophy of the Act*, p. 663.

101. Mead, "Scientific Method and the Moral Sciences," *Selected Writings*, p. 256.

102. Ibid., p. 255.

103. Ibid., p. 156.

104. Ibid., pp. 248–66.

105. Mead, "Scientific Method and the Individual Thinker," *Selected Writings*, p. 201.

106. Mead, *Mind, Self, and Society*, p. 289.

107. Mead, "Natural Rights and the Theory of the Political Institution," *Selected Writings*, p. 163.

108. As Mead states, "If you can make your demand universal, if your right is one that carries with it a corresponding obligation, then you

recognize the same right in everyone else, and you can give a law, so to speak, in the terms of all the community." *Mind, Self, and Society*, p. 287, n. 17.

109. Institutions are social habits. See, for example, *Movements of Thought in the Nineteenth Century*, p. 377.

110. Mead, *Mind, Self, and Society*, p. 286.

111. Ibid., p. 251.

112. Ibid., p. 352.

113. Ibid., p. 212.

114. Mead, *Philosophy of the Act*, pp. 496–97.

115. Mead, "Scientific Method and the Individual Thinker," *Selected Writings*, p. 211. Thus Mead illustrates the sense of felt creativity by reference to the creative effort involved in the scientist's search for a hypothesis. "The Definition of the Psychical," *Selected Writings*, p. 43.

116. Merleau-Ponty, *Phenomenology of Perception*, p. 408.

117. Ibid., p. 433.

118. It is precisely this significance of Mead's metaphysics, as well as the claim that it is in fact metaphysics, which is questioned by Joas, who takes a developmental approach to Mead's writings. *G. H. Mead: A Contemporary Re-Examination of His Thought*. See pp. 8 and 10 for his brief summary of this position.

BIBLIOGRAPHY OF WORKS CITED

PRIMARY SOURCES

George Herbert Mead

"Image or Sensation," *The Journal of Philosophy* 1, pt. 2 (1904).

The Individual and the Social Self: Unpublished Work of George Herbert Mead, ed. David Miller. Chicago: The University of Chicago Press, 1982.

Mind, Self, and Society, ed. Charles Morris. Chicago: The University of Chicago Press, 1934.

Movements of Thought in the Nineteenth Century, ed. Merritt Moore. Chicago: The University of Chicago Press, 1936.

The Philosophy of the Act, ed. Charles Morris. Chicago: The University of Chicago Press, 1938.

The Philosophy of the Present, ed. Arthur Murphy. La Salle, Illinois: Open Court, 1959.

Mead: Selected Writings, ed. Andrew Reck. New York: Bobbs-Merrill Co., 1964. The following essays:

"A Behavioristic Account of the Significant Symbol"

"Concerning Animal Perceptiion"

"The Definition of the Psychical"

"The Genesis of the Self and Social Control"

"Image or Sensation"

"The Mechanism of Social Consciousness"

"Natural Rights and the Theory of the Political Institution"

"The Nature of the Past"

"The Philosophical Basis of Ethics"

"A Pragmatic Theory of Truth"

"Scientific Method and the Individual Thinker"

"Scientific Method and the Moral Sciences"

"Social Consciousness and the Consciousness of Meaning"

"Social Psychology as Counterpart to Physiological Psychology"

"The Social Self"

Maurice Merleau-Ponty

Phenomenology of Perception, trans. Colin Smith. New York: The Humanities Press, 1962.

The Primacy of Perception, trans. and ed. James Edie. Evanston, Illinois: Northwestern University Press, 1964. The following essays:

"The Child's Relations with the Other"

"Eye and Mind"

"The Primacy of Perception and Its Philosophical Consequences"

The Prose of the World, ed. Claude Lefort, trans. John O'Neill. Evanston, Illinois: Northwestern University Press, 1973. The following essays:

"The Indirect Language"

"Science and the Experience of Expressions"

Sense and Non-Sense, trans. Hubert L. Dreyfus and Patricia Allen Dreyfus. Evanston, Illinois: Northwestern University Press, 1964. The following essays:

"The Battle Over Existentialism"

"The Film and the New Psychology"

"Hegel's Existentialism"

"Marxism and Philosophy"

"The Metaphysical in Man"

"Metaphysics and the Novel"

"The War Has Taken Place"

Signs, trans. Richard C. McCleary. Evanston, Illinois: Northwestern University Press, 1964. The following essays:

"Bergson in the Making"

"Einstein and the Crisis of Reason"

"On the Phenomenology of Language"

"The Philosopher and His Shadow"

"The Philosopher and Sociology"

The Structure of Behavior, trans. Alden Fisher, Boston: Boston Press, 1963.

Themes From the Lectures at the College of France 1952–1960, trans. John O'Neill. Evanston, Illinois: Northwestern University Press, 1970. The following essay:

"The Concept of Nature, I"

The Visible and the Invisible, ed. Claude Lefort, trans. Alphonso Lingis. Evanston, Illinois: Northwestern University Press, 1968.

SECONDARY SOURCES

Mitchell Aboulafia, *The Mediating Self: Mead, Sartre, and Self-Determination*. New Haven, Connecticut: Yale University Press, 1986.

Patrick L. Bourgeois and Sandra B. Rosenthal, *Thematic Studies in Phenomenology and Pragmatism*. Amsterdam: B. R. Grüner, 1983.

James Campbell, "George Herbert Mead: Philosophy and the Pragmatic Self," *American Philosophy*, ed. Marcus B. Singer. Cambridge: Cambridge University PRess, 1985.

John Dewey, "The Reflex Arc Concept," *The Early Works*, vol. 5, ed. Jo Ann Boydston. Carbondale: Southern Illinois University Press, 1972.

Martin C. Dillon, *Merleau-Ponty's Ontology*. Bloomington and Indianapolis: Indiana University Press, 1988.

Jürgen Habermas, *The Theory of Communicative Action, II*, trans. Thomas McCarthy. Boston: Beacon Press, 1987.

Hans Joas, *G. H. Mead: A Contemporary Re-examination of His Thought.* Cambridge, Massachusetts: The MIT Press, 1985.

John J. McDermott, *The Culture of Experience: Philosophical Essays in the American Grain.* New York: New York University Press, 1976. (Reissued by Waveland Press).

John J. McDermott, *Streams of Experience: Reflections on the History and Philosophy of American Culture.* Amherst: The University of Massachusetts Press, 1986.

Joseph Margolis, *The Persistence of Reality,* vol. 2, *Science Without Unity: Reconciling the Human and Natural Sciences.* Oxford and New York: Basil Blackwell Ltd., 1987.

David Miller, *George Herbert Mead: Self, Language, and the World.* Austin: The University of Texas Press, 1973.

David Miller, "The Meaning of Freedom From the Perspective of G. H. Mead's Theory of the Self," *The Southern Journal of Philosophy* 20 (1982).

Maurice Natanson, *The Social Dynamics of George H. Mead.* The Hague: Martinus Nijhoff, 1973.

Paul Pfuetze, *The Social Self.* New York: Bookman Associates, 1954.

Andrew Reck, *Persons and Community in American Philosophy,* ed. Konstantin Kolenda. Rice University Studies, vol. 66 (1980).

Paul Ricoeur, "The Question of the Subject: The Challenge of Semiology," *The Conflict of Interpretations: Essays in Hermeneutics,* ed. Don Ihde. Evanston, Illinois: Northwestern University Press, 1974.

Paul Ricoeur, "New Developments in Phenomenology in France: The Phenomenology of Language," *Social Research* 34 (1967).

Sandra B. Rosenthal and Patrick L. Bourgeois, *Pragmatism and Phenomenology: A Philosophic Encounter.* Amsterdam: B. R. Grüner, 1980.

John Sallis, *Phenomenology and the Return to Beginnings.* Pittsburgh: Duquesne University Press, 1973.

Beth Singer, "Rights and Norms." Forthcoming in the proceedings of the conference, *American Philosophy: Its Roots and Edges.* June, 1988 College Station, Texas: Texas A & M University Press.

Herbert Spiegelberg, *The Phenomenological Movement.* The Hague: Martinus Nijhoff, 1965.

H. S. Thayer, *Meaning and Action: A Critical History of Pragmatism.* New York: Bobbs-Merrill Co., 1968.

Ernst Tugendhat, *Self-Consciousness and Self-Determination,* trans. Paul Stern. Cambridge, Massachusetts: The MIT Press, 1986.

Norbert Wiley, "Peirce, Mead and the Internal Conversation." Paper presented at the American Sociological Association, August, 1989.

INDEX

P

transition 83, 113
triadic relation, meaning 34–38,
141, 179
truth 43–46
truth, agreement 45
truth, fitting 45
Tugendhat, Ernst 160, 204, 214, 119

U

Umwelt 47
unchanging 43
unexpected 153
unification 157, 158
uniformity of nature 41
unique 42, 63, 114, 144, 164
universal 35–37, 142, 143, 162,
163, 164, 215
universe 41, 42, 71, 76, 77, 78, 79,
82, 180
universe of discourse 89, 143, 144,
161
Ursprung 50

V

valuations, abstract 157
valuations, concrete 157
value 145, 151, 152, 153, 154–165,
211

value conflicts 161, 162
value laden 156
values, absolute, 161
values, fixed 145, 161
verification 77. *See* workability
vicious circle 37–38
vitalism 9
vocalization 141
voice 104
volitional 160

W

Watson 6, 141, 171
Weizsacker 13
Whitehead, Alfred N. 58, 59, 74,
188
Wiley, Norbert 203
workability 44, 45, 46, 108, 159,
160, 163, 165
working character 163, 164
working ideal 164
world 4, 9, 10, 14, 15, 20, 22, 24,
27, 40–43, 45–52, 49, 50, 59, 60,
61, 62, 63, 74, 75, 76, 77, 82, 85,
106, 107, 117, 124, 125, 137, 143,
144, 148, 151, 153, 162, 165
world-that-is-there 40–43, 45, 75,
77, 127
Wundt 137

ACT8704